RHYTHM IN ACTING AND PERFORMANCE

RHYTHM IN ACTING AND PERFORMANCE

Embodied Approaches and Understandings

EILON MORRIS

Bloomsbury Methuen Drama
An imprint of Bloomsbury Publishing Plc

B L O O M S B U R Y
LONDON · OXFORD · NEW YORK · NEW DELHI · SYDNEY

Bloomsbury Methuen Drama

An imprint of Bloomsbury Publishing Plc

Imprint previously known as Methuen Drama

50 Bedford Square
London
WC1B 3DP
UK

1385 Broadway
New York
NY 10018
USA

www.bloomsbury.com

**BLOOMSBURY, METHUEN DRAMA and the Diana logo are
trademarks of Bloomsbury Publishing Plc**

First published 2017

© Eilon Morris, 2017

Musical notation from *Alla ricerca dal teatro perduto* © Eugenio Barba 1965.
Reproduced by permission of Odin Teatret Archive

'What shall I do with the body I've been given' by Osip Mandelshtam, translated
by James Greene. Reproduced by permission of Angel Books.

British Library Cataloguing-in-Publication Data
A catalogue record for this book is available from the British Library.

ISBN:	HB:	978-1-4725-8985-9
	PB:	978-1-4725-8986-6
	ePDF:	978-1-4725-8988-0
	eBook:	978-1-4725-8984-2

Library of Congress Cataloging-in-Publication Data
Names: Morris, Eilon author.
Title: Rhythm in acting and performance : embodied approaches
and understandings / Eilon Morris [editor].
Description: London ; New York, NY : Bloomsbury Methuen Drama, 2017. |
Includes bibliographical references and index.
Identifiers: LCCN 2016048843 (print) | LCCN 2017010223 (ebook) |
ISBN 9781472589866 (pbk. : alk. paper) | ISBN 9781472589859 (hardback : alk. paper) |
ISBN 9781472589873 (Epub) | ISBN 9781472589880 (Epdf)
Subjects: LCSH: Movement (Acting) | Acting–Psychological
aspects. | Rhythm. | Drama–Technique.
Classification: LCC PN2071.M6 .M58 2017 (print) | LCC PN2071.M6 (ebook) |
DDC 792.02/8–dc23
LC record available at https://lccn.loc.gov/2016048843

Cover design: Louise Dugdale
Cover image © Vince Cavataio/Getty Images

Typeset by Integra Software Services Pvt. Ltd.
Printed and bound in India

To find out more about our authors and books visit www.bloomsbury.com
Here you will find extracts, author interviews, details of forthcoming events,
and the option to sign up for our newsletters.

For Charles

For Zoe

τοῦ ῥυθμοῦ πλείους εἰσὶ φύσεις καὶ ποία τις αὐτῶν ἑκάστη καὶ διὰ τίνας αἰτίας
τῆς αὐτῆς ἔτυχον προσηγορίας καὶ τί αὐτῶν ἑκάστη ὑπόκειται

There are many natures to rhythm. Of what quality is each these, for what reasons have they taken on the same name, and what is the meaning underlying each of these?

–Aristoxenus of Tarentum, *Elements of Rhythm*, 335–332 BC

「声を忘れて曲を知れ。曲を忘れて調子を 知れ。調子を忘れて拍子を 知れ」と云へり。… 拍子は初・中・後へわたるべし。

'Forget voice and know expression; forget expression and know pitch; forget pitch and know rhythm.' ... The rhythm must be understood throughout, at the beginning, in the middle, and at the end.[1]

–Zeami Motokiyo, *A Mirror to the Flower*, 1424

CONTENTS

List of Exercises xi
List of Figures and Tables xii
Acknowledgements xiii

PART ONE Establishing a Pulse 1

1   What Is Rhythm? An Open Question 7
The etymology of rhythm 8
Productive categories of rhythm 12
Reflections 23

2   An Epoch of Rhythm: Now and Then 25
Natural and organic rhythm 27
Mechanical and deterministic rhythmic aesthetics 30
Rhythm as a universal language 33
Authenticity and real time 35
A new epoch of rhythm 38
Reflections 41

PART TWO Stanislavski on Rhythm 43

**3   Tapping Emotions: The Ins and Outs
     of Tempo-Rhythm** 47
An aspiring opera singer 47
Psychophysical techniques 48
Eurhythmics and polyrhythm 52

Tempo and rhythm – ins and outs 54
Tempo-rhythm in training 59
Tempo-rhythm in rehearsals 66
Reflections 70

PART THREE Structure and Spontaneity 73

4   **Suzanne Bing: Music and Games in Actor Training** 77
Initial interests in rhythm 78
Children's school in Paris 80
Applying eurhythmics in actor training 83
Voice, movement and storytelling 85
Musique corporelle 87
Legacy of rhythm and play 91
Reflections 92

5   **Vsevolod Meyerhold: Rhythm Not Metre** 95
Form as a means to freedom 96
A rhythmic vocabulary 100
Rhythm versus metre 101
Tripartite rhythm 104
Reflections 107

6   **John Britton: Smashing the Ensemble Groove** 109
Musical accompaniment 110
Jazz as model for ensemble improvisation 111
Ensemble 113
Smashing the groove 114
The shape of an action 116
The energetic 118
Reflections 119

7   **Anne Bogart and Tina Landau: A Horizontal
    Viewpoint** 121
A non-hierarchical ethos 123

Musical accompaniment 125
Rhythm in Suzuki work 126
Viewpoints of time 127
Reflections 134
Reflections on structure and spontaneity 135

PART FOUR The Ecstatic Performer 137

8 Rhythm and Altered States of Consciousness: Entrainment and Communitas 143
Rhythmic entrainment 146
Group/ensemble rhythm 149
Reflections 151

9 Jerzy Grotowski: Seeking Pulse, Movement and Rhythm 153
Influences and sources 154
Exercises plastiques 158
Techniques of sources 161
Reflections 165

10 Nicolás Núñez: Becoming Present 167
Slow walking 168
Contemplative running 170
Cosmic verticality 173
'Here and now' 174
Continuity of effort and the sustaining of rhythm 177
Reflections 178

11 Eilon Morris: Orbits – Cultivating Simultaneity 181
Vertical time 182
Orbits 185
Running Orbits 190
Reflections 192
Reflections on polyrhythm and simultaneity 195

PART FIVE A Plurality of Voices 197

12 Rhythming Words: Where, How and Why 201

Meaning and rhythm 204
Reflections 208

13 Creating Spaces: Conversations with Judith Adams and Karen Christopher 209

Judith Adams 209
Karen Christopher 212
Reflections 215

14 The Poetry of the Breath: Conversations with Bruce Myers and Kate Papi 217

Bruce Myers 217
Kate Papi 220
Reflections 223

15 The Tune Is a Framework: A Conversation with Chris Coe and Frankie Armstrong 225

Reflections 229

PART SIX Reflections 231

Coda 238

Glossary 240
Notes 247
References 259
Index 271

LIST OF EXERCISES

Exercises

1 Outer tempo-rhythm 61

2 Movement score (Stanislavski) 62

3 Inner tempo-rhythm and given circumstances 63

4 Pranic breathing 64

5 Contrasting tempo-rhythms 65

6 Six levels of rhythm 68

7 The cat and the old rat 81

8 Ensemble voice and ball games 86

9 Duration of breath, text and movement 88

10 Mirroring and everyday tempos 89

11 Clapping rhythms and three group images 90

12 Tripartite rhythms in biomechanics 105

13 'The ball game' 116

14 'To' and 'against' 126

15 Tempo: 'the basics' 128

16 Duration and tempo 130

17 'Introducing Kinaesthetic Response' 131

18 'Introducing Repetition' 132

19 Movement score (Grotowski) 155

20 'Plastiques' 159

21 Slow walking (Grotowski) 162

22 Slow walking (Núñez) 169

23 Contemplative running 170

24 Departures, arrivals and journeys 186

LIST OF FIGURES
AND TABLES

Figures

9.1 Scored notation of physical actions, based on transcriptions by Barba (1965) 156

10.1 Energetic levels of cosmic verticality 173

11.1 Simultaneous and successive actions 182

11.2 Simultaneous tasks of an individual performer 184

11.3 Thirty-beat orbit form consisting of two-, three- and five-beat cycles 190

G.1 Musical and spoken accent symbols 240

G.2 Note values: European and American names 243

Tables

1.1 Characteristics of Greek metres 13

10.1 Rhythmic dramaturgies of attention in ritual and performance 179

ACKNOWLEDGEMENTS

This book and the research that contributed to it have involved the participation of a large number of people and groups, whose willingness, support and encouragement have contributed invaluably to my understandings of rhythm and the writing of this book. My thanks and appreciation to all who have been involved including Deborah Middleton, Liza Lim and John Britton for their supervision of my PhD; Judith Adams, Simon Warner and Jarvis 'Cockatiel' Warner-Adams of Whitestone Arts for all the warmth, hospitality, shelter and walks on the Moors; Helena Guardia, Ana Luisa Solis, Nicolás Núñez and the members of the Taller de Investigación Teatral for their openness and generosity of sharing knowledge and practice; the Duende Ensemble including Stacey Johnstone, Hannah Dalby, Eva Tsourou and Aliki Dourmazer for their participation in my research; Kate Papi and Oliviero Papi of the Au Brana Cultural Centre and the other members of OBRA Theatre Company including Hannah Frances Whelan, Pelle Holst, Unai Lopez, Ixchel Rubio and Fabian Wixe for their support and willingness to play; and Tray Wilson and the Wild Goose Theatre Laboratory and Victoria Firth from the Lawrence Batley Theatre for supporting my research sessions. My sincere gratitude goes to the Society of Latin American Studies for supporting my research in Mexico; Odin Teatret Archives for their help with the sourcing and providing permission to reproduce scores for Grotowski's rhythm exercises; Angel Books for their permission to use the translation by James Greene of Osip Mandelshtam's poem 'What shall I do with the body I've been given' in Chapter 14; for their assistance with sourcing research materials and translations I would like to thank Shawn Bodden, Sharon Carnicke, Thomas Hare, Yuki Kondo, Oliviero Papi, Vasiliki Syropoulou and Judita Vivas. Much thanks go to those who contributed valuable knowledge and personal insight through interviews and conversations: Judith Adams, John Britton, Karen Christopher, Bruce Myers, Kate Papi, Leo Warner, Frankie Armstrong and Chris Coe and Brian Pearson who hosted our interview in Chester. My dearest thanks go to my parents, Hana and Jonno, and all my family for their support, and to my partner Zoe Katsilerou for her attention, inspiration, patience and love.

PART ONE

ESTABLISHING A PULSE

In the making and training of performance, rhythm forms both the basis and the result of much that is done. In this context, the rhythms of life, play and ritual are pursued, encouraged and celebrated. Actors involved in cyclic and alternating actions and sounds warm up and train their bodies, voices and attention. We sense the pulsing of footsteps, the succession and duration of breaths, the poetry of language and the ebb and flow of dialogue; we are aware of the polyrhythmic coordination of an ensemble. The rhythms of music, architecture, light and sound are heard, seen and felt. We observe rhythm in the structuring and breaking down of scenes and actions into constituent parts and in the arrangement and flow of the dramaturgy and design of the performance. Whether conscious of it or not, rhythm informs almost every aspect of acting and performance.[1]

The theatre director Peter Brook observed: 'One cannot define rhythm; but nevertheless one can state that at the heart of a fine performance there is always rhythm' (Williams 1991:79). Despite (and possibly because of) the ubiquitous nature of rhythm, its meaning seems to evade us. There is little agreement amongst practitioners and theorists as to what rhythm is and how best it should be approached or understood within this field. And while many lay claim to its universality and capacity to unify the elements of performance, when we look closely at this topic, what we encounter is a broad range of differing (and at times contradictory) notions that change vastly from one context to another.

For the director Vsevolod Meyerhold, 'the gift of rhythm' was 'one of the most important prerequisites for a director' (Meyerhold cited by Schmidt 1978:79). Under attack from the RAPP (Russian Association of Proletarian Writers) for his supposed use of 'mechanical rhythm',[2] Meyerhold argued:

An understanding of rhythm in a production is one of the fundamental principles, as the Greeks would say. Here everything is turned around. We not only don't overvalue the meaning of rhythm, we undervalue it. We still haven't sufficiently studied its nature, the entire sphere of its influence on the work of the actor. But we already do it, whatever name you give it. ([1931] 1998:162)

While many acknowledge the centrality of rhythm in this field, there is still little that is openly discussed about the nature of rhythm, how it is approached, applied, embodied and understood, by performers, performance makers and those who train them.

Unsurprisingly, the ambiguity surrounding this term has left some with a sense that rhythm has become 'worn out', emptied of meaning and efficacy through its 'widespread and often indiscriminate usage' (Roesner 2014:83). Writing recently on the dominance of rhythm in the work of theatre practitioners at the beginning of the twentieth century, the theorist Rose Whyman suggested that 'the epoch's emphasis on rhythm is questionable now' (2008:242). Others have made similar assertions, querying the efficacy of this term within contemporary discourse. The philosopher Hans Ulrich Gumbrecht observed that the 'phenomenon rhythm has become an arbitrary (and thus worthless) offer to solve an (almost) arbitrary range of questions' (Gumbrecht 1988 cited in Roesner 2014:42).

We might ask, in this case, why bother discussing rhythm at all? I must admit that in my own experience as a performer, when a director mentions 'rhythm', there is a part of me that leans in with excitement and another part that shrinks back with a sense of dread. For seldom am I completely sure that I (or they) know precisely what they are referring to. Are they talking about the speed or the phrasing of my movement or voice? Am I being asked to make my work more structured and accentuated or more fluid, varied and dynamic? Or are they referring to any number of other specific technical, metaphorical or metaphysical meanings of rhythm, related to music, poetry, dance, nature, etc? Or are they commenting on a more general sense of timing or composition? As Curt Sachs said of rhythm, 'the confusion is terrifying indeed' (1952:384).

However, despite the confusion, this word still seems to stick, finding continued usage and interest throughout a broad range of practices and disciplines. Even though rhythm is seldom defined within the practical context of performance making, there often exists what might be best understood as a tacit knowledge that informs a performer's engagement with rhythm. As Brook and Meyerhold pointed out, even if we cannot define it, we still do it, or at least know when it is there or not. This is a knowledge that exists in the practice itself, in the doing and the making of performance and in the shared sets of understandings that emerge from the creative processes of collaboration. These embodied understandings resist definition and often take the form of shorthand remarks tossed about within a rehearsal process, evolving and integrating new meanings as the practices themselves change and develop over time. Instead of viewing rhythm as a fixed concept which we can point at and examine, rhythm might be better understood as a constellation of associations, understandings and embodied practices, of which we can enquire and explore.

Taking the latter approach, this book intends to address this topic by enquiring into the ways that actors, directors and other performance makers approach rhythm within their work and the contexts from which these practices emerge. Instead of examining rhythm as a top–down system of analysis and notation to be applied to performance, the aim of this book is to reflect on how rhythm is encountered in and emerges from the work of performance practitioners themselves. There is an intentional plurality to this endeavour. You will not be presented with a clean definition and systematic approach to understanding rhythm in performance. Instead you will be offered a collection of insights and reflections, some practical, others theoretical or poetic. Some may be stable and consistent, others highly changeable and open to interpretation and contradiction. There are some that will be familiar or easily grasped, while others might appear novel or perplexing. These are here to be drawn on, engaged with, realized and challenged both intellectually and practically. Taking this as a starting point, this book looks to build a richer and more informed discourse around this prevalent yet often overlooked aspect of our field.

1
WHAT IS RHYTHM?
AN OPEN QUESTION

Being difficult to point at or define in a specific or practical way, rhythm often receives little direct or detailed attention within this field. Attempting to define rhythm within acting, director Richard Boleslavsky stated: 'It is one of the hardest subjects to explain because it is so simple' (1987:108). The difficulty that emerges in any interrogation of rhythm is the inherent resistance it has to detailed analysis. Under scrutiny, the subject of rhythm reveals a nature that is both evasive and porous. In both theory and practice, rhythm shrinks from direct examination, having no substance of its own to which we can point or grasp. As Jacques Lecoq said, 'its essence eludes us when we try to penetrate it, just as the mystery of life does' (2006:88). The harder we try to hold on to or define rhythm, the further we find ourselves from understanding it.

Curiously, the opposite is also true. Rhythm is, at times, most noticeable in its absence, such as when things seem to be going wrong in a performance or when a structure is disrupted or eradicated. We are often struck by a problem with the rhythm of a performance, a disjuncture between performers or performance elements, or a lack of rhythmic clarity. The playwright Judith Adams states: 'It's always rhythm that offends me if it doesn't work' (interview with author, March 2016). When a sequence is flowing smoothly and all the parts of a performance work together as an effortless whole, then we seldom notice the presence of rhythm itself, focusing instead on the content or experience of the performance as a whole.[1] While performance practitioners repeatedly highlight the importance of rhythm within their practices, it is also easy to see how it can go unnoticed or unnamed.

The etymology of rhythm

Before moving forward with this discussion, it is worth taking a moment to examine some of the parallels between how rhythm was addressed in ancient Greek writings and the ways it has come to be applied within more contemporary contexts of acting and performance practice. While there are many elements that contribute to our understandings of rhythm in acting and performance, it is important to acknowledge that many of these are linked (explicitly and implicitly) to classical notions of rhythm, music and movement.

The term 'rhythm' comes from the Greek *rythmós* (ρυθμός). Derived from the word *rhein* (ρέω) meaning 'to flow', *rythmós* can be defined literally as a 'particular manner of flowing' (Benveniste 1971:286). Linguist Émile Benveniste suggested that the earliest known references to *rythmós* could be found in the works of Ionian lyric poets and scholars from the seventh century BC. These writers used *rythmós* to refer to a specific category of form or *schema* (σχῆμα). Yet, where in ancient Greece the term *schema* implied a fixed or static form, *rythmós* was used to describe something more transient:

> form in the instant that it is assumed by what is moving, mobile and fluid, the form of that which does not have organic consistency; it fits the pattern of a fluid element, of a letter arbitrarily shaped, of a robe which one arranges at one's will, of a particular state of character or mood. It is the form as improvised, momentary, changeable. (Benveniste 1971:285–6)

It is in this sense that dramatists and poets, including Aeschylus and Euripides, used *rythmós* to describe the 'impression' one has of an individual's disposition, mood, attitude or character. Early atomic theorists, including Democritus, also used this term to describe the way an object was formed from the 'characteristic arrangement' of its parts (Benveniste 1971:283). In these texts, *rythmós* related predominantly to a spatial configuration or mood, generally described as fluid and momentary. It is worth noting the contrast between these spatial qualities of physicality and changeability, and today's predominant understanding of rhythm as a temporal structure or form of musical sound. The concept of a 'rhythmic space' or 'rhythmic motion' may at first appear to be metaphoric – rhythm commonly understood as relating primarily to qualities of sound and time. However, if we look back to these early descriptions we see that this distinction can be easily dissolved or even reversed – temporal rhythm in fact being an analogy drawn from spatial rhythm or physical motion.

In looking to 'post-Socratic' theories of rhythm, which emerged in the fourth century BC, we can observe that it was only in this later period that *rythmós* came to be applied more specifically to the organizational properties and temporal aspects of music, poetry and dance. This trend is marked clearly in the works of scholars including Plato, Aristotle and Aristoxenus. In their writings, we see *rythmós* adopted as a structural device, whereby musical notes, spoken syllables and physical movements could be variously arranged into combinations of long and short units, formed into patterns and arranged into compositions. Emphasizing its bound nature, Plato defined *rythmós* as '*kineseos taxis*' (ordering of movement) (*Laws* sec. 665). This he saw as a gift 'given by the Muses … to assist us. For with most of us our condition is such that we have lost all sense of measure (άμετρος [a-metrical]), and are lacking in grace' (*Timaeus* sec. 47). A more technical understanding of *rythmós* was set out by Aristoxenus, who has been credited as the founder of musicology.[2] His aesthetic theories drew strongly on geometry, considering rhythm through the dimensions of space. Previously, scholars had been concerned with reducing music to a set of physical and mathematical properties. Aristoxenus was, however, primarily interested in the dynamic relationships between sounds, the ways they related to and informed one another. One of his most important contributions to our understanding of rhythm in performance is the notion that each musical part is defined, not by its individual characteristics, but by what it *does*, what it contributes to a composition as an organic whole. Similar to Plato, Aristoxenus defined *rythmós* as 'ordered movement', 'a dynamic species of form, signifying the internal structure of a moving thing' (Aristoxenus translated in Rowell 1979:68). In both Aristoxenus and Plato's writings, *rythmós* often took on the characteristics of a verb; it was something done to movement, to sound or to time itself. It was attributed with the capacity to control, discipline and shape the movements of the body, emotions and the soul. Through the act of bringing 'order', *rythmós* was also seen as cultivating forms of insight and knowledge, transferable to other fields such as philosophy, ethics, aesthetics and the sciences. Aristotle brought attention to the compositional nature of spoken prose. He identified *rythmós* as a device that had 'migrated' from poetry to prose, with the distinction that, in the case of prose, 'speech must have rhythm, but not metre; otherwise it will be a poem' (1991:230). Aristotle claimed that if spoken language is overly metrical, then it is distracting and unconvincing, seeming to be artificial. However, without any rhythm to bind the language together, speech risks becoming chaotic and unintelligible: 'for what is unbounded is unpleasant and unrecognisable' (1991:230). The relationship between rhythm and metre will be discussed in more detail later in this book (Chapter 5), but for now it is worth noting that for Aristotle, metres were not seen as distinct from rhythm, but as a 'species of rhythms (μόρια τῶν ῥυθμῶν)' (*Poetics* 1448b:20–2). While on the one hand, Aristotle sought cohesion and clarity through measurement and numbers, he also encouraged a quality of complexity, seeking to avoid obvious and predictable forms of repetition and metered form. As with Plato and Aristoxenus, Aristotle highlighted rhythm's capacity to control and give 'order' to what would otherwise be 'unbounded' and, therefore, 'unpleasant'. Through the arrangement of long and short durations and their numeric ratios, what was raw material and unformed matter was given boundaries and definition of shape.

Many conceptions of rhythm in music, poetry and prose maintain strong ties to these post-Socratic frameworks. As such, rhythm is often seen as a system for structuring actions and sounds into units, groupings and patterns to which meanings and organizational properties can be ascribed. In these models, rhythm is also often arranged systematically and hierarchically built on the basis of a series of regular beats, pulses, syllables, units or poetic feet, which can be grouped and organized into various patterns of music or poetic composition. Writing in 1962 on the use of rhythm in theatre direction, Lael Woodbury defined rhythm as 'a pattern imposed on stimuli, a recurrent alternation of thesis and arsis, or, in art, a regular recurrence of like features in a composition' (1962:23). As with many definitions, it is the imposition of regularity and repetition which is emphasized here. Similar understandings were also expressed clearly in Stanislavski's attempt to define rhythm as 'a combination of moments of every possible duration which divide the time we call a bar into a variety of parts' ([1938] 2008:466). Evoking Platonic descriptions of rhythm as a 'bound' quality of motion and time, director Richard Boleslavsky offered a definition of rhythm as 'the orderly, measurable changes of all the different elements comprised in a work of art' ([1933] 1987:112). A definition given more recently by theatre director John Martin further emphasizes the principles of organization and repetition, stating: 'Rhythm is the division of silence and stillness into organized and repeatable units' (2004:82).

Yet, it is perhaps in the performance theories of Patrice Pavis that we encounter the clearest example of rhythm as a systematized structuring of time. Here he defines rhythm as 'the linking of physical actions according to a precise schema' with these referring to 'a rhythming of time within a defined duration' (2003:149). For Pavis, rhythm describes a fixed and stable element of performance. It marks out the durations and forms within which the performers find their own qualities of timing and flow.

While such models form the basis of a large proportion of the general usage of the term 'rhythm' today, it is worth noting that references to earlier (pre-Socratic) notions of *rythmós* have, and continue to populate many areas of performance discourse, gaining popularity also within fields of philosophy and poetry (Michon 2011). Clear examples of this can be found within many contemporary performance practices. Here we often see rhythm used as a way of describing the 'character' or the disposition of a role, as well as the application of rhythm as an expression of the dramaturgical 'arrangement' of a performance. In these instances, significance is given to both the spatial and the temporal aspects of rhythm, as well as to the fluid/malleable qualities of a performance. These rhythmic aspects can also be noted in many forms of acting practice, particularly where the emphasis lies on the vital, spontaneous and subjective. Writing about the movement of actors in the mid-nineteenth century, François Delsarte stated: 'Rhythm is that which asserts, it is the form of movement, it is vital' (Shawn 1954:55). This vitalist conception of rhythm persists in the language of more recent theatre scholarship, with Mel Gordon proposing that rhythm 'springs from a specific individual activity' (Gordon 1988:196) and Bella Merlin defining rhythm as 'the intensity with which you execute [an action]' (Merlin 2007:139). In these examples rhythm is something that arises from physical action, being dynamic and momentary, while also having a sense of existing in both space and time. The physical dimensions of rhythm and its sense of shape are important aspects in many understandings of rhythm in performance. Eugenio Barba describes the 'actor or dancer' as 's/he who knows how to carve time. Concretely: s/he carves time in rhythm, dilating or contracting her actions' (Barba and Savarese 2006:241). Referring to ways rhythm is formed through changes in physical motions through space, Janet Goodridge defines rhythm as 'a patterned energy-flow of action, marked in the body by varied stress and directional change' (1999:43). As with earlier definitions of *rythmós*, it is more the spatial, rather than the temporal characteristics of rhythm, which are highlighted by these descriptions.

Within today's performance discourses we can observe the continued presence of this broad range of perspectives. While there are many instances of rhythm taking on a highly structured quality of containment and order, there are equally numerous contexts in which the spontaneity and momentary nature of rhythm is given emphasis and description. The key principle that continues to find voice in contemporary performance practice is the active characteristic of rhythm: the sense of agency or action attributed to rhythm.

Productive categories of rhythm

Writing about musicality in theatre practices, David Roesner suggests that to gain a better understanding of rhythm in this field we should look 'at rhythm as a *productive* category that influences training, acting, directing, designing and devising processes' (2014:41, italics in original). Here the emphasis is not so much on what rhythm *is*, but on the ways it is used and approached within performance practices themselves. Instead of examining rhythm as an aesthetic object or perceptual phenomenon, it is useful to ask what can we *do* with it and what it can *do* to us within this field. Amongst rhythm's productive roles in acting and performance, we can list its use as a tool for the following:

- accessing specific qualities of expression and mood
- communicating with an audience
- building ensemble

- developing an individual and shared performance language
- establishing expressive territories

There are many crossovers between these categories, and clearly other areas in which rhythm has and is applied within performance. For now though, this list will offer a useful starting point from which to begin considering rhythm as a productive ingredient of performance.

Qualities of expression, mood and meaning

The use of rhythm as a means of tapping into and directing particular energetic/emotional qualities or meanings is a tool that has been used both explicitly and implicitly in a wide range of twentieth-century approaches to acting, including those of Stanislavski, Meyerhold, Copeau and Grotowski. However, this is by no means a modern concept. Links between qualities of rhythm and descriptions of mood and character can be found within the studies of music, poetry and dance, dating back to ancient Greece.[3] Table 1.1 presents some of the characteristics and moods associated with different Greek metres.

While such a formalist approach to classifying and attributing character to rhythm may seem overly simplistic, rhythm's capacity to affect the mood of a performance and convey meaning to audiences is a principle that continues to be acknowledged today. Voice practitioner

Table 1.1 Characteristics of Greek metres

Iambus	Short–long	Masculine, aggressive, energized
Trochee	Long–short	Feminine, graceful, calm
Dactyl	Long–long–short	Grave, serious, solemn
Anapaest	Short–short–long	Simple march, sense of advance, moderate temper
Cretic/Peon	Long–short–long	Excitement and foolishness or terrifying and pitiable
Ionian	Long–long–short–short	Violent agitation or profound depression

Note: based on Laban 1980:123.

Cicely Berry identifies the centrality of rhythm as a source of meaning in performance:

> For the writer, the essence of the meaning is locked in the rhythm – whether smooth or broken, it is in the length of the phrases and how they knock against each other – be it Shakespeare or Rudkin, Jonson or Pinter, Massinger or Beckett. Meaning is rhythm, rhythm is meaning. (Berry 2013:17)

Equally, the physical rhythms of movement and space have been identified as key mechanisms for establishing mood and meaning in performance. Writing about the rhythm and timing of movement in dance, Janet Goodridge notes: 'Frequent, irregularly recurring pauses may have an uncertain or hesitant effect, or if the recurrence is regular, pauses in the movement may contribute to a more relaxed, calm mood' (1999:152).

A large part of how the audience reads a performance comes down to the structure and flow of its rhythms. These can be intentionally manipulated as in Goodridge's example of generating a hesitant or relaxed 'effect', but often these qualities can and do occur unintentionally, without the performers necessarily being conscious of their use of rhythm on stage. A performance can be seen as having a fluid continuity and or a clear sense of rhythmic development. Or we may feel a sense of unease due to the flow being disrupted or the timing of the performance seeming to lack synchronicity – the rhythm said to be 'out'.

Observing the movements of his actors, director Jacques Copeau noticed a distinction between 'two types of action'. The first he called 'discontinuous'. This seemed 'intentional, artificial, theatrical'. The second type was described as 'continuous', giving the impression of 'portentousness and inner sincerity, real life and power' (1990:34). For Copeau, a key obstacle to 'sincere' acting was a performer's inability to enact 'continuous actions' or to 'follow-through' with an action. Describing this quality of gesture, he wrote 'to be silent, to listen, to answer, to remain motionless, to start a gesture, follow through with it, come back to motionless and silence, with all the shadings and half-tones that these actions imply' (1970:222).

Copeau observed that developing continuity of movement and qualities of slowness was seen to establish a condition for the actor to play more powerfully and sincerely. Yet, this relationship was also observed from another perspective. The sincerity of the performers was seen to produce a quality of continuity in their actions. Here, clarity of thought was reflected in clarity of movement, framed by stillness. Copeau noted that inhabiting an action with calmness and power brought with it a sense of certainty and a quality of being 'natural'. Not in the sense of being naturalistic but of having a 'feeling' that appeared 'true' (Copeau 1990:33–4) what might be described as a sense of authenticity.

These notions of sincerity and the link between actions and a psychological state were to a large extent inspired by Stanislavski's own interests in psychophysical theories of movement and emotion. In rhythm, Stanislavski saw a psychophysical tool that could be used by performers to access emotions and generate complex characters. Working with different rhythmic qualities and tempos of movement, Stanislavski exploited the interrelationship between performers' 'external' movement qualities and their 'internal' dynamics, including the rhythms of thoughts, emotions and intentions. These approaches drew on Stanislavski's own observations as a director and actor, as well as reflecting the contemporary scientific theories of his time such as those of Theodule Ribot and Wilhelm Wundt. In his research, Wundt identified a direct relationship between rhythm and emotion, with these seen as existing within a continuum.

The feeling of rhythm is distinguished from an emotion only by the small intensity of its moving effect on the subject, which is what gives 'emotion' its name. And even this distinction is by no means fixed, for when the feelings produced by rhythmic impressions become somewhat more intense ... the feeling of rhythm becomes in fact emotions. (Wundt 1897:186–7)

The influence and application of these theories will be discussed in more detail in Part Three, while the links between rhythm and altered states of consciousness will be given specific attention in Part Four of this book.

Connecting with an audience

Another role often attributed to rhythm is that it provides a direct link between the performer/performance and the audience. Meyerhold spoke of the need for 'a *pattern of movement* on stage to transform the spectator into a vigilant observer' (1991:56). Similarly, Jacques Lecoq noted: 'The theatrical communion between the audience and the author through the intermediary of the actor is a rhythmical agreement' (2006:88). Here rhythm forms a meeting point, a site of communion and empathy, a shared experience which often transcends the use of a specific performance language or aesthetic.

Describing his experience of Grotowski's production, *Akropolis* in 1968, Peter Brook observed 'Something in me was disturbed, aroused like in jazz, but what beats in jazz is a limited part of one's organism. In a much more complete way, something began to beat until I had a physical feeling of contact with the performers' (2009:15). Brook suggests that it was 'an understanding of certain rhythms' that allowed these performers to break through the barrier of 'rational communication' and access something deeper. In the hands of a skilled actor, rhythm is described as surpassing the limits of music or words, of communing with its audience through a direct language that speaks to the very core of their organism.

Equally, the rhythms of a performance can also be blamed for disengaging an audience, for dulling their attention or putting them to sleep. Theatre director Eugenio Barba describes:

> One kind of fluidity is continuous alternation, variation, breath, which protects the individual tonic, melodic profile of every action. Another kind of fluidity becomes monotony and has the consistency of concentrated milk. This latter fluidity does not keep the spectator's attention alert, it puts it to sleep. (Barba and Savarese 2006:241–2)

Finding the right quality of rhythm is a significant part of any performance making process. While it is difficult to define what it is that constitutes the 'right' or 'wrong' rhythm for a performance, as observers and performers we often have an intuitive sense of when this is realized, and perhaps a stronger sense of when it is not. Without clarity of rhythm, a performance can be difficult and potentially impossible to follow or access. To a certain extent, it is the rhythm that sustains and directs the audience's attention. It gives emphasis to some moments over others and establishes a sense of progression and anticipation that helps the focus to move from one event to the next, or between multiple events.

Many directors refer to the need for a certain tempo or pace in a production. When the tempo is 'wrong', we might say that a performance is lagging or being rushed. Disturbing the flow of a production, this can produce a sense of incongruity between the elements of a performance. For an audience this might also bring about a sense of lethargy or awkwardness, a sense of being disengaged and separated from the performance material. However, it would be wrong to assume that the 'right' tempo for a performance is always the most comfortable or familiar one. There are many instances when an irregular pace or patterning is used intentionally to promote a sense of unease, intensification or emotional detachment. Bertolt Brecht, for example, encouraged the use of unconventional tempos in the delivery of some of his texts and often intentionally drew on irregular rhythmic forms within his writings. These approaches will be discussed further in Chapter 12.

Building ensemble

Rhythm's capacity to generate unity and a sense of camaraderie within a group is another aspect often drawn upon within performance and training. This is an attribute that has been observed across a range of contexts. We can note examples of this in the sense of a common or shared rhythm observed in social interactions and gatherings. Similar forms of rhythmic cohesion have also been identified in exchanges between parents and infants, as well as in the qualities of camaraderie and *communitas* which form through organized rhythmic activities such as military marching, manual labour, ritualized chanting and movement (McNeill 1995; Feldman 2007; Malloch and Trevarthen 2008). Actor trainer Phillip Zarrilli discusses the way a group, who train together over an extended period, forms an energetic/perceptual link based on a shared sense of rhythm:

One of the most important things to emerge in the psychophysical process of breathing/moving/training together is a sense of how the tempo-rhythm appropriate to the exercise becomes manifest and 'forms' an energetic/perceptual link to others in this space between as the exercise is being performed. (2013:374)

Zarrilli explains that through the repetition of daily training, the 'appropriate' rhythm for each task/action emerges. Here rhythm is seen to be relational, forming in moments of interaction, existing in the spaces between performers as well as in the spaces, stillness and silence between their actions. Through the process of moving together a link is formed: a 'dynamic coupling of movements' (2013:374). Overtime, the group learns to 'tune into' this sense of a shared rhythm – a type of rhythmic entrainment in which no single individual is leading or directing the group. This is not an imposed sense of rhythm, but rather an emergent form of mutual synchronization. These aspects will be discussed in more detail in Parts Four and Five of this book (see Glossary for a more detailed explanation of entrainment).

This notion of an 'ensemble rhythm' also raises some ethical questions regarding the relationship between the rhythms of individual performers and the emergent rhythms of the group. From my experience of performing within and training a number of ensembles, I have observed a range of responses to the process of subordinating or surrendering to a group rhythm. Some performers feel empowered by a sense of shared rhythm – their actions being supported and enhanced in a way by their connection with the group. Yet there are others who shrink from the thought of losing their personal identity or sense of agency, feeling that in giving over rhythmic autonomy they are also surrendering their creative control and will.[4] With this in mind, it is interesting to reflect on how Stanislavski viewed an actor's capacity to 'tune' into and work with the ensemble's rhythm as paramount to a successful production. Meyerhold on the other hand was openly critical of this aspect of the Moscow Art Theatre's (MAT) work, stating: 'Once everything became subordinated to "the ensemble", the creativity of every actor was stilled' ([1913] 1991:33).

Understanding rhythm's capacity to generate unity or independence within a training process or production is a valuable tool for any director, educator or performer. Part of this is about understanding when and what types of control it is useful for the performer to give over to the group. It is also very useful for performers to learn how to inhabit an ensemble rhythm while remaining attentive to their individual rhythms, maintaining a sense of their own presence within the group. These principles will be discussed in more detail in Chapters 6, 8 and 11.

Rhythm as territory

While performers often think of rhythm as something that they make, it can be equally useful to consider the ways that rhythm makes us, or at least the territories that we inhabit. As stated by Gilles Deleuze and Félix Guattari: 'Territorialization is an act of rhythm' (1988:346). Often this occurs unconsciously. We establish patterns of behaviour and idiosyncrasies that help to mark a space of familiarity just as an animal distinguishes its territory through a process of demarcation. Describing this tendency in children, Deleuze and Guattari noted: 'A child comforts itself in the dark or claps its hands or invents a way of walking, adapting it to the cracks in the side-walk, or chants 'Fort-Da' … Tra la la' (Deleuze and Guattari 1988:330).

Rhythm establishes the boundaries of when/where one thing ends and another begins; it creates spaces and identifies these spaces. This is done through qualities of expression and the differences that form between these. We express our'selves' and establish our territories through our qualities of rhythm and the musicality that informs our actions.

Performance is one of the ways we mark out a space, a time, a sense of shared or fragmented identity through rhythm. A change in rhythm can mark the beginning or the end of a performance; it can also indicate where one scene, event, phase, theme, character, action or thought concludes and another begins.

The performance maker Robert Wilson provides a clear example of how rhythmic territories can affect not only the succession of events but also the way we relate to simultaneous rhythms occurring on stage. Describing Wilson's intentional use of isolated rather than unified rhythms within his performances (leading up to the mid-1980s), Erika Fischer-Lichte writes:

> Each system of theatrical elements followed its own rhythm: the lighting changed in the fraction of a second while the performers moved in slow motion. Voices, sounds, music, and tones became interwoven into a sound collage which produced its very own rhythm. Rhythm de-hierarchized the elements, and made them appear in isolation. It established a separate temporal structure for each one, which differed perceptibly from each other. In this sense, the spectators experienced different temporalities simultaneously. Their

perception was de-synchronized and became sensitized to each individual effect of the various performance elements. (2008:134)

A disruptive, desynchronous use of rhythm is identified here. Wilson exploits rhythm's power to establish distinct perceptual territories, which the audience can shift between and interpret as entities in their own right, rather than parts of a compositional whole. Yet, even where such approaches seek to fracture the rhythmic ecology, the performance remains a container for the synthesis of these elements, a location in which meaning is formed through the ways the audience relates one rhythm to another (through harmonious agreement or oppositional contrast) and forms their own sense of composition from these diverse elements. In this sense, even isolation can be seen as a form of relationship – even a cacophony produces a composition, be that a disturbing or fragmented one.

The idea of rhythmic territory can also be applied to the ways we think about constructing a character. In their work on a role, actors may start by embodying a collection of rhythmic qualities: a rhythm of walking or gesturing, a characteristic pace, a way of structuring sentences, pauses, durations and shifts of attention, rapid or sustained thoughts, shallow or deep breathing, regular or irregular patterns of movement. We can observe the sense that each individual has their own unique rhythm by which they can be identified and distinguished. Often we can recognize who someone is even from a distance simply by the sound or movement of their walk, long before we see their face. Stanislavski described his own default rhythm as that of a 'camel' or 'ox' (1952:134) and strove to break away from what he saw as its 'dead' rhythmic quality. Yet there are many instances in which we see actors exploiting their unique personal rhythmicities, thus establishing their 'trademark' quality. Discussing the role of tempo in performance, Patrice Pavis identifies the ways that 'actors mark their enunciation of text and a role with their own stamp and internal tempo'. Pavis analyses this by examining the individuality of how performer use: 'pauses, silences, and interruptions in the action, as well as mechanisms used to slow things down or speed them up: vocal delivery, movement, changes in tempo in relation to the cultural norm or a previously adopted system' (Pavis 2003:157).

Tapping into an individual's rhythm can also be seen as a means of embodying their identity. Aristotle spoke of musicians, dancers and poets as artists who imitate rhythms, suggesting that the actor 'by the rhythms of his attitudes, may represent men's characters, as well as what they do and suffer' (*Poetics*, i). Performer Karen Christopher describes how she often uses recordings of other people as a basis for generating performance material. Playing the late comedian, Lenny Bruce in one production, she explains how working with his rhythm offered her a simple and direct way to approach this role:

> he was very combative in the way that he talked and he had quite a particular kind of rhythm in his voice. So it was very easy for me to learn his lines because they were in this rhythm and all I had to do was remember the rhythm. (Interview with author, February 2016)

Here rhythm acts as a 'placard' that signifies the identity, or terrain of the character. Christopher describes this as a process of 'referral, not imitation (Schmidt 2009 cited in Cull 2012:198). She points to Lenny Bruce through his rhythms, evoking a sense of the territory he once occupied.

Pavis also indicates the ways a performer's rhythmic qualities or their tempo are often read in relationship to an established sense of normality, or a 'previously adopted system'. Choosing to work within or against these adopted frameworks strongly affects how a performance or an individual within a performance is identified. When does a character or a production conform to their expected rhythms and when do they break or challenge these?

All performance to some extent is 'tied to the conceptualization of time that it shares with its audience' (Shepherd 2006:91). As such, the rhythmic expression and organization of time within a performance depends on the interaction between the established temporal norms/ frameworks of a culture/audience and those generated and expressed by the performance. The ways time is enacted and portrayed within performance can be seen as a way of negotiating, confirming or contradicting an audience's 'assumptions about time' (Shepherd 2006:93). Challenging or promoting these temporalities is a further means by which rhythm is used as a way of establishing the territory of a performance. Through the use of shared or distinct rhythms a performance territorializes a time/space that can encompass the performers and audience alike or establish independent temporalities, which may exist in parallel or contrasting relationships.

Development of a performance language

As has been observed in the previous examples, how some performance makers use rhythm, the compositional choices they make and the shared rhythmic awareness they acquire through experience and training contribute strongly to the development of their performance aesthetic and the ways this is experienced by performers as well as audiences.

In characterizing the work of particular practitioners or companies, the dominance or lack of certain rhythmic elements is of particular significance. Observing the ways a performance generates its own rhythmic aesthetic, or identity, we can examine the strong presence of regular or irregular patterns, the sense of continuity or fragmentation, the propensity or lack of polyrhythm and the dominant pace or tempo, amongst other rhythmic elements that help define the quality or style of a performance. These aspects may contribute strongly to our overall sense of a production, as well as to an ongoing aesthetic that is carried through the work of a particular company or individual. For example, in the work of Meyerhold, Roesner observes the use of 'drastic and abrupt changes in rhythm as a trademark of his musicality', contributing to Meyerhold's aesthetic of 'the grotesque' (2014:89). While the repeated use of particular rhythmic qualities or motifs will often establish a sense of the characteristics or style of a performance, even the decision to continuously vary one's use of rhythm, can in itself, contribute to the formation of a particular sensibility – an aesthetic of unpredictable rhythmicities or irregularities.

It is also important to note the link made by Pavis regarding our reading of tempo in relation to a 'cultural norm' or 'adopted system'. As audience members, our expectations of rhythm are strongly affected by the rhythmic customs of our culture (Goodridge 1999:74). Our sense of a performance being fast or slow is affected by our expectations and the performance tempos that are most familiar to us. Lee Strasberg recounts the initial challenge of being unfamiliar with the tempo of a Japanese Noh Drama:

It was so slow that you almost push forward. You want to make it faster. Your muscles push to get the actors going. Instead as it goes on they become even slower, and by the very fact that it becomes slower and slower, before you know it you are completely caught up; whereas if it goes in the way you first wanted it to go, you would remain on the outside as an onlooker. (1965:244–5)

As with the formation of a *group rhythm*, different forms of actor training can also shape an ensemble's rhythmic aesthetics. Emphasis given to rhythm in training and rehearsals can be seen as a means of enculturating a particular relationship to time, a way of preparing the actor so that when it comes time to perform they have a sense of what is and is not rhythmically 'appropriate' within the context of this particular ensemble, production or cultural setting. How an actor trains and the discourse used in training contribute strongly to a *sense of rhythm*, by both revealing instinctual capacities and by shaping and refining a sense of what is *appropriate* or *right* in that performance context.

Reflections

While our understandings of rhythm are to some extent formed by ideas and concepts, much of how we comprehend rhythm in this field is the result of practical and embodied knowledge. This is possibly the reason why when we come to explain rhythm in words we often become tongue tied. Viewing rhythm as a productive act through which we create performance shifts us away from the concept of rhythm as an object or thing to be studied and establishes a sense of rhythm as a process through which performance is generated. Through an enquiry into the ways rhythm is used for creating qualities, characters, ensembles, shared and exclusive territories as well as a direct engagement with an audience, the performer/performance maker is offered a valuable collection of tools.

From my experiences as a performer and teacher, approaching rhythm as a creative territory can be an important step in learning to work *with*, as distinct from working *on* or *to* rhythm. The (far too common) experience of performers feeling threatened, oppressed or simply confused by rhythm seems often to be the result of individuals trying to understand and control rhythm before they have given themselves time and permission to experience and play with it. There is a certain irony to writing this in a book, but I think the principle still holds. Instead of attempting to reduce rhythm to a set of definitions, this book offers up a collection of ways in which rhythm is approached and worked with. This includes some of the ideas, metaphors and associations attributed to rhythm, as well as the practical means by which performers have looked to develop rhythmic qualities within their work. Before this book exams a number of specific practices in more detail, the next chapter will address some of the common metaphors and principles applied to rhythm in this field, as well as the ways these have been shaped by practical and cultural understandings over the last century.

2
AN EPOCH OF RHYTHM
NOW AND THEN

At a conference held in London in April 2016, titled *Rhythm as Pattern and Variation*, Pascal Michon in his keynote presentation reflected on the fact that studies of rhythmic phenomena and the use of rhythm as an operating concept have become increasingly prevalent and embedded in many paradigms of thought and practice. He observed a growing interest in rhythm that began in the 1990s, as seen in the arts as well as the human and social sciences.

> Whereas 30 year ago, rhythmic studies were very few, and confined to sociology, economics, philosophy, musicology and poetics. They both multiplied and then spread in new disciplines. And for the past twenty years, rhythmic research has been developing in psychiatry, psychoanalysis, cognitive science. ... It emerged in anthropology, history, geography, urbanism. We saw it rising in linguistics and communication science ... Management and education science. ... To make it short, we are witnessing a quite remarkable blooming of studies on rhythm, or [studies] using rhythm as a tool. (2016)

This 'blooming' of interest and discourse is reminiscent of an earlier wave of attention given to rhythm, which emerged in Europe, Russia and North America a century earlier, spanning a period from the 1890s to the 1940s. Attempting a survey of rhythm studies in 1913, experimental psychologist Christian Ruckmich wrote:

> The experimental investigation of the perception of rhythm has grown so extensive and, at the same time, so indefinite in scope that

the writing of an introduction which shall be adequate to the general problem is now altogether out of the question. (1913:305–6)

Ruckmich explained that the subject of rhythm had been carried over into many fields. In the field of psychology alone, he noted how researchers were investigating the role of rhythm in 'attention, work, fatigue, temporal estimation, affection and melody', and in other areas, rhythm was being frequently mentioned in regard to 'music, literature, biology, geology, gymnastics, physiology and pedagogy' (1913:305–6). This historic period also corresponds with the emergence of new fields of science including experimental psychology and psychophysics, along with a growing fascination with human physicality and well-being in general. This cultural phenomenon of physical idealism came to identify the human body as a location and signifier of personal, cultural and racial identity and as a basis for self-cultivation and morality. Woven through these philosophies was the notion of rhythm as being the product of our biological make-up, arising from the fundamental structures and processes of the body which were also seen as the basis of racial and gender identities. These body-based cultural movements gave rise to many new forms of collective physical exercise including forms of 'gymnastics' and 'drill', which gained popularity throughout Europe and North America. Alongside this, growing industrialization led to a focus on the efficiency and rhythmicity of labour and production. In this way, the metaphors of clocks, tools, devices and mechanics came to populate many discussions of rhythm. It was from within this cultural milieu that a strong focus on rhythm and physical expression took hold across a wide range of art forms, including modern dance, poetic and dramatic writing, and the staging of theatrical productions. Of key significance to this book are the ways that rhythm came to form a central principle within many of the influential approaches to directing and actor training which emerged during this period.

Reflecting on his formative experiences as a young director in Kiev in the 1920s, director Grigori Kozintsev offered an insightful explanation of the key position given to rhythm in this 'epoch's' search for new forms of expression:

All our experiments, all these quests for new forms came because we had an intense feeling of an extraordinary renewal of life. We felt profoundly the impossibility of translating this sensation of the marvel and importance of events through the means offered by the art of the past, which to our eyes appeared dreadfully academic and naturalist. Thus in our production of *Marriage* [1922], a predominant place was accorded to rhythm, because the novelty of things was initially felt not in themes or characters, but in rhythm. *Art had changed rhythm.* The new epoch had found its first expression in rhythm. ... If this atmosphere is forgotten or neglected, then the art of those times remains incomprehensible. (1987:100, italics in original)

It is important to understand the ways that many of the attributes, aesthetics and vocabularies we apply to rhythm today are linked to the cultural and scientific movements that ran through this period of history. While some of these principles may appear dated and problematic when viewed from an early twenty-first-century perspective, many of these understandings and approaches nonetheless continue to inform the ways practitioners and audiences interpret and apply rhythm within performance.

Natural and organic rhythm

Looking to the vitalist philosophies of the mid-nineteenth century and classical models of aesthetic beauty, pedagogues such as François Delsarte, Ruth Saint-Denis, Émile Jaques-Dalcroze, Rudolf Laban, Sergei Volkonski and Isadora Duncan drew strongly on notions of 'natural' and 'organic rhythm' in their theories and teachings. With its association with the biology of the body and the phases of nature, rhythm offered these practitioners a means of tapping into qualities of performance that were seen to be essential and universal. Viewed as an organic phenomenon, rhythm was also seen to offer unity, both in regard to achieving harmonious relationships amongst the elements of a production and as a means of facilitating the unity of the performer, bringing together their mind, body and spirit. Approaching performance from this holistic perspective, these practitioners and theorists located and described the rhythms of physical movement and language as part of a wider field of natural phenomena.

While many practitioners have made reference to concepts of natural and organic rhythm in their work, Laban was one of the few to define this concept directly. Laban's understanding of natural rhythm encompassed the 'formation, growth and movement' of living and non-living things, including humans, crystals, plants and animals, with all of these 'subject to the same spatial laws of tension' (1920:32). He stated: "Every phenomenon [*Erscheinung*], including those which are perceived by us as immobile, is in constant motion, and it is therefore intrinsically rhythmic' ([1921] 2014:76). These rhythms were said to be caused by natural 'forces' (*teilspannungen*), which generated structures and qualities of regularity, symmetry, harmony and proportionate flow. Laban categorized these 'natural' movement qualities with the term *eurhythmy*,[1] taken from ancient Greek (ευρυθμία), meaning 'a beautiful or harmonious flow of movement [*wohlfluss*] perceivable through our senses' (2014:75). *Eurhythmy* emerged both from the characteristics of a movement and from our perception of it.

When our organs of perception perceive these chains of events with a spatial arrangement, speed, amplitude and intensity appropriate to their perceptivity, we gain the impression of something ordered, comprehensible and clear, and then we speak of understanding, beauty, positive flow – eurhythmy. (Laban 2014:76)

Central to Laban's understanding of 'natural rhythm' was the sense of an alternation of tension and relaxation or effort and recovery. Reflecting a fundamental pattern found throughout nature, these oppositional processes and their rhythmicity were seen to allow for the flow of energy and life (Hodgson 2016:187).

Notions of organic and living rhythm also had a strong influence on theatre aesthetics and the progressive approaches to actor training being pioneered in Russia and France. In their search for qualities of sincerity and spontaneity, directors including Stanislavski, Copeau and Vakhtangov looked to the motion of the body as a basis for rhythmic understanding. Searching for a practical means of approaching these qualities through rhythm, these and many other theatre directors at this time initially turned to Dalcroze's methods of training musical rhythm through physical movements (Chapters 3 and 4), as well as other dance and gymnastic techniques including those of Isadora Duncan and Rudolf Bode.

Meyerhold also drew strongly on musical rhythm as a means of coordinating actions as part of his training and performances, using live and recorded music to help his performers find 'greater precision' in their acting (Meyerhold 1998:161).

Pianist Lev Arnshtam explained that despite common misconceptions, this was not intended as an oppressive form of control, but rather as a way of bringing a quality of freedom and flow to the action: 'Free movement of the actor should be laid out over an entire musical phrase. ... Not to be subordinate to the music, but to breathe it, to live it – repeatedly he reiterated this' (Leach 1993:113). This association between breath and the vitality of rhythm in performance is prevalent throughout many systems of actor training, informing approaches to movement, text and dramaturgy. In the rhythms of the breath we encounter a sense of alternation and repetition as well as spontaneous fluctuation and variation. As a physiological process the breath relates to both the voice and the muscularity of the performer's movements. It has a liminal quality, being a process that often occurs intuitively, while being available to conscious control. For Copeau, breath was also seen as a means of bringing the actor into contact with the intentions of the playwright, viewing this as a key tool for approaching initial work on a dramatic text.

What remains in the director's mind, and not only in his mind but within reach of his senses, so to speak, is a feeling of general rhythm – the breathing, as it were, of the work which is to emerge into life. (Copeau cited in Rudlin 1986:31)

The 'breathing' of a text was seen as a way of tapping into some trace of the author, a way in which the actor could access a text's hidden meaning and communicate this to an audience.

Many of these concepts have been carried through into contemporary approaches to performance, with terms such as 'natural', 'organic', 'authentic' and 'real' rhythm, continuing to be used and evolved within current practices, along with metaphors of 'breath', 'pulse' and 'flow' which have found voice throughout the work of a broad range of practitioners.

In a text written in 1972, Eugenio Barba presents a clear example of how these concepts have been inherited within more recent studio practices. Describing the process of developing Odin Teatret's approach to training, Barba explains:

> In the first period of our existence all the actors did the same exercises together in a common collective rhythm. Then we realized that the rhythm varied for each individual. Some have a faster vital rhythm, others a slower one. We began to talk about organic rhythm, not in the sense of a regular beat but of variation, pulsation like that of our heart as shown by a cardiogram. This perpetual variation, however minute, revealed the existence of a wave of organic reactions which engaged the entire body. Training could only be individual. (1972:52)

It is worth observing the ways Barba distinguishes organic rhythm from the 'regular beat' and 'common collective rhythm' of the group. Here organicity is associated strongly with the notion of the individual, each possessing their own distinct and personal rhythmicity. We can also note how 'organic' is located in opposition to the more structured and fixed aspects of rhythm, such as beat or metre. This is a theme that will be developed in more detail later in this chapter and throughout the following sections of this book.

Mechanical and deterministic rhythmic aesthetics

Organic rhythm is often defined in contrast to the mechanic rhythms of machines and industrialized labour. Where organic rhythms have often been characterized by variety, spontaneity, responsiveness and vitality, taking on associations with primitive, archaic, ecstatic, irrational and feminine aspects (Roach 1993:163; Koritz 2001:554), mechanical rhythms have been described as deterministic, repetitious, ordered and segmented, being associated with musical concepts of metre and tempo, along with rational thinking and mass production (Roach 1993:161; Cowan 2007:231). Speaking in 1968, on the distinction between the 'organic' and 'mechanic' in performance, Jerzy Grotowski stated:

> The 'Organic' springs from a seed within which exists [as] a 'cause' which is allowed to be acted out. It is something that comes, as

it were from the roots, and is permitted to exist – not something springing from some conceptual model and duplicated blueprints going toward some final point. ([1978] 1989:7)

Grotowski highlighted the product-driven quality of the mechanical. This was something pre-determined, based on an existing model or concept. In contrast, the organic sprung to life from its own source, growing from its 'seed' or 'roots'. It was given permission to exist rather than being produced or reproduced in accordance with a design or 'blueprint'.

Although many practitioners have, and continue to use the word 'mechanical' to suggest an undesirable or superficial quality of performance, the presence of mechanistic elements, metaphors and aesthetics have also been widely exploited in this field. Alongside the growing popularity of vitalist philosophies and aesthetics in the early twentieth century, research into the 'mechanics' of rhythm also gained currency within the growing industrial cultures of Russia, Europe and North America. Writing at the end of the nineteenth century the German theorist Karl Bücher stressed that the technical advances of his time would not have been possible without the ever-increasing division and organization of labour. The rapid increase in productivity witnessed at this time was seen to be orchestrated and facilitated by rhythm, operating at every level, from the rhythms of the worker's bodies to the structure and management of the industrial corporations (Golston 2008:22). Bücher commented that this 'Machine Age' was fuelled by an economy based in 'the rhythmisization [rhythmisierung] of affordable work' (Bücher 1899:379 as translated in Golston 2008:22). Through rhythm, physical labour could be analysed and automatized, regulating movement and rest patterns, as well as the systematic timing of the factory as a whole. Here rhythm enabled the workforce to function both socially and productively, just as 'lubrication keeps the machine going' (Bücher cited in Golston 2008:22).

At the beginning of the twentieth century, the 'management' theories of the American scientist Frederick Taylor also gained popularity, inspiring others, like Alexi Gastev in Russia, to set up laboratories for researching movement efficiency and productivity. In England, Laban collaborated with management consultant Fredrick Lawrence to develop a new system of 'effort analysis' and published an instructional booklet on this theme (Laban and Lawrence 1942). Metaphors of production and capital were also extended into the 'economy of attention', where rhythm was seen as an evolutionary tool that allowed mental acts to become automatic, facilitating the expansion and productivity of perception and memory (Miner 1903:20). These repetitive aspects of rhythm were not only seen to make work more easeful and efficient but were also identified as providing aesthetic pleasure.

In line with these ideas, Stanislavski suggested that through repetition, '[w]hat is difficult becomes habitual, what is habitual becomes easy, what is easy is beautiful' (Stanislavski and Rumyantsev 1998:63). Highlighting the aesthetic qualities of physical labour, Meyerhold also drew directly from theories of movement efficiency adopted in Russian factories. In 1909 he wrote:

> If we observe a skilled worker in action, we notice the following in his movements: (1) an absence of superfluous, unproductive movements; (2) rhythm; (3) the correct position of the body's centre of gravity; stability. Movements based on these principles are distinguished by their dance-like qualities. (1991:98)

Here, rhythmic efficiency and organization were translated from the economic productivity of the factory into an aesthetic productivity that could be realized by an actor through the organization of their own physicality. Here the body became an 'instrument', a 'tool', a 'raw material' that could be worked on, used and shaped.

Weaving together the biological and the mechanical, along with the processes of evolution and automation, a new artistic philosophy based on rhythmic efficiency and determinism sprung into being. Inspired by these ideas, directors and theoreticians turned to the machine and the factory as a model for building new approaches and aesthetics. Jean D'Udine, a disciple of Dalcroze, spoke of the human as a 'dynamo' through which rhythmic impulses pass. Every emotion had a corresponding body movement, and it was through that movement that a work of art could express or 'transfer' emotions. To achieve this effectively all movement and sound had to be rhythmicized and segmentary, forming a *'series of consecutive propositions'* (D'Udine 1912:100, italics in original[2]). Effectively fusing the organic and mechanic, D'Udine described art as *'the transmission of emotion by means of stylised natural rhythm'* (1912:220). These theories synthesized elements of Delsarte's system of semiotics with the music-movement approaches disseminated by Dalcroze, forming a basis for new approaches to acting, film-editing and dance. In early twentieth-century theatre and actor training practices, rhythm took on the metaphors of a mechanism, tool, instrument, sign, trap and trigger. And as a technology, the attributes of rhythm were exploited in accessing, achieving and actualising the aspects of a performer's work that otherwise seemed to evade direct engagement or manipulation. Following this trend, directors including Boris Ferdinandov, Lev Kuleshov and Stanislavski adopted metronomes and flashing stage lights as a means of shaping their actors' rhythms and luring emotions.[3] Through the mechanics of rhythm, actors were seen to be able to unify their audience to a synchronized ticking pulse. Explaining this, Stanislavski described the actor as a 'large clock', moving confidently, beating every minute and second, and resounding loudly on the hour. In contrast, the audience were all 'small clocks', with weak beats, their rhythms of minutes and seconds, barely audible. The task of the actors was to bring the rhythms of the audience into sync through the rhythm of their performance, 'getting all the small clocks in unison and rhythm with their hours' (Stanislavski 1986a:230).

Rhythm as a universal language

What unites both bodies of thought (mechanic and organic) is their insistence on the universality of their principles. At the beginning of the twentieth century, many in the arts and sciences considered rhythm and music to be innate and universal aspects of humanity, Dalcroze stating, 'We have all of us muscles, reason, and volition; consequently, we are all equal before Rhythm' (Jaques-Dalcroze 1967:119). Following a similar line of thought, Michael Chekhov stated:

It is impossible not to perceive rhythm. The thought might not reach the audience but rhythmical action definitely will. ... Rhythm is a universal language. Thought is a hight-falutin curlicue ... But everybody understands rhythm. (Chekhov 1926 cited in Kirillov 2015:54)

As in earlier examples, the 'universal language of rhythm' is what allowed for a direct communication between performer and audience, circumventing the difficulty of expressing thoughts (Chapter 1).

Attempting to codify the expression of rhythm, Delsarte had gone as far as formulating a 'rhythmic law of gesture' – a system of semiotics, which he linked to the fundamental 'rules' of nature. His 'law of rhythm' related the movements of the body to the swinging motions of a pendulum, stating: 'the rhythm of a gesture is proportional to the mass to be moved' (Delaumosne et al. 1893:62). Applying this law directly and systematically to the use of gesture within acting, he instructed actors that their torso and legs should for the most part remain calm, while their upper body and the eyes were free to move at a much faster pace. Later, drawing from Delsarte's laws of movement, Isadora Duncan stated: 'All movement on earth is governed by the law of gravitation, by attraction and repulsion, resistance and yielding; it is that which makes up the rhythm of dance' (1928:90). While attempts to associate aesthetic principles with natural laws may appear to be a dated approach, a number of contemporary theories in both the arts and sciences continue to emphasize links between gravitational effects and the rhythmic aesthetics of timing in movement and music (Rosenbaum 1998; Maffei et al. 2015). As perhaps the most widespread of all the rhythmic principles, the effect of gravity on physical movement can be observed equally across all cultures and contexts (on the surface of earth at least). Relating the principles of physical motion to those of music, Mine Doğantan-Dack has recently proposed that

> we experience and make sense of musical phenomena by metaphorically mapping the concepts derived from our bodily experience of the physical world onto music. Accordingly, listeners hear the unfolding musical events as shaped by the action of certain musical forces that behave similarly to the forces behind our movements in the physical world such as gravity and inertia. (Doğantan-Dack 2006:450)

Here the basis of our rhythmic aesthetics is seen to be formed (or informed) by our experiences of movement in the world around us and in the ways our bodies move through space and time. Linking our sense of rhythm to our bodily processes, others have also argued that our experience of rhythm is based primarily on neurological systems that group and characterize certain patterns of experience within a hierarchical or a metric/non-metric framework (Sakai et al. 1999). Such theories suggest that our experiences of rhythm are predominantly shaped by perceptual constraints and the ways these lead to the organization of our experiences at a neurobiological level.[4]

The influence of yogic philosophy on the work of Stanislavski offers another perspective on the universality of rhythm in acting. We encounter an example of this in his instructions to his students, suggesting that by mastering the rhythms of their body they would come to realize

> the whole universe exists in accordance with a definite rhythm and that you as a fraction of it, are also subject to the laws of rhythm. Having grasped the fact that not only yourself, but everything that lives, is an eternally moving rhythmic entity, you, the actor and teacher, will yourself, as you analyse a part, be able to detect the rhythm of every part and every performance as a whole. (1967:44)

Adopting this metaphysical viewpoint, Stanislavski located the actor within a rhythmic universe in which the 'laws of rhythm' were seen to guide everything from the microcosm of their internal bodily rhythms to the macrocosm of planetary orbits. From this perspective, rhythm governed not only the creation of art and performance but also the patterning of everyday social interactions and the natural world. Subject to these 'laws', the performer or director was given the task of sensitizing themselves to these rhythms and using this awareness to help 'detect' the 'correct' rhythm or tempo for their actions, character and production as a whole. Rhythm in this sense was seen to be the key to creating a holistic theatre in which the elements of movement, music, text, lighting and scenography could be synthesized into a singular art form.

Authenticity and real time

As with notions of organic, natural and universal, the claiming of 'real' or 'authentic', in relationship to time or rhythm, is another common framework adopted by acting and performance practitioners. This often has the effect of prioritizing certain qualities and forms of relationship over others. The naming of a particular rhythm as being more (or less) 'realistic' can be seen as a brash means of justifying one's aesthetic choices by linking them to a seemingly preordained or universally shared system of behaviour. Writing from a materialist feminist perspective, Lauren Love problematizes the ways that Stanislavski's principles of 'organic' and 'natural' acting have come to be normalized within the context of American actor training, effectively privileging certain understandings of emotion and the body over others: 'By way of its reliance on Freudian precepts, the organic method encourages unquestioning obedience to dominant, normalized modes of thinking and doing' (Love 2002:280). Growing from Stanislavski's emphasis on organicity within the development of his acting 'system', many 'naturalistic' approaches to performance have claimed qualities of 'psychological truthfulness' and 'authenticity', along with the notion of a 'fourth wall', as fundamental conventions of 'truthful acting'. As Love points out, many approaches claiming the status of 'natural' and 'organic' also encourage the performer to prioritize their psychological experience over their awareness of physicality and movement on stage and seek to avoid aspects of 'artifice' or direct address within performance. By adopting such terms, a practice establishes a framework by which a certain view of reality, truth and authenticity is defined and promoted within performance and training.

Describing the use of improvisation as a common film-making technique used to 'bring life to a scene', actor trainer and director John Abbott explains: 'If the actors are skilful in the technique, then the film can really take on the textures and rhythms of reality' (Abbott 2007). We once again encounter the ways in which rhythm is used to evoke a quality of 'realness' and 'sincerity' in acting. Here, improvisation acts as a tool for accessing a particular quality of spontaneity that is seen to bring with it a sense of truth and vitality. Working outside the restricted forms of a script, the performer is encouraged to tap into a more personal and sincere quality of rhythm. In this case, the actor's 'technique' involves learning to recognize and draw on these spontaneous rhythmic qualities in their improvisation and find ways of bringing these into their later performances when working to a script or fixed series of actions.

This aesthetic delineation between qualities of rhythm being real or unreal is not exclusive to naturalistic or modernist approaches to performance. The use of the term 'real-time' within live art and postdramatic theatre carries its own collection of assumptions and value judgements which prioritize certain rhythms over others. As a performance device, 'real-time' is sometimes used to describe a quality of temporal immediacy as experienced through elements such as 'live streaming' or the use of ear pieces worn by performers in 'verbatim theatre'. Laura Cull explains how various approaches to performance and live art have looked to differentiate themselves from 'dramatic' and 'theatrical' approaches to time in performance, by emphasizing the concept of a 'shared time' between performers and spectators (Cull 2012:184–5). This differentiation has been encouraged by the dismantling of conventional approaches to organizing time in performance, including 'curtains, intervals, scenes, acts, plot and narrative, or in terms of audience expectation with respect to standard lengths of performance, speeds of speech and movement, and dominant desires for particular rhythms of action and entertainment' (Cull 2012:195). While attempting to move away from the conventions of naturalistic acting, these approaches have, in their own ways, sought many of the same rhythmic qualities aspired to by modernist theatre practitioners of the early twentieth century, seeking the ephemeral, immediate and experiential qualities of rhythm in their performance events.

In reflecting on the use of these rhythmic qualities in performance, it is important to recognize the ways that terminologies can be used to promote dominant ideologies and establish notions of otherness or cultural segregation. In regard to rhythm, this may take the form of a blanket application of certain cultural forms (i.e. the use of Western musical models as a basis for studies of rhythmic perception) or claims as to the universality of a reading of certain rhythms as being truthful, authentic or real. In using these terms, it is worth considering when such descriptions clarify a desired quality of rhythm in performance and when they further the establishment of cultural stereotypes or preconceptions of normality.

What is significant here are the ways in which we attribute meaning to rhythm. This book is not in a position to prove or disprove any of these theories. Nor is it my aim to distinguish which meanings are rooted in our biology and which are the results of cultural associations. What interests me here is the ease with which rhythm takes on metaphorical associations relating to nature, daily life and or technology. Often, unintentionally and unconsciously, we absorb and apply our experiences of rhythm in the world around us and in our own bodies to the ways we engage with and create performance. This application of experience takes place both in regard to the language we apply to rhythm and in regard to our aesthetic sense of these forms. Whether or not we identify this as a cultural bias or a universal principle, it is worth considering rhythm's strong capacity to provoke associations in performers and audiences and the ways it effectively draws on and merges with other systems of behaviour and meaning. The way rhythm evokes in us a sense of life and feelings of familiarity, or on other occasions produces a sense of coldness or detachment, is another of the creative roles it plays in performance. Learning to be aware of these associations and the ways they are formed is a critical aspect of understanding how rhythm operates within this field.

A new epoch of rhythm

Finding ourselves in the midst of yet another supposed 'epoch of rhythm', it is worth reflecting on the metaphors and models of thinking that have dominated the discourses of rhythm in performance in more recent times. To what extent do we still draw from classical and modernist concepts of rhythm and what other frameworks have we developed or adopted from different fields or contexts of practice and theory?

Within contemporary actor training we can observe the enduring nature of many classical and modernist notions of rhythm, with concepts of determinism and universality still being widely adopted. The Alba Emoting Technique, developed by neuroscientist Susana Bloch, provides a clear example of links between early approaches to actor training and modern science. This approach has been described as a 'psychophysical tool [which] allows the actor to explore and experience the physiological changes that occur during emotion'. As the outline for an introductory workshop run by Jessica Beck explains:

> During the workshops you will identify six basic emotional patterns (anger, tenderness, fear, sexual love, joy and sadness) along with their corresponding bodily responses, which are universal to all human beings. By reproducing three aspects of these patterns – breathing, posture and facial expression – an actor can access and express genuine, organic emotion at will. The group will then explore

using these patterns to engage with text, objects and fellow actors. (SCUDD 2013)

In this description from 2013, we can observe clear echoes of the semiotics of Delsarte and Volkonski, as well as notions of 'sincere' and organic expression aspired to by Stanislavski and Copeau. While the science underpinning Alba Emoting may be more contemporary, the terminology and ethos remain closely linked to the discourses of early twentieth-century theatre and acting. This illustrates the degree to which these models have become embedded within this field, remaining relatively stable despite considerable changes in aesthetics and scientific understandings.

In reflecting on other aspects of rhythm in performance, we can note the influence that new forms of technology (from tape/video editing to digital audio-visual design) have had on the ways we describe durations and transitions in performance. Words such as 'cross-fade', 'jump-cut', 'loop' and 'decay' have found their place within acting and performance vocabularies. Playing a central role in the development of performance art and 'happenings' in the 1950s, John Cage and Merce Cunningham's work also marks a clear shift in perspectives regarding the rhythms of performance. Rather than talking about the structure of movement and sound in terms of musical phrases, beats or tempo, Cage and Cunningham often worked to the precise timing of a stopwatch, introducing the concept of 'time brackets'.[5] Cunningham remarked: 'What is rhythm? You are going to say that rhythm is simply giving a metric beat? Rhythm is what anybody does in terms of physical action, it's what anybody does in time' (1980 cited in Goodridge 1999:42). With the growth of performance art in the 1960s came a clear shift in perspectives on rhythm. Erika Fischer-Lichte suggests that previously, rhythm – although central to the creation of performance – had been subordinate to the 'dominant logic of the plot'. In the development of performance art, 'rhythm became the guiding, superior, if not sole principle of organizing and structuring time' (Fischer-Lichte 2008:133).

As design elements within performance become increasingly sophisticated, we can also observe the ways that elements such as lighting, sound, video and set design can often influence and even shape the rhythms of a performance. Rather than simply following the rhythm set out by the script or the dramatic action on stage, these elements contribute their own sense of structure and momentum to a production. Director and designer Leo Warner identifies lighting as one of the main rhythmic elements of performance. Commenting on the work of lighting designer, Paule Constable, Warner states: 'She just has an instinct for it. And [she] lends a rhythm, lends a pace, a visual pace of things which is the fundamental binding agent of the entire production in a lot of cases' (interview with author, February 2016).

The growing use of projection and video design within live productions has also had a strong impact on the ways rhythm and temporality are being approached. Describing his work with projection for opera and dance productions, Warner comments on the challenges of marrying the technological elements of his designs with the 'organic rhythms of live performance'.

> In order to make it work in a live environment and to match the organic rhythms of live performance – which of course change to some extent from night to night, but change massively over the course of a rehearsal process – we have to build things in an extremely modular, and therefore arhythmical way. So we build [what are] almost like packets of data, packets of visual information that we then need to weave back into a rhythmical context, using cues – effectively. And for the most part, when there is a live orchestra those cues will be run or called by a stage manager reading off a score but also following the conductor. So building a kind of organic fluid element into something which is effectively quite linear and rigid, to the point where it feels like it's not linear or rigid anymore, but it's part of the fabric of a rhythmical construction, is one of the most difficult and specific skills that we use all the time. (Interview with author, 2016)

In this work we can observe techniques of deconstructing and compartmentalizing the 'fluid' rhythms of the performance. Beginning with breaking a sequence up into individual 'packets', the job of the designer and technician is then to 'weave' these back into the flow of a live 'organic' process. Warner is often looking to bring together, rather than isolate, the organic from the mechanical (or technological) elements of performance. Yet, this does not necessarily mean that these elements always share the same rhythms. While often there is an intention to create a seamless unity between the live and the mediated elements of the performance – with video, lighting and projected material woven into the dramatic rhythms – on other occasions qualities of 'rhythmical juxtaposition', 'counterpoint' and 'dovetailing' are intentionally sought. What is critical here is not that all the parts necessarily merge into one, but that they are able to effectively speak with and inform one another. It might be worth distinguishing between the unintentional desynchronization of elements (i.e. projections anticipating or lagging behind live performances or vice versa) and the intentional use of polyrhythmic approaches (i.e. the layering or separating of elements through the use of distinct rhythms, as observed in the work of Robert Wilson). Where the former may impede an audience's engagement with a performance, the latter looks to enhance and intensify this experience. As with many of the examples found throughout this chapter, the separation of the 'organic' from 'mechanical' is not always clear-cut. Approaching the fluid qualities of 'organic rhythm' can often involve the paradoxical use of arhythmical processes.

Opening out to the wider field of contemporary performance theories, we can observe the ways that new scientific models (such as quantum, chaos, fractal and systems theories), as well as philosophical models (including immanence, temporality and plurality), have come to challenge many of the dualistic, structural and system-based concepts that dominated previous rhythmic paradigms (Michon 2011; Cull 2012; Ikoniadou 2014). As part of these trends, we encounter the growing use of terms and concepts such as 'emergence', 'entrainment', 'synchronicity', 'simultaneity', 'time-frames' and 'non-hierarchic', all of which have an influence on the ways rhythm is considered and approached within performance practices. These concepts will be discussed in more detail within the individual case studies found throughout the remainder of this book.

Reflections

While the terms we use to describe rhythm continue to evolve and take on new metaphors and associations, there remain various streams of thought which feed into the ways rhythm is approached and discussed within this field. Reflecting back on the etymology of rhythm discussed previously (Chapter 1) we observe that many notions of organic rhythm reveal close associations with earlier usages of *rythmós*. These metaphors emphasize the fluid, variable and individualistic nature of rhythm. While mechanical metaphors applied to rhythm often focus on aspects of order, structure, containment, segmentation and mathematical symmetry, linking rhythm to post-Socratic and Platonic theories. Such metaphors offer us a language for describing various qualities of rhythm, but ultimately it is also important to understand their limitations. There are many instances of 'organic' or 'natural' processes whose qualities are highly structured and ordered. Similarly, mechanical processes and the actions of manual labour can take on qualities of fluidity and dynamism often associated with nature.

As we go on to examine the approaches and application of rhythm in the work of various performers, performance makers and educators from the beginning of the twentieth century to the present day, it is worth observing the ways these different currents run through and inform one another within these practices. At times one understanding or approach may dominate, or two or more may run side by side. There are also many instances in which multiple, at times seemingly contradictory, notions of rhythm can be seen to form a single stream, coalescing a range of rhythmic notions and frameworks into a single body of work.

PART TWO

STANISLAVSKI

ON RHYTHM

Few other theatre practitioners present us with as broad and detailed an understanding of rhythm as Stanislavski.[1] In part, this is due to the immense body of documentation and scholarship that surrounds his work. But more than that, it was his sustained interest in rhythm and the significant ways in which he applied rhythm to the processes of directing and actor training, that make his work central to our understanding of rhythm within acting practices.

Stanislavski identified rhythm as 'the foundation of the whole of our art' (1967:93) and on another occasion declared, 'You cannot master the method of physical actions if you do not master rhythm' (Toporkov 1998:170). Commenting on the significance of rhythm in the work of Stanislavski, Meyerhold defended his own use of rhythm, arguing, 'I would like to see a genuine director who disregards the importance of rhythm. Say that to Stanislavski and he would throw you right out the door' ([1931] 1998:162). Yet despite the significance that Stanislavski himself attributed to rhythm, few theorists have discussed or examined this aspect of his work in much depth or rigour.[2] Instead, many have focused primarily on his interests in attention, 'affective memory' and other psychological aspects, while neglecting the foundational role and influence of rhythm and music in the development of Stanislavski's approaches to acting and directing (Carnicke and Rosen 2013:121–2).

Far from being a peripheral theme, rhythm became a central mechanism underpinning Stanislavski's pursuit of psychophysical techniques and the building of complexity within his training and directing. Rhythm offered him a means of approaching complex relationships between what were seen as the internal and external aspects of performance, providing a practical framework through which he could explore the unified, as well as contrapuntal relationship of these aspects. From his earliest experiences of performance to his last work on physical actions, his interest in rhythm remained central to his work. The following chapter will discuss the various ways that Stanislavski approached rhythm in his work as both an educator and director and highlight the key sources of influence that shaped these practices.

3

TAPPING EMOTIONS

THE INS AND OUTS OF TEMPO-RHYTHM

An aspiring opera singer

As a young man in his early twenties, Stanislavski would rush home enthusiastically from work to receive singing lessons from the renowned opera singer and professor, Fyodor Komissarzhevsky. Stanislavski was fascinated by the complexity of rhythmic awareness that was required of opera singers, their ability to 'unite several completely different rhythms in the same breath' (1952:134). As part of their lessons, Stanislavski and his teacher engaged the services of a pianist skilled in improvisation. With the accompaniment of live music, they undertook their own practical research over a series of evenings in which they 'lived, moved and sat in rhythm' (1952:134). In these formative experiences, we can observe the template for what would later become the basis of his work on 'tempo-rhythm' and 'physical actions'. Stanislavski had dreamed of working as Komissarzhevsky's assistant in a rhythm class at the Moscow Conservatoire teaching 'physical rhythm' to opera singers, and had aspired to become a professional opera singer himself. Though he never made a profession from singing, Stanislavski did realize his ambition of teaching opera singers; the last phase of his career focused predominantly on teaching and directing opera and music-based productions.[1]

Looking back on his initial experiments with rhythm, Stanislavski observed that where he had begun from a 'primitive' use of 'outward rhythm', over time he came to discover a 'more true and fundamental inner rhythm' ([1921] 1952:134). The beginnings of these developments are reflected in his descriptions of working on the operetta *Lili* in 1886:

This was real success in a way, for if I did imitate, it was not the stage I imitated, but life. Feeling the national characteristic of the part, I found it easy to justify the tempo and the rhythm of my movements and my speech. This was no longer tempo for the sake of tempo, rhythm for the sake of rhythm, but this was an inner rhythm. (1952:125)

Here we can note Stanislavski's growing interest in experiences of 'daily life' (rather than theatrical conventions) as sources of inspiration for acting, as well as the primary role that he attributed to inner 'justification', particularly in relationship to external physical characteristics and actions. These discoveries marked an important turning point in Stanislavski's approach to his own acting and the formation of the 'system' of acting which he went on to teach to others. Yet what is perhaps more critical to the development of an understanding of rhythm in acting are the ways Stanislavski's approach to outer and inner rhythm evolved over the latter parts of his career. During this period, he increasingly focused on the relationship between these elements rather than their distinctions. We can see in this a shift from a binary understanding of external versus internal approaches, to a way of working with rhythm as part of a continuum that connected inner experience to outward expression.

Psychophysical techniques

Seeking to better comprehend what he saw as a relationship between the inner (psycho) and outer (physical) aspects of acting, Stanislavski drew from the emerging scientific fields of psychophysics and experimental psychology, along with elements of yogic philosophy and practice, which arrived in Russia with the growing interest in occultism and spiritualism at the turn of the century (Zarrilli 2007:637). These concepts offered Stanislavski a framework for describing the ways in which a performer's 'inner' and 'outer' actions related to one another. Writing between 1936 and 1937, he described the interconnected relationship of these aspects:

the link between body and mind is unbreakable. The life of the first engenders the life of the second and vice versa. In each physical action, if not purely mechanical but brought to life from within, there is inner action, experiencing. ([1936-7] 2010:57)

Here it is the performer's inner 'life' that is seen to distinguish the 'organic' and 'living' from purely 'mechanical' 'external' form. Even as Stanislavski progressed into his later work on physical actions and active analysis, he continued to emphasize the importance of sensing what he described as the 'life of the human spirit'. Having developed an 'unbroken line of physical actions', the performers were encouraged to listen and begin to sense the formation of another 'parallel' line forming inside of themselves.

The more often I sense these two lines coming together, the more I believe the psychophysical truth of that state of mind, the more I am aware of the two levels. The life of the human body is good soil in which to plant a seed that will grow into the life of the human spirit. (2010:58)

These observations also reflected many of the scientific theories of Stanislavski's time, including those of Theodule Ribot and Ivan Pavlov. Stanislavski drew on these theories, both as inspiration and as a means of constructing a theoretical framework to support his existing theories of acting practices. Regarding rhythm, Ribot had proposed that '"transformation" of pleasure into pain, and pain into pleasure, is only the translation into the order of affective psychology of the fundamental rhythm of life' ([1914] 2006:56). In this way the rhythms of sound and movement were understood to 'act directly on the organism, and indirectly on the vital functions' (Ribot 2006:104). Theories such as these proposed an analogous relationship between the experience of emotion and the internal rhythms of the human body. In this way, emotions were also seen to be directly (and indirectly) influenced by the rhythms perceived in music and in one's environment. Explicit references to these and other similar theories can be found throughout much of Stanislavski's later writings on tempo-rhythm and physical action.

Venturing into the world of clinical psychology, Stanislavski discussed the distinction between the rhythms of attention in a normal individual and those of a 'madman':

A normal man's attention can be graphically represented by -.-.-.- and so on. That is to say, in a normal man there is always an interval of rest and reflection between each moment of attention. During these intervals the work of attention, no doubt, goes on, but it does not emerge from the layers of subconsciousness to the active brain centres which relay the action to the outside world....

In a mentally unbalanced man the rhythm of attention is broken. The intervals of rest, or the time during which attention relays its vibrations to the subconscious mind and gathers them together afresh, as the lungs inhale the air so that life can go on, do not exist so far as he is concerned. For him only the dashes exist, or in other words, attention, attention, and again attention, and his words pour out of his mouth without conveying any meaning to normal people. The speech of a madman is just a dance of thought without rhythm or control. ([1918–21] 1967:141)

Here Stanislavski lays out a complex description of the rhythmic workings of the conscious and subconscious mind, and the ways these relate not only to an individual's well-being but also to the ways we communicate with one another. A rhythmicity of thought is seen here to correlate with a clarity of mind and a capacity to communicate one's thoughts to another or to an audience.

Stanislavski went on to apply concepts of psychophysical unity directly to the relationship between tempo-rhythm and 'feeling', stating: 'There is an indissoluble link between Tempo-rhythm and feeling, and conversely between feeling and Tempo-rhythm, they are interconnected, interdependent and interactive' (2008:502).

Operating as a tool for actors, tempo-rhythm became a reliable and effective/affective means of approaching emotions and feelings, which were otherwise seen to be unreliable and difficult to access within performance. By establishing a link between the technical elements of rhythm and tempo and the more ambiguous terrain of human feelings and emotions, Stanislavski lays out an accessible framework by which an actor could begin to explore principles of psychophysical unity within the context of training and performance.

Stanislavski's understanding of internal and external rhythms was also strongly influenced by his interest in yoga, and in particular the concept of *prana*. Ramacharaka (Stanislavski's main source of knowledge regarding Hindu philosophy) defined *prana* as:

A universal principle, which principle is the essence of all motion, force or energy, whether manifested in gravitation, electricity, the revolution of the planets and all forms of life. (Ramacharaka [1904] 2007:152)

Stanislavski adopted this term during his work at the First Studio, referring to *prana* as a form of 'vital energy' that could be generated by a performer's 'inner rhythm' and could be directed into the space around the performer in the form of *pranic rays*. These were seen as a form of communicative energy that could pass between fellow performers as well as between a performer and their audience. Combining psychophysical theories with yogic philosophies, Stanislavski also applied the concept of *prana* to explain the ways that rhythm and music could communicate with a listener through the transmission of *pranic rays* (1986b:229). As a framework for understanding the ways that energy was transferred and communicated between performers and within an individual performer, the concept of *prana* was used here as a way of understanding the relationships between movement, emotion, rhythm and thought. Along with the theories of Ribot and Pavlov, these yogic principles helped Stanislavski to locate the biological rhythms, emotions and imagination of the performer within a psychophysical continuum (see Exercise 4 later in this chapter).

While some of Stanislavski's descriptions of inner and outer tempo-rhythm seem to suggest a mechanical or deterministic relationship between rhythm and emotion, with one aspect triggering the other, in practice this relationship appears to be more complex. The actor had the task of bringing this relationship 'to life from within' (2010:57). In this sense the correlation was not seen to be entirely deterministic. The actor's inner experience was not simply the result of a 'mechanical' process triggered by external rhythms. Rather, it involved a more 'organic' relationship, cultivated through the performer's sensitivity and imagination. These processes are hinted at by Stanislavski's earlier reference to the body as 'soil' or 'seeds' for bringing to life the 'human spirit', and in the emphasis he placed on imagination and sensitization within these training practices.

Eurhythmics and polyrhythm

As well as turning to yoga for inspiration, Stanislavski also looked to a number of other practices for guidance in developing approaches to rhythm in acting. One of the main sources that Stanislavski drew from directly was the pedagogical approach developed by Émile Jaques-Dalcroze. As an instructor in music and harmony, Dalcroze had originally set out to address the rhythmic difficulties and lack of coordination that he observed in his students. He identified these as being primarily the result of 'insufficient coordination between the mental picture of a movement and its performance by the body' (Jaques-Dalcroze 1912:28). In response to this insufficiency, he developed a collection of movement exercises designed to promote greater muscular and nervous coordination, and sensitivity to rhythm and tempo. This work grew into a pedagogical approach to movement and music training, which developed vast popularity throughout Europe, Russia and the United States and came to be known as eurhythmics.

Whereas traditionally, European rhythm and movement training had focused on single lines of rhythmic phrasing or the unified movements of large groups, eurhythmics consciously encouraged a capacity for polyrhythmic music and movement. Dalcroze saw the development of rhythmic independence between the limbs as a crucial part of musical training, in terms of learning both to enact and to effectively perceive polyrhythm. He explained that for a student to develop a sense of simultaneous rhythm:

> it is indispensable that he should be made to execute, by means of different limbs, movements representing different durations of time. … One limb, for example, may execute the quarter-values of the time, another the eighths, a third the sixteenths – or, by way of variation, one the quarter-values, another the same in syncopation – and by this means he will attain the necessary facility in dissociating movement to enable him to practice and observe polyrhythm. (Jaques-Dalcroze 1967:43)

Although this work was principally intended as a musical pedagogy, many theatre and dance practitioners recognized the potential value in this training and sought to apply these methods within their own fields.

Extending beyond the realms of music training, these practices were used for developing muscular coordination, while also being seen as immensely beneficial in aiding the development of concentration and awareness. Adolphe Appia, a theatre designer and theoretician, was one of the first to observe the benefit that this work could have for actors. He wrote that eurhythmics 'accords a natural harmony to the body, which will benefit the purity and flexibility of acting and will give it the sensitivity necessary for any style' (1911 cited in Beacham 1985:156).

In a collaboration that began in 1906 and lasted through to the beginnings of the First World War in 1914, Appia and Dalcroze established a centre for eurhythmics in Hellerau, Germany. Over its relatively short existence the Eurhythmics Studio of Hellerau played host to many key figures of twentieth-century theatre, with Stanislavski amongst them.[2] Following this wave of interest in Dalcroze's teachings, eurhythmics was adopted as part of Stanislavski's actor training programme at the Moscow Art Theatre (MAT) from 1911,[3] with Dalcroze and his students also visiting and demonstrating their work at the Art Theatre in 1912.

Eurhythmics has been cited as forming the basis of Stanislavski's work on outer tempo-rhythm (Rogers 1966:127–30; Benedetti 1982:68), with Stanislavski's interest in layering multiple rhythms within performance also potentially inspired by Dalcroze's own work in this area. While Stanislavski (along with many of his contemporaries) openly drew inspiration from Dalcroze's practices, over time he began to move away from what he saw as the more formal aspects of this training. Copeau and Meyerhold shared similar views regarding the direct application of eurhythmics within acting practices. Copeau, having introduced eurhythmics to his company's training, eventually stopped these sessions feeling that the work was too specialized and idiosyncratic and at risk of dehumanizing the actor (Copeau [1921] 1990:64). Similarly, Meyerhold questioned what he saw as an oversimplification of the relationship between music and movement (both these perspectives will be discussed in more detail in the following chapters). Stanislavski, although less openly critical of eurhythmics, often found this work to be overly 'mechanical', lacking the internal and imaginative aspects that he encourage in his own practices. Looking to address these concerns, he expressed the need for 'inner justification' and a detailed awareness of movement throughout his work with rhythm (Benedetti 1982:68).

Observing his actors undertaking rhythmic hand exercises, Stanislavski exclaimed:

> I don't understand just what you are doing now.... If you are trying to make beautiful movements in space by using your softly curvaceous arms while your imaginations are fast asleep and you don't even know it, then what you are indulging in is empty form. Try to fill it up with something out of your imagination. Give each exercise some purpose of its own. (Stanislavski and Rumyantsev [1922] 1998:7)

Even within the most elementary of technical exercises, he insisted that nothing should be done 'in general' or 'just for the purpose of going through a form' (Stanislavski and Rumyantsev 1998:7). Instead the actor needed to maintain a continuous awareness of the relationship between 'inner' experience and 'outward' expression, and to always seek the imaginative life within their physical actions.

Tempo and rhythm – ins and outs

It is very difficult to identify a single definition of tempo, rhythm or tempo-rhythm that can be applied consistently across all of Stanislavski's work. It might be for this reason that those writing about tempo-rhythm seldom (if ever) offer the same definitions. Each author effectively presents his/her own perspective and set of understandings relating to these terms. There are, however, certain aspects that many of these definitions share. Here I will unpick some of these common threads and explore what ties them together.

Used on its own, tempo is most commonly associated (in Stanislavski's work) with terms such as 'speed', 'pace' and 'rate'. These words deal with quantitative aspects of time, measurable in numbers and units. Linked in this way to the mechanics of clocks and metronomes, tempo has often been associated with an objective sense of time. Definitions of rhythm, on the other hand, include terms such as 'pattern', 'individual', 'action', 'intensity', 'stress', 'effort' and 'accent'. These are more descriptive of the quality of a sound or action, rather than simply being a measurement of speed. Other commonly made assertions regarding rhythm are that it should be perceived from 'within' the performer, with many scholars linking notions of rhythm directly to a performer's sense of 'inner' experience and to concepts of 'organic life' and 'vitality' (see Chapter 2).

In reference to Stanislavski's work at the First Studio,[4] Mel Gordon describes rhythm as being primarily an internal phenomenon, with the 'major difference between Rhythm and Tempo' being 'that the latter derives from the outside environment' (1988:111). Following this logic, he defines tempo as a 'general pace of life that is found in a shared physical or cultural environment', with rhythm seen as arising 'from a specific individual activity', being something that 'varies from person to person' (1988:196). In a similar vein, Rose Whyman has suggested that 'we can think of the tempo (or speed or pace) of the external movement and action or speech, and rhythm as the internal state' (2013:126). Establishing a dichotomy between tempo and rhythm, Whyman then indicates that these aspects are essentially reintegrated through the concept of tempo-rhythm. While these aspects can be approached separately, ultimately Whyman sees these as being 'inextricably bound within the human being' (2013:126). Here Whyman seems to be making reference to Stanislavski's statements cited earlier, regarding the 'indissoluble link between Tempo-rhythm and feeling', these being 'interconnected, interdependent and interactive' (2008:502).

The writings of director and student of Stanislavski, Yevgeny Vakhtangov, offer further insight into the ways rhythm and tempo operated within Stanislavski's practices. Vakhtangov was a student of Stanislavski as well as Meyerhold and had strong involvement in the First Studio before going on to establish his own career as a director. Vakhtangov stated: 'To perceive the rhythm of a character means to understand the role. To find the rhythm of the drama is to find the key to its presentation' (1947:122). In his teaching of rhythm, he emphasized the importance of freedom, lightness and spontaneity and insisted that rhythm 'must have an *inner justification* proceeding from nature' and must follow 'organic and not mechanical laws' (1947:121). Discussing the role of rhythm in actor training, he went on to explain:

> The feeling of rhythm is not only the primitive ability to subordinate one's physical movement to a rhythmic count. The actor must subordinate his whole being, his whole organism to a given rhythm – the movement of his body, of his mind and his feelings. Rhythm must

be perceived from within. Then the physical movement of the body will become subordinated to this rhythm spontaneously. The task of the school consists in training the pupil in this sensitivity to rhythm, and not in teaching him to move rhythmically. (1947:121)

Focusing on an embodied sense of rhythm, Vakhtangov also looked to distinguish his own approaches from what he saw as the 'mechanical' techniques of imposing rhythm from the outside. Commenting on the work of his contemporaries, he observed that often 'actors who study rhythmic gymnastics diligently and successfully become non-rhythmic on stage'. Identifying the discrepancy between the skills acquired through rhythmic gymnastics or dance training and those required by the actor, he noted that an actor having learned to perform 'the most difficult dancing steps moves on the stage in a non-plastic manner' (1947:121). Vakhtangov felt that the cause of these problems lay in the actor's attempt to perform these rhythmic exercises 'correctly', in a technical or mechanical sense, rather than using these exercises as a means of encountering a manifestation of the general 'laws' of rhythm and plasticity.

This 'internal' sense of rhythm, however, did not constitute a closing off from the external world. While rhythm was understood to be rooted in the inner experience of the actor, the performer's timing and pace was linked to their immediate 'circumstances'. A performer or a character may have a 'habitual state' or 'characteristic rhythm'; yet this could, and was often seen to be affected by changes in circumstances, these resulting in an increase or decrease in 'energy'. Vakhtangov described this in terms of tempo and offered the following example:

if I am accustomed to having my dinner in a particular tempo and someone tells me I must be somewhere else in ten minutes without fail, my tempo will change. (1914 cited in Malaev-Babel 2011:186–7)

In line with this, Vakhtangov gave a number of other examples of 'circumstance' that could be used to bring about an increase or decrease in the tempo/energy of an individual's actions. These included a demand from a friend, a bell announcing an imminent train departure or somebody making you cook fried eggs (Malaev-Babel 2011:186–7).

The actor Zygmunt Molik, a member of Grotowski's Laboratory Theatre, made a similar assertion regarding the way an environment could change the rhythmic qualities of a performer:

it's normal, natural, that the way you move is influenced by the circumstances in which you are. And if you are, for example in the middle of a field, full of sun, you must be light; you must do the same action, but like a butterfly. The rhythm depends on the circumstances in which you are. (Molik and Campo 2010:14)

There is a sense in both Vakhtangov and Molik's descriptions that performers need to be sensitive and aware of the ways an environment can influence their tempo and rhythm. While Vakhtangov insisted that ultimately a change in tempo/energy occurs inside the performer through a change of 'inner justification', these changes do not take place in isolation but grow out of a relationship between the inner rhythm of the performer and the affective quality of the circumstances he or she inhabits. Rather than a mechanical description of an imposed external tempo, what we find here is a more ecological understanding of tempo and rhythm. These aspects are seen as elements that interact and influence one another, as with the relationship between an individual and the world around them.

Making reference to Stanislavski's tempo-rhythm, Patrice Pavis offers a distinct perspective on this theme. In his writings on tempo, he emphasizes the changeable and individual nature of this aspect within performance, defining it as 'subjective', 'invisible and internal'. In contrast, he refers to rhythm as 'the sense and direction of time', an aspect that is 'quantifiable', 'objective' and 'external' (2003:156). This definition is informed by a mechanical reading of rhythm. Here, this aspect is viewed primarily as a structural mechanism made up of fixed elements, which an individual performer may realize through a range of tempos. In this sense, adding his or her own qualities to a performance, an actor may extend or shorten the duration of a pause or accelerate or decelerate the pace of an action or piece of text, effectively changing the tempo, of an otherwise consistent rhythmic form. This interpretation correlates closely with the way a musician might approach a musical score. Here the notes may be fixed, but the speed at which a performer plays these notes is open to interpretation and may vary from musician to musician and from one performance to another.

We can observe, that although rhythm may often be associated with inner experiences and subjectivity, and tempo with outer environments and objectivity, these dichotomies are by no means absolute. Even though many forms of music approach tempo as being a relatively stable element, in relationship to which the rhythm may be fluid and variable, there are many instances in which rhythm can equally be presented as a fixed element and the tempo as a variant. Similarly, a performer may choose to focus on an 'external' source of rhythm or tempo, while at other times an 'internal' awareness of either or both these elements might be more useful. There are no clear-cut or definitive rules here, and there seems to be no particular reason why we would need there to be. Rather than valuing internal rhythm over external, or changeable qualities over fixed, it might be more useful to understand performance as taking place in the meeting of these aspects.[5]

From within, each actor brings to the performance their own physical presence; their rhythmic sensibilities, qualities and habits; their thoughts, emotions and understandings; their inner dynamism, imagination, intensity, intentions and impulses; their vitality and inner momentum. Regarding external qualities and stimuli, the performer might choose to work with an awareness of physical form and movement directions; the use of a text or other performance scores/choreographies; or focus on the quality of a space (lighting, sound, size, structure, intensity); a fictional circumstance or the specifics of their environment; the actions of the other actors; the dynamics of the ensemble as a whole; or the presence of the audience. The rhythm and tempo of a performance emerges through the interactions of these aspects. Sometimes these follow one another almost seamlessly. Other times they exist independently or in contrast to one another. While there might be instances where it is effective to use the terms 'tempo' and 'rhythm' as ways of naming and separating out these relationships – given the vast range of interpretations applied to each of these terms – this can often lead to more confusion than lucidity.

It is worth noting that in his own work, Stanislavski offered few concrete definitions of tempo or rhythm, and that as his career progressed he increasingly referred to both rhythm and tempo as being internal and external elements. It is also important to observe that on the few occasions when he did attempt to define these terms, he promptly dismissed these definitions in favour of practical exploration – insisting that his students 'simply play with rhythm', 'enjoying it easily, freely, lightheartedly … playing with it like a toy' (2008:465). Perhaps, more than any definition, these instructions tell us something about how Stanislavski viewed and approached rhythm and tempo within his work.

Tempo-rhythm in training

Although an interest in tempo and rhythm was present throughout Stanislavski's career, the notion of 'tempo-rhythm' as a tool within actor training and rehearsals seems to have only taken form in his later productions and writings. The introduction of this term also coincided with a shift from work that had predominantly been concerned with the actor's 'inner experience' to a practice that centred on 'physical action' and the use of external form. Writing about the changes that took place in Stanislavski's Studio around 1921, Vakhtangov observed:

> Until now, the Studio, true to Stanislavski's teachings, has doggedly aimed for the mastery of inner experience. Now the Studio is entering a period of search for new forms – remaining true to Stanislavski's teachings, which search for expressive forms, and indicate the means to be used to achieve them (breathing, sound, words, phrases, thoughts, gestures, the body, plasticity of movement, rhythm – all these in a special, theatrical sense founded on an internal, natural basis). (1921 cited in Allen 1999:72)

A large part of this development grew from Stanislavski's exploration of rhythm in his work on operas and other musical productions at the Bolshoi Opera Studio (from 1918) and the MAT's Music Studio (from October 1919). The majority of these initial rhythmic training approaches grew out of drill-like exercises derived from Dalcroze and Isadora Duncan's work with movement and music. Overtime these practices evolved into a more integrated approach to actor training, with Stanislavski developing an understanding of tempo-rhythm, 'not as something separate from or ancillary to action, but as a crucial aspect of action itself' (Blair 2008:32).

Jean Benedetti's descriptions of training exercises undertaken in the last phase of Stanislavski's career, between 1935 and 1938, offer a clear perspective on how approaches to tempo-rhythm came to relate to both inner and outer aspects and the ways these were applied more specifically to character development and scene work (1998:80–6). Benedetti divided this work into the following six categories:

1 Outer tempo-rhythms

2 The influence of outer tempo-rhythms on mental states

3 Inner tempo-rhythms

4 The influence of mental states on outer tempo-rhythms

5 Contradictory inner and outer tempo-rhythms

6 Varying tempo-rhythms

The following examples drawn from Benedetti's text as well as other documented sources offer us valuable insight into some of the practical ways that inner and outer tempo-rhythms were approached during this period.

Outer tempo-rhythm exercises

As identified earlier, many of Stanislavski's outer tempo-rhythm exercises came directly from eurhythmics. These practices had already been strongly established as part of the MAT's core training (Rogers 1966:127–30; Benedetti 1982:68). Drawing from this body of work, Stanislavski began his teaching of outer tempo-rhythm by introducing actors to a number of basic musical elements, including note values, tempo measurements, time signatures and rhythmic phrasing. Starting from this technical basis, this work eventually led to the actors exploring the ways that external tempo-rhythms could affect qualities of emotion, imagination and character.

EXERCISE 1: OUTER TEMPO-RHYTHM

Participants began with basic musical exercises designed to help them understand the relationship between the tempo of a regular steady beat and its various rhythmic subdivisions. Dividing into four groups, the first group began by clapping one beat per bar (establishing a stable tempo), the second joined in clapping two beats per bar (double the speed of the first group), the third group then joined, clapping four beats per bar and finally the fourth group, clapping eight beats per bar. Following this, similar rhythms were then explored through walking, with the actors taking note of the different qualities associated with each subdivision of the beat (Benedetti 1998:81–2).

Building on these exercises, participants were instructed to perform tasks (such as passing an object, serving drinks or putting on make-up) at various rhythms over a sustained fixed tempo. Starting with the group working to a single shared rhythm, these tasks would eventually be done with each actor taking on a distinct individual rhythm. Eventually the actors were also free to change their own rhythms while continuing to work in relationship to a shared tempo. Throughout these exercises participants observed the emotions and 'given circumstances' that arose from and were associated with changes in outer tempo-rhythm (Stanislavski 2008:274–281).

To begin with, the tempo was indicated by the ticking of a metronome (or metronomes), yet as the performers began to develop their own sense of timing, these support mechanisms were removed. Working without an external guide, the actors were encouraged to maintain a sense of an 'imaginary metronome' while continuing to perform their actions and interact with each other (Stanislavski 2008: 480).

Here we can see how the concept of a stable tempo provided these actors with an opportunity to explore ways of varying their rhythms while still keeping an awareness of and relationship to an underlying pulse.

Building on these principles, students also performed action sequences to fixed rhythmic scores. These exercises where often set to a specific number of beats, working with various fixed tempos.

EXERCISE 2: MOVEMENT SCORE (STANISLAVSKI)

Benedetti gives the following example of a movement score for training actors:

> Actions (in bars of 4/4). Fix the tempo.
> Pick up a book – 2 beats.
> Open it – 2 beats.
> Read a page – 4 beats.
> Turn the page – 1 beat, read 3 beats
> Stop reading – 1 beat, listen – 3 beats (Benedetti 1998:82)

Sequences such as these were performed at various tempos and in different metres, the actors analysing the experiences that these changes produced. This notion of 'scoring' a physical sequence can be seen in the work of various practitioners including that of Meyerhold and Grotowski.[6]

These exercises offered a clear means by which actors could develop awareness and sensitivity to the pace of a scene (identified here as tempo), as well as the timing and intensity of specific actions within a sequence (rhythm). This 'scoring' of movement also offered actors the opportunity to recognize and break their habitual uses of tempo and rhythm and enabled them to experience the effects that specific rhythmic choices could have on their internal state, associations and emotions. Further, by experiencing how they could share a single tempo while each performing a different rhythm, performers were given the opportunity to discover more complex ways of working as an ensemble.

Inner tempo-rhythm exercises

Having established a basic understanding of outer tempo-rhythm, Stanislavski began to introduce exercises involving rhythmic phenomena found inside the body. These exercises were based on the psychophysical premise that 'our feelings and thoughts ... have a particular Tempo-rhythm, according to the situation we are in' (Benedetti 1998:83).

EXERCISE 3: INNER TEMPO-RHYTHM AND GIVEN CIRCUMSTANCES

Participants in these exercises imagined themselves in a variety of given circumstances. For example, 'a dark night, on an empty street, you hear footsteps approaching' (Benedetti 1998:83). At the same time, they were instructed to observe the ways these 'circumstances' altered their experience of internal biological rhythms including breathing and heart rates. There is a strong similarity between these exercises and those described by Vakhtangov in the previous section, suggesting that many of these exercises were inspired by work undertaken within Stanislavski's earlier studio practices.

While outer tempo-rhythms where described through a collection of technical musical structures and terms, the concept of inner tempo-rhythm often addressed a less tangible and more enigmatic body of phenomena. As discussed earlier, Stanislavski's understanding of 'inner rhythm' was strongly linked with the yogic concept of *prana*, which he referred to as 'vital energy'. Looking at some of the ways Stanislavski worked with *prana* offers a further understanding of his approaches to inner tempo-rhythm.

EXERCISE 4: PRANIC BREATHING

In his lecture notes for the MAT, Stanislavski described rhythmic breathing exercises that could be used as a way of 'receiving' *prana*. Here he instructed that 'in order to receive more prana', one should inhale over six beats of the heart – hold the breath for three beats of the heart – and exhale over six beats (1986b:220). Stanislavski explained that in his opinion, the movement of *prana* was created by 'internal rhythm' and that this could be accessed through a range of exercises (1986b:221). A further example involved the loose swinging of the legs or arms while at the same time raising and lowering the toes or fingers. Other suggestions included observing different qualities of walking and searching for qualities of smoothness and regularity, along with balance and poise (Stanislavski 1986b:220).

Such exercises were used as a way for actors to work with and further generate an inner dynamic or energetic state, which could then be expressed or directed externally to another actor or to the audience. In these ways, *prana* and inner tempo-rhythm provided Stanislavski with valuable links between thought and emotion and a way of relating the imagining/experiencing of a 'given circumstance' and 'emotional state', with the physiology of body rhythms (breath, heartbeat, thought patterns) and vice versa.

Contrasting inner and outer tempo-rhythm

Having opened up the performer's capacity and awareness of the relationship between inner and outer tempo-rhythm, Stanislavski went on to experiment with how these elements could be related to and contrasted with one another. Here he explored ways of generating a sense of conflict or complexity by setting up oppositional and contrapuntal relationships between different layers of tempo-rhythm.

Techniques such as these were also seen as producing a heightened quality of presence in the performer. As Michael Chekhov explained: 'An outer slow tempo can run concurrently with a quicker inner tempo, or vice versa. The effect of two contrasting tempos running simultaneously on the stage unfailingly makes a strong impression on an audience' ([1953] 2002:75).

Despite Stanislavski often referring to these inner and outer aspects as being indissolubly linked, there are many instances in which he looked to separate these out as a way of achieving further complexity or dramatic tension in a character or scene (Stanislavski 2008:479). Actor-singer Pavel Rumyantsev commented that while working with Stanislavski to establish a physical score for his actions, the question arose, 'how to relate the rhythm of external movement to the inner rhythm of feeling'. Stanislavski's response was simple: 'They may coincide or not' (Stanislavski and Rumyantsev 1998:312). Stanislavski explained this concept by suggesting that a character who is resolute and single minded in thought and action should have a single, 'dominant' tempo-rhythm. But in the case of a character whose 'resolution wrestles with doubt' (the example offered by Stanislavski in this instance was Hamlet), then multiple rhythms must be employed, working side by side and in opposition to one another (Stanislavski 2008:479).

As a tool for both the performer and director, this opened up the potential for more layered rhythmic relationships within a single character or across an ensemble, with performers embodying rhythms that might work in opposition to an existing tempo, a dominant character, or an established ensemble rhythm.

EXERCISE 5: CONTRASTING TEMPO-RHYTHMS

As mentioned previously, the polyrhythmic nature of this work may have been influenced by Dalcroze's movement coordination exercises. Examples of polyrhythmic exercises similar to those used in eurhythmics can be found in Stanislavski's lesson plans. In one example, Stanislavski asked his students to synchronize their internal state with the rapid beat of a metronome, while at the same time externally enacting physical actions to slower more sustained 'whole' and 'half note' rhythms. Stanislavski also reversed this relationship, with the students being asked to enact rapid actions in 'eighth', 'sixteenth' and 'thirty-second notes', over a relatively slow tempo (Stanislavski 1986b:288).[7]

Examples of a more psychological approach to contrasting tempo-rhythms can be found in Benedetti's descriptions. Here students are instructed to work within a 'circumstance' that might provoke a set of contradictory behaviours: 'Someone is telling you a very long and very boring story and you are almost jumping with frustration but you remain outwardly polite'. Or you are being interviewed for a part in a play. 'You are tense and nervous but you want to appear relaxed' (Benedetti 1998:85).

While each of the exercises listed here looks to work with contrasting tempo-rhythms, they take different approaches to achieving this. Where the earlier examples look to build a performer's capacity to layer multiple rhythms by working on technical tasks and musical concepts, the emphasis in Benedetti's examples lies in the psychological justification of these contrasting elements established through the use of an imagined circumstance.

Tempo-rhythm in rehearsals

It is important to acknowledge that while many of Stanislavski's theories appear to draw strongly on musical concepts and terms, when we look more closely at his practical application of tempo and rhythm within his rehearsals and notebook entries, a far more flexible and at times poetic set of interpretations emerges. In these descriptions we find many examples in which the term 'rhythm' is used in a less technical and more general sense. At times Stanislavski refers to the rhythm of a scene, an environment or an ensemble, describing what might be understood more technically as the tempo or pace.

Often, rather than looking to distinguish tempo from rhythm, these terms were discussed 'side by side', in conjunction with one another. In his notebooks he described the distinct 'rhythm and tempo' needed in performing Chekhov and Turgenev's plays. Reflecting on his 1909 production of *A Month in the Country*, he explained: 'Chekhov has a slow rhythm and tempo', his plays requiring a high level of attention and focus. In contrast Turgenev has a 'completely different tempo and rhythm', his work requiring a less sustained focus (1986a:350).

Describing the first act of *The Cherry Orchard,* he wrote of the 'rhythm and tempo' brought about by the arrival of Ranyevskaya and other characters:

> [They] give a new tempo and rhythm to the play. This rhythm and tempo is the first pulse, the tuning-fork for the following scene. If any of the participants could just keep their ear open to this tuning-fork and, having taken hold of it, tune their internal temperament and energy, then subsequently their external rhythm and tempo of movement also [would be tuned]. (1986a:349)[8]

Through the metaphor of 'a tuning fork', Stanislavski describes here the way that a key moment within a play can act as a catalyst, establishing the rhythms and tempos of the subsequent scenes. The actor's job is to be open and responsive to these elements of a production, to 'tune' into them in order to find the appropriate tempo and rhythm for each scene and to know the critical reference points within a play which sets out its rhythms. Here, we can observe how instead of using the term 'tone' (as was commonly used during this time to describe the external energetic/emotional quality of a scene), Stanislavski adopts the more technical terms, tempo and rhythm.

Similar uses of the term 'rhythm' can be seen in other descriptions of Stanislavski's rehearsals. While working on a dinner scene for his production of *Dead Souls* (1931), he instructed his actors to work with six different rhythms:

EXERCISE 6: SIX LEVELS OF RHYTHM

Rhythm 1 – Quiet conversations; their voices are low and velvety.

Rhythm 2 – Voices sound a little higher in pitch.

Rhythm 3 – Voices still higher and tempo faster; listeners are beginning to interrupt those talking.

Rhythm 4 – Voices still higher and tempo faster and somewhat broken; listeners no longer pay attention to what is being said but only look to interrupt the speaker.

Rhythm 5 – Most guests talk at the same time; their voices are high-pitched and the tempo of their speech is jumping and syncopated.

Rhythm 6 – highest level of sound and maximum syncopation; no one listens to anyone; each seeks only to be heard. (Toporkov 1998:146–7)

A much broader meaning of rhythm is adopted here, including aspects such as tempo, syncopation, dynamics, pitch, counterpoint and timbre. In this instance, the term 'rhythm' relates to both the individual parts and the emerging energetic state, or group dynamic within the scene. Stanislavski makes no attempt here to separate out these elements and instead clumps them all together under this simple umbrella term.[9]

A further example of Stanislavski's diverse uses of rhythm can be seen in his rehearsals for *The Embezzlers* (1928). During one scene, Stanislavski commented on an actor's stance, stating: 'You are not standing in the correct rhythm!'. The confused actor queried Stanislavski, explaining that he did not understand what he meant by 'rhythm'. In response, Stanislavski explained:

In the corner, there's a mouse. Take a stick, lie in wait for it and kill it as soon as it jumps out. No, that way you will miss it. Watch it closely, closely. As soon as I clap my hand, hit it. Now, you can see, you were too late. Try again … and again. Concentrate and try to make the blow coincide with the clap. Now, you see, your standing in a different rhythm from before. Can you feel the difference? Standing and watch the mouse is one rhythm, watching a tiger creep up on you is another. (Toporkov 1998:62)

Here again rhythm takes on another set of meanings: an intensity, a charged quality of relationship between the actor's intentions and their environment. We get a sense here of Stanislavski's understanding of internal rhythm and *prana*, as a way of describing a performer's 'vital energy' manifested on stage.

Examples of how Stanislavski looked to apply contrasting tempo-rhythms can be seen in his approach to directing the opera *Boris Godunov* (1928). Here the performers were working with a musical composition that was in a slow regulated tempo. Despite the slow tempo of the music, Stanislavski insisted that underpinning the scene was a growing sense of agitation, 'nervous tension' and 'inner turmoil'. He instructed the performers:

The scene is in essence a revolt. You sing in quarter notes but inside you are throbbing in eighth notes or sixteenths. Don't interpret this rhythm externally, in terms of gestures. What you must find is the rhythm of your feelings. It is as if you had a metronome inside you. One move is ready to move on into several accelerated ones; whole notes threaten to break up into thirty-second notes. It is only by combining your rapid inner rhythm with your slow external rhythm that you can transform a quiet scene into a tempestuous one. It is a complex job, but if you can achieve this you will always be at ease on stage. (Stanislavski and Rumyantsev 1998:312)

In this example, we again come across Stanislavski's image of an inner clock/metronome. We can also see here the application and adaptation of various principles taken from Dalcroze's eurhythmics: the concepts of shifting the subdivision of the beat, of polyrhythm and counterpoint, and most particularly, the capacity to feel a rhythm internally without expressing it through the movement of the limbs. For the performers to realize a score such as this required that they have not only a detailed (musical) understanding of rhythm but also (and more importantly) a sensitivity to the relationships between inner experience and external expression and a capacity to inhabit this complex relationship with conviction and ease. This was a process of play and personal enquiry, rather than being purely about musical technique and exactitude. The performers were encouraged to explore for themselves how best to combine and approach the layering and opposition of rhythms.

Stanislavski went on to explain to these performers that if they had difficulty finding the 'right rhythm for their feelings', they could begin by intentionally externalizing their rhythms and then discover their inner justification through their actions or vice versa. Stanislavski summed this up by saying: 'If you wind up a watch it will go of its own accord ... Forget about any system of acting then, *for such a system's sole purpose is to give nature a free rein*' (Stanislavski and Rumyantsev 1998:312). These recommendations suggest that far from prescribing a fixed system or set of terminologies, Stanislavski was seeking a means of awakening in the performer what he saw to be a fundamental process. Here the performer was encouraged to explore and experiment with rhythm and tempo (both inner and outer) and discover for themselves the approaches that best worked for them.

Reflections

We can observe that where in Stanislavski's theoretical writings he often attempted to distinguish between the characteristics of tempo and rhythm, in practical accounts, these were often seen to be part of the same process – both terms at times appearing to be interchangeable and analogous.

These examples and observations highlight the complex relationship between theory and practice within Stanislavski's work as an actor, teacher, director and scholar, and also raise a number of questions regarding the ways Stanislavski intended these terms to be used and understood by other practitioners. Is tempo-rhythm best understood as a single aspect of performance or as a relationship between two distinct, yet interrelated, elements? If (as many scholars seem to suggest) it is the later, through what means do we distinguish and locate these elements within the work of the actor?[10]

Far from answering these questions, Stanislavski's use and descriptions of tempo-rhythm demonstrate the difficulty of defining one's terminology from within a practice that is constantly changing from day to day and from one context to the next. In attempting to analyse this work, we must take into account the experiential and tacit nature of these exchanges. How these terms are understood is ultimately tied to the practices in which they are used: the experiences and techniques formed through training, the metaphorical and poetic associations from which they are drawn and the intuitive immediacy of the exchanges between actors and directors working through the specific demands of their practice.

One of Stanislavski's intentions in the development of his work with tempo-rhythm was to move away from what he saw as the ambiguity and technical imprecision with which rhythm and tempo were being approached by actors and directors. While he may not have clarified the precise meaning of these terms, he was successful in creating a collection of training tools and a body of work, in which rhythm and tempo were applied effectively. These processes offered actors and directors a technical means of working with rhythm as a tool by which they could communicate directly with an audience and a means of shaping the internal/external dynamics and composition of performances. Ultimately what this work offers us is not a closed 'system' of ideas, but an open enquiry into how rhythms and tempos both inside and outside of us interact and feed into the work of performers and ensembles.

PART THREE

STRUCTURE AND SPONTANEITY

A common theme amongst the practitioners discussed in Part Three of this book is their use of improvisation as a key mechanism for training performers. Improvisation has been defined as a 'particular mode of performance activity', Frost and Yarrow stating: 'It issues as *performances* (the product of work which is made "on the spot", or is explicitly open to amendment during performance)' (Frost and Yarrow 2007:1). In this sense improvisation reflects a performer's capacity to inhabit and respond to the immediacy of the present moment. As a 'mode', it can be found in all forms of performance, from the most highly rehearsed production through to a spontaneous creation of work not previously conceived by performer or audience. In the examples that follow, improvisation is often applied as a tool for cultivating qualities of spontaneity, awareness and immediacy in performers, with the aim of applying these qualities to both the act of generating performance material and performing existing material.

In this sense, improvisation also foregrounds the dialectic relationship of *structure and spontaneity*, which is at the heart of many discussions of rhythm in performance. Identifying the need to balance these elements, Grotowski stated 'improvisation really begins when the performer chooses certain very concrete and precise limits' (Grotowski in Barba and Savarese 2006:269). While the spontaneous and novel aspects of improvisation are often highlighted, it is also worth reflecting on the fact that most forms of improvisation are informed (to some extent) by rules, either explicitly defined or implicitly understood by the performers involved. Even in so called 'free improvisation' we can observe the emergence of structures and devices by which the performers negotiate their relationships with one another as well as their audience, setting out a performance language and set of expectations that are either realized, transgressed or left unfulfilled.

One of the challenges of improvisation is the process of drawing on existing skills and knowledge while simultaneously being open to the unexpected and the new. The improviser often inhabits the dual experience of knowing and not knowing, of remembering while forgetting. As flautist and scholar Ellen Waterman points out, improvisation involves a 'delicate negotiation of trust and risk' (2014:60). For these reasons training through improvisation often requires both the development of familiarity (with the ensemble and/or the performance material) and the encouragement to take risks, to disrupt or disturb (the form or the relationships within the ensemble). In this context, performers work in two directions: seeking to build empathetic relationships, shared knowledge and understandings, while also seeking to challenge and transcend the limits of defined structures and preconceptions.

The practices described in this part of the book include those of Suzanne Bing, Vsevolod Meyerhold, John Britton, Anne Bogart and Tina Landau. These practitioners have approached the relationship between structure and spontaneity in improvisation through a variety of means:

- by the use of games and play;
- by establishing clear structures in which spontaneity can be encountered;
- by developing shared principles and terminologies through which an ensemble can negotiate their relationships;
- by encouraging performers to work outside the limitations of what might feel familiar or comfortable;
- by deconstructing hierarchies, both in regard to the relationships between performers and directors, and in terms of the status given to individual aspects of performance (i.e. script, music, physicality, staging, etc.).

Over the next four chapters, these themes will be discussed in more detail and in relationship to the practices from which they are drawn.

4
SUZANNE BING
MUSIC AND GAMES IN
ACTOR TRAINING

While a considerable amount of scholarship has focused on Jacques Copeau's role in the formation of French theatre and contemporary approaches to physical theatre, only marginal attention has been given to the work of Suzanne Bing, who was one of Copeau's key collaborators, the main teacher within his school and a lead performer in his theatre company, the Vieux-Colombier. Bing was a central figure in the realization of Copeau's vision of a new approach to acting and theatre, playing a crucial role in bringing together his principles and applying these to the formation of a 'coherent method of actor training' (Evans 2006:26). Of particular interest here are the ways that Bing worked to integrate music and rhythm into the training of actors through the use of 'theatre games' and improvisation.

Discussing improvisation, Bing wrote: 'The actor can become through his own movement the director's collaborator and render the latter's work more and more useless' (Bing cited in Baldwin 2013:77). Training the actor's ability to improvise, Bing looked to shift the performer's role from simply being the puppet of a director's vision to becoming a collaborator in their own right. In this way the actor was empowered to make creative choices and bring their own sensibilities and understandings to the act of performing, as well as to the processes of devising and rehearsing. Jane Baldwin remarks that while Copeau's persona and role was mostly that of an authoritarian director and teacher, Bing in contrast 'emphasized creativity, spontaneity, choice, and independence, within limits' (Baldwin 2013:80). Her development of a range of pedagogical approaches offers us clear examples of some of the challenges, risks and potential benefits of integrating rhythmic and musical principles into the training practices of actors.

Initial interests in rhythm

A primary source of inspiration for both Copeau and Bing regarding rhythm in acting was the work of Jaques-Dalcroze (Chapter 3). Reflecting on these practices, Bing wrote: 'The possibility of using music for exercises in bodily technique has been confirmed by Dalcroze's Gymnastics and made clear through constant attendance' (Bing 1920:1). At first these approaches were embraced by Bing, seen as valuable tools for training performers. However, as they began applying these practices more directly to the training of young actors, it became clear that there was an 'incompatibility' between what Bing identified as a 'conventional form of gymnastics and the hidden musical feeling to be developed in sensitive instruments' (Bing 1920:1). She explained:

> This difference is not theoretical, nor is it the feeling that one method is better than another. On the contrary, the perfection of Dalcroze Method as such has prevented me from pursuing my experiments any further and allowing them, as yet, to become a method. This is a factual and natural difference. (Bing 1920:1)

To understand this 'difference', it will be useful to look back to the sources of Copeau's initial interest in rhythm and the work of Dalcroze. This stemmed primarily from his desire to develop a new approach to training actors, one that would reflect the needs of the 'new theatre' that he envisaged. Copeau commented: 'We cannot speak of a renaissance, or even envisage its possibility, as long as we have not begun at the beginning, that is the creation of a school and of a teaching which will restore its working conditions' ([1921] 1990:27). To achieve this, he began by looking outside the conventional frameworks of his profession, searching for individuals and approaches that would encourage what he described as a 'natural instinct' for performance. At first, outdoor gymnastics and various forms of callisthenic exercise were adopted by the Vieux-Colombier. While these were seen to provide the actors with a general level of fitness and athletic exuberance, they did not lead to the level of integrated plasticity or the quality of expression that Copeau was seeking. The answer, Copeau believed, lay in rhythm. Yet he remained frustrated that he did not have access to a form of rhythmic training which would result in expressive actors rather than specialized dancers or gymnasts (Rudlin in Copeau 1990:55).

In the spring of 1915, Copeau came across a pamphlet in English titled *The Eurhythmics of Jaques-Dalcroze*. He commented that reading this was 'a veritable revelation' (1990:57) and took extensive notes and quotations from this text. Finding that many of Dalcroze's ideas around education, music and movement resonated strongly with his own, he copied various sections of this text into his own note book, underlining key phrases:

> technique should be nothing but a means to art, that the aim of musical education should be, not the production of pianists, violinists, singers, but of musically developed <u>human beings</u>, and that therefore the student should not begin by specialising on any instrument, but by developing his musical faculties, thus producing the basis for specialized studies.[1] (Copeau 1990:57; Copeau's underlining, retained here and elsewhere)

Initially seeing eurhythmics as a non-specialized form of training, this work held great appeal to Copeau in his search for new ways of training actors outside the confines of what he saw to be genre-specific approaches to acting taught elsewhere. In eurhythmics, rhythm provided a way of approaching the quality of immediacy which he sought in his actors. Dalcroze had claimed that performers needed to learn to express what they heard with their ears, through movement, without hesitation or analysis, just as with reading where words are comprehended and spoken without the sense of a mental process. Copeau saw a strong correlation between these concepts and his own initial attempts at training performers to be more supple and responsive in movement and speech. Approaching acting from the basis of musical sensitivity, Copeau felt that the performer would be given a sense of universality and greater plasticity. Stripped back to what he saw as its essence, Copeau felt that it was primarily rhythm that should guide the work of the actor, rather than the specialized forms of artistic expression he had observed in the so-called 'great' actors of his time (Copeau 1990:58).

With many of the Vieux-Colombier's members recruited to fight in the First World War, Copeau put his efforts into gathering research for the development of a new pedagogy for actors and a model for establishing a school. He travelled to Italy to meet with Gordon Craig in September 1915 and continued on to Switzerland where he met with Dalcroze and Adolphe Appia. Observing the work of Dalcroze in person, Copeau wrote: 'I am sure from what I saw in Geneva, of the value of general rhythmic training as a basis for the professional education of the actor' (1990:62). It was in part Dalcroze's own playfulness that appealed to Copeau, the ways he integrated musical principles into game-like activities. Copeau noted from his observations:

> Dalcroze lets them play. He has them execute the simplest movements collectively, rapidly and joyfully. Everything must begin with the child's play... Everything must come from him; nothing must be imposed or taken away. Helping him without his noticing it. (Copeau [1915] 1990:61)

He observed the ways Dalcroze used simple storytelling devices to explore musical elements. On one occasion his students acted out episodes from *Snow White* while he narrated the story through words and rhythms. These observations provided Copeau with rich inspiration and greater confidence to peruse his ambitions of working with rhythm as a basis for training actors.

Children's school in Paris

Following on from these travels, Copeau returned to Paris and opened a drama school, which was initially set up for small children. Although Copeau was officially the director of the school, he acknowledged that in reality it was run 'under the complete direction' of Bing, with Copeau teaching only occasionally (Copeau 1990:35). Where Copeau began this endeavour with limited practical knowledge of acting and theatre making, Bing was already a trained and accomplished actress with an existing understanding of the value of improvisation and 'theatre games' as a way of working with actors.[2] In contrast to Copeau's emphasis on 'results', Bing gave attention to the children's own processes, looking for inspiration in the ways they played and drawing on their spontaneity as a basis for devising improvisation exercises. Observing the children in their initial sessions Bing commented:

> We started teaching them one of Dalcroze's rounds and singing it with actions. They were a little embarrassed by that, but those whose gestures were natural, retained them when the others did not follow. Then, rhythmics ... it is coming along well, they put their whole heart into it, and the three older girls are doing very well. (Copeau and Bing [1915]1920:2).

In April of 1916 Copeau returned to Switzerland to visit Dalcroze's school, this time accompanied by Bing and his daughter. They observed Dalcroze teaching, talked with his students and saw a performance presentation of the 'dance of the Furies' from Christopher Glück's *Orphée*. There they observed what they saw to be an effective means of integrating movement and music, as well as a functioning model for their school. However, one of the tendencies they noted in Dalcroze's students was the difficulty they had in playing human emotions. Looking for ways to address this in their own training, Bing explored ways of approaching human characterization through the observation of animals and natural processes. She led her students in voice exercises that began with imitating animals and sounds from nature, gradually leading to the application of these qualities in the development of human sounds, speech and characters (Kusler 1974:51).

EXERCISE 7: THE CAT AND THE OLD RAT

Integrating Dalcroze's storytelling techniques with their work on animal movements, Copeau and Bing worked with the children at their school on enacting a fable by Jean de La Fontaine, *The Cat and the Old Rat*. First Copeau read through the story and then guided the children in developing various ways of walking and moving, inspired by the characters in the story. Bing wrote the following description of this process.

First, the cat; how does a cat walk? They simply crawled around on all fours, not good. And how does a dog walk? Understanding there was a difference, they timidly made the dog walk a little more strongly. And now how does a cat walk? They had understood, and a few of them succeeded in doing a silent elongated walk. Why? The one who did it best, answers: so as not to make any noise: yes, so that mice won't hear him. With these few words, they were already into the drama of the fable ... The cat enters: you remind him that he is Attila and at the same time we should not hear him come in. Several times we have to tell the mice to hide themselves better. We bring a bench into the middle of the room on which the cat can climb and stand on ... The mice lift their noses in the air, showing their heads a little, then return to their rat holes – in haste and panic as your tone of voice suggests. Then they scamper out and form a half-circle around the cat; he bounds into their midst, and they run away; he chases one, and we stop there. (Copeau and Bing [notes made December 1915] 1920:5)

Bing noted how the students seemed changed by this work, elated and full of enthusiasm to play at being the characters in the story. In these exercises, the children were led through a process of discovering particular rhythmic qualities and character traits through the use of their imaginations and play, rather than through drill-like exercises. Working with enthusiasm and amusement the children quickly discovered ways of moving quietly like a cat and marching like dogs. They explored the differences between moving timidly and moving with more strength and commitment (Kusler 1974:51). In this work Bing and Copeau also observed the excitement that the children brought to their improvisations and saw in this a sense of the immediacy that they wanted actors to be able to bring to the stage.

We can see in these simple activities the beginnings of an approach that went on to be developed and refined. In exercises that Bing later developed with older students, she encouraged them to work from real-life observations of animals and applying these physicalities to the building of characters. These story-led exercises also established a model for guiding improvisations as they occurred through a form of 'side-coaching'. Again this was an approach that went on to be developed in much of Bing and Copeau's later improvisation exercises.

Applying eurhythmics in actor training

From the school's beginnings, Copeau established eurhythmics as part of the main curriculum. Paulet Thevenaz led classes from 1915 to 1916, and in 1917 Jessmin Howarth[3] was employed to assist with further integrating eurhythmics into the practices of the Vieux-Colombier company. Joining the theatre company on their tour of the United States, Howarth was based with them in New York from 1917 to 1919. Despite Copeau's enthusiasm for eurhythmics, the troupe's first contact with these practices seems to have met with some resistance and at times open rebellion. Bing observed that Howarth had difficulty convincing the actors that her classes had anything to do with theatre. Ultimately, it was felt that eurhythmics carried with it the same sense of 'specialization' and 'dehumanization' that they were seeking to get away from in conventional forms of actor training (Copeau [1921] 1990:63–7).

Bing commented that rather than training the actor to embody a general sense of rhythm, eurhythmics used the model of 'modern musical notation' and attempted to instil an equivalent model of notation in the form of physical movement. For Bing this was 'equivalent to translating what was audible into the visible bodily notation' (1920:1). As a system, she saw musical notation as imprisoning and impoverishing the actor. She wrote: it 'dries up the inner feeling of the Rhythm found in declamation and Gregorian chant, and the ways the Actor should come upon it in the great texts' (Bing 1920:1). She continued:

> It is not the number (and variety) of rhythmic combinations which can favour rhythmic sense ... This sense must come from the inside. Exercises are always unsatisfactory if they are not used exclusively to exercise the outer manifestation of the inner sense that one wants to develop. (a feeling that a grouping is needed)
> ...

With Dalcroze, Music is reduced. Our art is not reducible to numbers and signs. The Music we are trying to express by cultivating ourselves as instruments is the same one we may hear between an architectural form and its environment, and the movements born from them. When Dalcroze speaks of music, he means music reduced to its instrumental function. When he deals with the human body, it is in order to incorporate what he has learned from this music by means of a conventional muscular translation of that music's conventional signs. In this way, there is also a reduction of bodily expression: a kind of graphics. (Bing 1920:2 [underlinings by Copeau])

In her writings Bing articulated in detail the reservations expressed by various practitioners regarding the direct application of conventional models of musical rhythm onto the work of the actor. Echoing Stanislavski's concerns (Chapter 3), she highlighted the risks of developing a 'bodily technique' based purely on external form without a deeper 'inner' understanding and sensitivity to rhythm. While she indicated the possibility that these objections were only relevant to the 'pupil-actor', she insisted it would be 'dangerous' to ignore these risks.

During the two years that the Vieux-Colombier company spent in New York, Bing also had the opportunity to encounter new trends in children's education, observing and briefly teaching at a Montessori-based school run by Margaret Naumburg.[4] There she experienced a learning atmosphere that was both creative and open. She also had the opportunity to lead sessions with the children, offering her a space to explore and develop her pedagogical skills. In these classes, she drew on her knowledge of working with games, animal movements, pantomime, dance and story dramatizations. Although some simple rhythmic and musical games were played, Bing made a point of not using any eurhythmics exercises in these sessions. Commenting to another teacher about her disappointment with these methods, she explained: 'I do not want music to be the base, the point of departure, after what I know of the results of the Dalcroze method' (Bing 1918 cited in Kusler 1974:94). In looking to develop her own pedagogical approaches, Bing wanted to find ways of working with rhythms that were not based primarily in music but rather came from a sense of play and observation.

Despite this general rejection of eurhythmics as a training approach for actors, Howarth's work with the company and her introduction of rhythm, dance and pantomime to their training, played an important role in the evolution of Bing and Copeau's pedagogy. These experiences also had a strong influence on the work of other company members including Charles Dullin who went on to use elements of these rhythm exercises in his own practices, with Howarth herself supervising some of this training at his school.[5] Initial exercises run by Howarth in pantomime – using the senses and imitating people's 'character silhouettes' and rhythms – became the basis for a large part of the training at the Vieux-Colombier School in the years that followed (Kusler 1974:64).

Voice, movement and storytelling

The company's return to Paris in 1919 marked a shift away from eurhythmics as a training approach for actors. Instead Bing and Copeau looked to develop a more integrated use of music, movement and text within the school and company's training programme. In 1920, a first attempt at a school for teenagers and young adults was set up, with Bing responsible for a large proportion of its teaching. Baldwin describes the school as initially a 'one-woman operation', Bing teaching twelve students throughout the entire day. These classes involved text analysis, oral interpretation, basic sound and movement, gestural expressiveness, and elementary improvisation (Baldwin 2013:77).

With the official opening of the Vieux-Colombier School in 1921, Bing continued to experiment with new approaches to training actors. Much of the initial work undertaken at the school focused on developing skills for working with spoken text and physical movement. The emphasis through many of these exercises lay in simplicity, play and the building of ensemble. A broader curriculum was also established, which included classes in theatre history (with a particular focus on ancient Greek theatre), acrobatics, dance and music studies (including choral singing, music theory, musical culture and history). Throughout this period Copeau's role was limited to giving theoretical lectures, monitoring teaching, critiquing and guiding the students in their work and end of year projects.

As part of this programme Bing ran classes in 'Dramatic Instinct', which combined games and improvisations, with the aim of integrating the various specialist skills the students were learning in their other classes. In classes focused on the delivery of text, Bing encouraged the students to take their time as they read, all the time looking to incorporate the feelings and inner experiences of their characters. In one exercise, she instructed actor Jean Villard to read each phrase with a new breath, intentionally addressing each of these to a different person[6] (Kusler 1974:73–4). Voice work was also approached through the use of games. These were developed as a way of encouraging the students to work as an ensemble and to integrate their work on voice with elements of movement.

EXERCISE 8: ENSEMBLE VOICE AND BALL GAMES

A game described as 'telephones', involved two groups sitting in rows facing one another. Each group had to pass an exclamation down their line, with these sounds evolving as they were passed from one student to another. The same formations were also used for exploring *crescendos* and *decrescendos*, as well as musical scales. Here, with each exchange, the volume or pitch of the voice would either go up or down as it was passed along the lines.

In another exercise, the students had to make three vocal exclamations and movements, performed in unison as a group, each one bigger and louder than the one before it. Sometimes they were also given a context or scenario in which to play these actions, such as news of a scandal. Another common exercise involved students throwing balls between themselves, working with a fixed pattern, 'maintaining a rigorous rhythm and dynamics' (Kusler 1974:74). This work with balls had been explored earlier by Copeau in his initial research with children in 1915. In these sessions he focused on using the ball to promote a 'promptness of decision', gradually increasing the speed of these exercises until they could be performed 'very rapidly' (Copeau and Bing 1920:6). A more detailed discussion of ball games can be found in Chapter 6.

In working with these teenage and young adult students, Bing and Copeau continued to utilize the work they had developed with children in 1915–16. In particular, the work with improvised enactments of short stories and fairy tales. These provided an effective framework for training the students in ensemble and compositional awareness. Barbara Kusler describes the ways musical elements were integrated in these improvisations:

> Students began to create simple characters, for example, by dramatizing the song 'Frère Jacques' thus utilizing music, dance and ensemble elements: the actors playing Jacques mimed being 'asleep' and paid no attention to the group at first. They sang louder to wake him, increasing the size of their movements as the sound augmented. The group also improvised their own version of 'Sleeping Beauty', emphasizing its rhythmic elements. (Kusler 1974:74–5)

Kusler describes how the work on 'Sleeping Beauty' developed into a small production, this providing the students with a way of integrating musical principles as well as qualities of improvisation and movement into their performances.

> The first scene was an improvisation in dynamics of movement and sound as the palace guards, cooks, ladies and gentlemen fell asleep. The 'tree' regulated the rhythms and intensity; as women made the sounds of knitting, the sounds of games and songs came in and gradually voices grew louder and movement more active – all following a similar movement, getting softer and more quiet as they all fell asleep (Kusler 1974:139).

Here musical elements were woven into a narrative structure that took on game-like qualities. The students were also given the opportunity to find ways of incorporating their work on improvisation into a more structured performance context. While this work was seen to have a positive effect on the student's performances, there was still a sense that it remained incomplete.

Musique corporelle

Elements of music were given even more priority as the school developed over the next few years. Between 1921 and 1923 students received music tuition in singing and instrumental studies, alongside classes in Classical and Greek music theory. They were also given tuition in gymnastics and lessons in various dance styles. Yet even with this exposure to a broad range of music and dance studies, the students still struggled to apply much of this work directly in their performances. As before, it was mostly Bing who was responsible for finding ways to bring together and apply these principles, as well as weaving aspects of their instrumental and singing training into their productions.[7]

During this period, Bing ran a course, named *Musique Corporelle*. This focused on further integrating the principles of music, text and physical movement, attempting to discover how these elements could be incorporated within dramatic performances. Each session explored a particular theme. These included 'space, time, shape, force, speed, volume, intensity, weight, duration'.[8] Classes were mostly practical, with students exploring each theme through movement, voice and language, while also engaging with these themes through analysis and discussion.

Time

The first principle examined in this course was *Time*.

EXERCISE 9: DURATION OF BREATH, TEXT AND MOVEMENT

Bing instructed students to fill particular durations with their breath and then to explore improvising movements over the same durations. In a similar way, students also played with filling a time sequence (or a series of beats) with actions or improvised dialogue. Looking to apply these exercises to dramatic performances, they worked with starting a particular action and then interrupting these actions with brief movements.

Tempo

In the following classes the theme of *Tempo* was introduced. These exercises had some similarities to the eurhythmics exercises discussed in Chapter 3. However, Bing made a point of students accompanying themselves predominantly with their own voices rather than relying on external music.

EXERCISE 10: MIRRORING AND EVERYDAY TEMPOS

The students worked on the juxtaposition of two tempos, one in the arms and the other in the feet, while they accompanied themselves with their voices. Students also played 'mirroring' games and 'follow the leader', using these as ways to explore performing actions in the same tempo. In these sessions they sometimes worked with live piano accompaniment.

In these classes Bing often worked with everyday associations rather than musical expressions when describing tempo. For example, a sewing machine was used to represent a quick tempo and the movement of an elevator offered an example of a slow sustained action.

Bing's focus on physicality and voice offered an effective means by which the students could embody these rhythmic elements and locate them within a dramatic context. Working from their own understandings of tempo in daily life, rather than drawing on musical terms and timing concepts, also marks a shift from the more specialized approaches associated with eurhythmics and those referred to in Stanislavski's outer tempo-rhythm exercises (Chapter 3). Approaching rhythm through the use of the students' voices also further reflects Bing's insistence that rhythm should emerge from an internal personal awareness rather than from an externally imposed form.

Rhythm

In the classes that followed, students examined the role of *Rhythm* across a range of contexts, observing the use of repetition at regular intervals in drawing, language, architecture and music. The students made comparisons between these and noted the similarities and differences in rhythmic qualities found within these contexts.

EXERCISE 11: CLAPPING RHYTHMS AND THREE GROUP IMAGES

They played with clapping different rhythms and then replacing claps with vocal exclamations such as 'Ah!'. They examined how several rhythms could be joined together to form a unified succession or layered to create polyrhythms. Following on, these compositions were performed in silence with the rhythms being embodied within their physical movements. In addition, they continued to work with various ball games, using these as a way to explore how their actions could work in obedience to a particular rhythmic pattern. A more complex exercise in phrasing involved the students working in three groups. The first group would run into the space and take up a position, the second would then join them, taking a complimentary position and finally the third group would complete the image. This would then be done with eyes closed, the students looking to recall their original pathways and positions.

Students discussed the similarities and differences between phrases of spoken language, movement and music. They also talked about the differences between movements choreographed to music and those performed in silence, the performers maintaining an internal sense of rhythm without music supporting their actions. Here they commented on the fact that music brought a 'greater purity and abstraction' to their movements, 'but often blurred the dramatic sense' (Kusler 1974:131).

They identified that in music and spoken language, rhythmic phrases could be formed through the use of accents, silences and contrasts, while in movement, rhythm might come from 'changes in direction, weight, duration, levels, [and the] use of body parts' (Kusler 1974:167).

Despite the technical nature of many of the *Musique Corporelle* classes, Bing stressed the importance of imagination, as well as the development of continuity and unity of direction. Here she built on Copeau's principles of 'follow-through' and sincerity (Chapter 1). Building on Copeau's theories regarding the significance of the stillness that proceeded and followed actions, Bing worked with students to analyse and explore the relationships between the emotional qualities of gestures and the rhythm of their preparation.[9]

Legacy of rhythm and play

As testimony to the significance of rhythm in both Bing and Copeau practices, many of the companies and practitioners whose work grew out of the Vieux-Colombier and its school continued to apply and evolve these training principles and approaches to rhythm. These include Charles Dullin, Étienne Decroux, Jean Dorcy, Jean Villard and Michel Saint-Denis, and following on from these, Jean-Louis Barrault, Antonin Artaud, Marcel Marceau, Jacques Lecoq and Philippe Gaulier. Describing the use of exercises derived from Copeau and Bing in his own teaching, Lecoq explained:

> We play people, elements, plants, trees, colours, lights, matter, sounds – going beyond their images, gaining knowledge of their space, their rhythm, their breath through improvisation. (Lecoq cited in Frost and Yarrow 2007:157)

As with Bing's own practice, the focus here is not on attempting to reproduce the image of the animal, plant or person, but rather to discover their rhythmic and spatial qualities and to bring these to life through improvisation. Another example of the continuity of these approaches can be found in the training programme of the London International School of Performing Arts (LISPA). Echoing many of Bing's principles, they explain in their 2016 course brochure that students 'will explore the fundamental principles of theatrical complicity, construction and creation through a highly physical approach to rhythms in nature and urban life, as well as in architecture, music, painting and poetry' (Prattki 2016). Reflecting the ethos set out by Bing, these approaches seek to explore rhythm, not simply as an aspect of music, but as an element of life in nature and in everyday experiences. Approaching rhythm in this broader sense, the actor's process is one of synthesis (at times synaesthesia). They observe and bring together a sense of rhythm in motion, sound, image, text and daily life and seek to internalize and integrate these aspects within their dramatic performances. Moving beyond a musical framework, these understandings of rhythm invite performers to find their own sense of rhythm, resulting from a sense of play and personal enquiry.

Reflections

Throughout Bing's teachings, we can see clear attempts to balance the more formal aspects of Dalcroze's approaches to rhythm and composition with a continued search for ways of translating these principles into a performance language applicable to actors. We can also observe the value that play and improvisation brought to the processes of discovering and embodying rhythmic qualities. One of the key principles in Bing's approach was the significance given to the student's own discoveries from within the processes of exploration and improvisation. Rather than attempting to impose techniques or musical concepts onto these actors, Bing instead looked to provide a context in which these principles could be played with and encountered through simple game-like activities.

Bing's work with rhythm reveals both the challenges and the benefits of incorporating musical elements into actor training and the importance of play, exploration and imagination within these processes. Yet despite the significant pedagogical developments that emerged from this work, Bing often found herself frustrated by the inability of her students to fully engage with these principles, feeling that ultimately 'the problem of integrating music and dance into actor training was never fully resolved' (Kusler 1974:181). It is hard to conceive precisely what such a 'resolution' would entail, and there remain very few notes or detailed documents outlining Bing's vision of actor training. We can, however, catch a glimpse of this vision in the little that is available to us.

We can see running through this work a paradoxical relationship between rigour and freedom. On the one hand, Bing sought to develop a strong technical and conceptual understanding of rhythm in her students, while on the other hand, there is the sense of childlike exploration and discovery that was consistently encouraged. The actors looked to know while not knowing, to hold on while letting go, to find precision in their play. In Bing's practices, we are reminded of Stanislavski's insistence that his students approach rhythm as a child approaches a toy: to be curious and open, to simultaneously seek understanding and to embrace naivety. Play can be seen here as a model for both improvisation and rhythm in performance. In playing with rhythm, we are required to follow the rules while also learning to bend them to our will – we work within structures while also grasping opportunities and facing the challenges of the moment. The next chapter will examine the spontaneity of rhythm in relationship to the structured elements of a performance in more detail, discussed in regards to the work of Vsevolod Meyerhold.

5

VSEVOLOD MEYERHOLD
RHYTHM NOT METRE

Jonathan Pitches proposes that for Meyerhold, 'rhythm is the glue which binds all the other skills of the actor together' (Pitches 2003:115). Operating as a central principle throughout his career, rhythm informed almost every aspect of Meyerhold's work as both a teacher and a director. On the one hand, rhythm and music offered Meyerhold a means of establishing a unique and precise performance aesthetic, while also bringing a sense of spontaneity and dynamism to his work with fixed movement sequences. In these ways, Meyerhold's notions of improvisation and rhythm differ slightly from others presented here. Meyerhold defined improvisation as 'the free combination of previously prepared elements' (1998:180). Where most of the examples of improvisation in this book refer to the spontaneous creation of performance material, the emphasis in Meyerhold's training and performances lay more in the discovery of spontaneity within existing performance structures and forms.

This approach to improvisation is common in the field of music. Within many musical styles, there exists an understanding that 'improvisation is part of a dialectic relationship between premeditated composition and different degrees of deviation from a given template or model' (Roesner 2014:71). A musician often begins by studying scales, modes, chord progressions, rhythmic phrases and other compositional devices and then looks to discover a quality of spontaneity and immediacy through which these elements can be brought to life. Whereas in many forms of actor training we encounter the reverse of this. Actors often begin by exploring and finding spontaneity through games and improvisations and then look to build fixed performance material or apply these qualities to existing material. Following a similar model to that of classical music education, Meyerhold looked to train his performers through rigorous exercises and movement studies (referred to using the musical term *etude*). Having mastered the technical aspects of these sequences, the actors then improvised within these forms, discovering rhythmic variations and a sense of sympathy between co-performers. Meyerhold's understanding of rhythm was also more technical than many of those found within this book. His use of rhythm drew clearly from his own musical background as a violinist, as well as his interest in the physical rhythmicity and coordination of factory workers (see references to Taylorism in Chapter 2). Searching not only for a precision of action but also an efficiency of movement in performance, Meyerhold strove for a detailed and subtle understanding of rhythm within his actors. In line with these understandings, Meyerhold's approach to rhythm and the language he used to discuss it were distinctly systematic and precise, especially when compared with Stanislavski and Bings's often fluid interpretations of tempo and rhythm.

Form as a means to freedom

In looking to cultivate qualities of 'musicality'[1] in his performers, Meyerhold drew strongly on the use of musical accompaniment (both live and recorded). In training, this was often used as a means of encouraging a more precise and compositional relationship to time. Meyerhold observed that the work of his performers was greatly enhanced by the use of musical accompaniment, stating:

> Supported by a rhythmical background of music, the actor's playing acquires precision... The actor needs a musical background of music in order to train him to pay attention to the flow of time on stage. If an actor is used to playing with a musical background, then without it he will sense time completely differently. (Meyerhold 1998:161)

Meyerhold linked this concept to what he had observed in Asian performance practices, including Chinese Opera and Noh Theatre.

In this regard, he noted how in 'Eastern theatre', stage assistants struck percussively on a board to both mark the climax of an action and help the performers find more precision in their movements. When the celebrated Chinese actor Mei Lanfang performed in Moscow in 1935, Meyerhold was struck by this artist's subtle mastery of rhythm. He exclaimed 'the rhythm demonstrated by this great stage master has not been felt on our stage'. While the Russian actors marked their performance in terms of minutes, Meyerhold made the observation that Mei Lanfang 'counts every one sixtieth of a second' (Meyerhold cited in Tian 2008:71). Applying his own aesthetic principles to this work, Meyerhold's descriptions emphasized the exactitude of these rhythms rather than their expressive potential.

> We have built all our performances from musicals to drama in such a way that none of our actors was inspired with the necessity of keeping an eye on the time on stage. We do not have a sense of time. Strictly speaking, we do not know the meaning of using time economically. (Meyerhold cited in Tian 2008:71)

It is in this sense that we can observe some of the differences between Meyerhold's approach to rhythm and those of his contemporary, Stanislavski. While there are some similarities between Meyerhold's use of musical rhythm and the 'outer tempo-rhythm exercises' used by Stanislavski, there is a marked distinction between the ways each of these directors drew on external rhythmic forms in relationship to the actor's internal experience. Where Stanislavski used rhythm as a way to access and 'lure' emotions, Meyerhold saw rhythm as primarily a means of coordinating performers' actions and disciplining their temperaments. Meyerhold looked to avoid the emotive techniques he had observed at the Moscow Art Theatre, viewing these as a form of 'self-hypnotic narcosis' (Roach 1993:197). Rather than using tempo and rhythm as means of tapping into personal emotions, for Meyerhold, these were seen as ways of preventing actors from being distracted by their individual feelings or habits. As he explained: 'In most cases the art of the naturalistic actor lies in surrendering to the dictates of his temperament. By prescribing a strict tempo, the musical score frees the actor in music drama from the demands of his own temperament' (1991:85).

Offering actors a framework on which to hang their performance, the musical score was seen here to liberate them from their habitual rhythms and tempos helping them achieve clarity and precision in their actions. This use of precise 'form' as means of freeing the actor may on the surface appear contradictory. Yet, rather than viewing form as a restriction placed on an otherwise free and liberated performer, Meyerhold proposed that through the imposition of certain rhythms or tempos the performer had a chance to break away from the limitations of their habits. As composer and director Heiner Goebbels has more recently pointed out, without an imposed form, performance often risks falling into conventional and quasi 'natural' forms of acting:

> There are so many conventional habits in body language, in expressive gesture, in speech training, in 'that's how we do it'. But in order to avoid being a victim of the conventional, 'natural' idea of theatre any form is helpful. (2012:114)

Like Goebbels, Meyerhold's use of form was intended as a means of breaking away from the naturalistic conventions that dominated his time. As a formal mechanism, music offered Meyerhold a way of structuring the flow of a performance and shaping its aesthetic. This has at times generated an impression of Meyerhold as a dictatorial puppeteer or conductor, using music as a mechanism by which to control his actors 'note for note'. In practice, however, Meyerhold strove for a more complex and personal relationship between musical form and acting. He stated: 'The actor's art consists in far more than merely acquainting the spectator with the director's conception' (Meyerhold 1991:50–1). Distinct from the orchestral musician, who was valued for their virtuosic technique and depersonalized enactment of the conductor's will, the actor 'assimilates both the director and the author and then gives of himself [or herself] from the stage' (Meyerhold 1991:51).

For Meyerhold, it was through rhythm that the actor was seen to grasp this spontaneous and improvised quality in their performance:

> It is precisely in the possibility for the actor to improvise that drama is distinct from opera. In opera the conductor does not permit the extension of any temporal sections, and only the tempi can be extended ... I will never renounce the right to stimulate an actor to

improvise. The only important thing in improvisation is that secondary concerns do not overwhelm the main thing, which is the matter of timing, and of the interdependence of temporal sections on stage. (Meyerhold cited in Schmidt 1978:79)

The actors were given 'licence' to improvise but with a strict regard for how their timing related to the other elements of the performance. Here again rhythm was seen to both free the performers and contain (or guide) their choices on stage.

Part of Meyerhold's interest in improvisation also came from a desire to break away from a direct correspondence between the actions of the actor and the music. Meyerhold observed that in the work of Jaques-Dalcroze and Isadora Duncan, as well as in Chinese and Japanese theatre, there was a dominant sense of unity between music and action. Actions occurred for the same duration as a musical phrase, and stillness often coincided with silence. Distinguishing his own approaches from these (particularly in his later productions), he was openly dismissive, making reference to the 'balleticism' and 'mere prettiness' in Dalcroze and Duncan's work. While in his earlier production Meyerhold had often insisted on a direct correspondence between music and action, as his career progressed, he looked to find more complex relationships between these elements, rejecting what he saw to be a simplistic unification of music and movement, lacking 'sub-text' and 'vitality' (Meyerhold 1998:131).

Whereas in Tristan I insisted on the actor's movements and gestures synchronizing with the tempo of the music and the tonic scheme with almost mathematical accuracy, I tried in The Queen of Spades to allow the actor rhythmical freedom within the limits of the musical phrase (like Chaliapin), so that his interpretation, whilst remaining dependent on the music, would have a contrapuntal rather than a metrically precise relationship to it, sometimes even acting as a contrast, a variation, anticipating or lagging behind the score instead of simply keeping in unison. (1991:247)

Meyerhold's approach to developing a more complex relationship to musical rhythm also informed the ways he trained his actors. They started by exploring 'elementary movements' done to simple rhythms, gradually building to more complex phrases and the ability to layer these over what was described as a 'canvas of metre'. This training worked towards 'free rhythmical movement', with the ultimate goal being the 'mastery of free movement according to the laws of unrestricted counterpoint' (Erast Garin cited in Leach 1993:114). Once students had developed their capacity to work their rhythms independently of a metrical framework, they then moved on to coordinating their own rhythms with a partner and also applying these principles to working with objects and props. Again, a comparison can be made between these processes and those of a student musician – beginning with basic rhythmic and metric exercises and gradually building to more complex forms of rhythmic expression.[2]

A rhythmic vocabulary

Unlike Bing, who looked to avoid musical concepts and terms in the training of actors, Meyerhold embraced musical rhythm and its language as a tool for cultivating a musical sense of time in the actor, as well as directing the overall musicality of his productions. He commented: 'Musical terminology helps us a great deal. I love it because it possesses an almost mathematical exactness' (Meyerhold 1981:154). In order to communicate and fix the various rhythmic qualities of an action or sequence, Meyerhold developed a vocabulary of terms that helped both him and his actors articulate the musicality of their movements. Some of these were basic terms taken from music, including *legato* (smooth, flowing), *staccato* (shortened, separated) and *luft-pause* (breath, suspension).[3] Meyerhold also made regular references to tempo descriptions, marking his scripts like musical scores with terms such as *grave* (very slow, solemn), *andante* (moderate walking speed), *allegretto* (fairly quick), *scherzando* (playful, joking) and *capriccioso* (free and lively).

In addition to these terms, Meyerhold also looked to sources outside of music and theatre for rhythmic terms that could be applied to performance. One term often used in training and rehearsals was *tormos*. This literally translates as 'brake', a mechanical term which referred to 'slowing the action of the machine by offering a resisting counter-force' (Pitches 2005:79). This was a way of exerting control over an action as it was performed, allowing an action to be elongated or at its extreme brought to a point of dynamic stillness. Describing this energized quality of stillness, Meyerhold used the term *rakurz*, taken from the French *raccourci* (translated as shortcut or switchblade). This term was adopted from fine arts and was also used within Copeau's work to describe a concentrated gesture (Pavis 1999:333). These instantaneous moments of dynamic stillness further emphasized the arresting quality of rhythm, 'cutting up' an action or sequence while still maintaining a quality of forward motion. Illustrating this, Meyerhold explained: 'When you look at a bridge, you seem to see a leap imprinted in metal, that is, a process and not something static' (1998:124).

Rhythm versus metre

Two key terms used by Meyerhold where rhythm and metre. Insisting that an actor's movements should not be bound to the metre of music, Meyerhold stated 'all music is based on rhythm, the task of which is to conceal the regular metrical divisions' (1991:283). The challenge for these actors was to work with the rhythms of the music, while at the same time not revealing to the spectator its metrical structures.[4] For Meyerhold, this distinction between rhythm and metre was critical to the work of the actor:

> I still have to deal with actors, who use the word 'rhythm' where one should speak of 'metre' and *vice versa*. An actor needs to have knowledge in this area – In the area of mimesis he needs to learn how to move his muscles, has to pay attention to the vectors of power triggered by movement, and know the effect of weight, gravitation, path, velocity. What is the difference of legato and staccato? If the actor doesn't distinguish between metre and rhythm, then he doesn't know the difference between legato and staccato either. (Meyerhold cited in Roesner 2014:78)

He explained that this distinction is not simply theoretical, but rather something that must be learned through the doing and experiencing of bodily movement. Although Meyerhold often drew on musical terminology as a means of teaching and scoring the rhythmic aspects of his performances, he was also keen that the performer embodied a sense of rhythm that was rooted in their physicality and their sense of movement.

As observed in the previous discussion on rhythm and tempo (Chapter 3), attempting to separate rhythm from other temporal aspects of music and acting is not always a clear-cut procedure. In the field of acting and performance we also have to contend with two prominent sources of understanding regarding metre (musical metre and poetic metre), whose functions and definitions differ in various ways. It is beyond the scope of this book to properly address these vast fields of understanding and ongoing debates.[5] Yet for now, I believe it will be useful to set out some general distinctions commonly made between metre and rhythm and reflect on some of the ways Meyerhold and others have looked to apply these to their practices.

Philip Hobsbaum writes: 'Metre is a blueprint; rhythm is the inhabited building. Metre is a skeleton; rhythm is the functioning body. Metre is a map; rhythm is a land' (2006:7). Regarding metre, what is most often highlighted is its sense of regularity and stability, which is seen as distinct from the changeable and fluid nature of rhythm. Following this line of thought, metre generally describes a regular beat, pulse or unit of time (either heard or felt) that can be grouped into a repeatable sequence. In contrast, rhythm often implies a more complex or individual form of expression or perception, one that is experienced as being free or variable.

Meyerhold explained that while circus performers may find it useful to work to a strict metronomic metre, for the actor it was more useful 'to work rhythmically within musical phrases' (Leach 1993:113). Meyerhold described how for circus performers a steady beat was essential for synchronizing their routine. Actors, on the other hand, needed to go beyond simply counting out the beats and find a quality of expression that could transcend this metric framework.[6]

Building on Meyerhold and Hobsbaum's metaphors, we can imagine metre as a 'canvas' or framework, providing the context and structure on which an individual can express themselves through rhythm.

Rhythm is what 'overcomes', 'disputes' and 'conceals' the metre (Meyerhold 1998:135). We might understand this as a relationship between a performance's underlying structures and the performers' own spontaneous journeys through those structures.[7] While the former has a sense of pre-existing as a framework or container, the latter emerges moment by moment, moving with an intentionality that carries its own momentum or force. In performance, these elements speak to and inform one another. The structure/score/text provides the resistance, stability and context in which actors can discover the spontaneity of their expression. Here actors can play and explore subtle shifts in timing and establish an immediate and nuanced relationship to their performance material and their fellow performers.

Conversely, we might also consider metre not only as a basis for rhythmic expression but also as a product of this expression. We can take note of the ways that the rhythms of a performer's movements or speech themselves evoke or suggest a sense of structure. A rhythm may imply an underlying pulse or establish the expectation of repetition without directly or overtly marking these out for an audience. As the film director and student of Meyerhold, Sergei Eisenstein pointed out, rhythm may bring about a sense of uniform movement or approach regularity while in itself remaining fluid and vital (Eisenstein 2010:320). A useful distinction to be made here is between moments of 'productive repetition' (i.e. repetition that generates a sense of development or progression) and what Deleuze and Guattari refer to as 'reproductive meter' (implying a sense of uniformity and mechanical reproduction) (1988:346). There are times when a metric pattern or repetitious sequence can produce a sense of motion, development or expression. Even the metrical ticking of a clock or the mechanical flashing of a car's indicator can evoke a sense of rhythm, a variation of beats, a quality of music or poetry.[8]

For Meyerhold, the concept of 'sub-text' is also important in regard to rhythm. The job of an actor – like a good conductor – is not simply to perform the score (or the text), but to bring the spaces between the notes/words/actions to life through their rhythmic interpretation, in a sense, allowing these to breathe. Here, the actor's capacity to convey, what Meyerhold identified as the 'sub-text', 'lies in mastering the empty moments between rhythmic beats' (Meyerhold 1998:135). Viewing sub-text through a rhythmic (rather than psychological) lens opens up the notion that rhythm and meaning emerge from the intervals between one action/word and another – literally 'reading between the lines'. As Eisenstein proposed 'the agent of rhythm is not voluntary acts, but that which lies between consciously fixed metrical intervals'. Here rhythm (and meaning) is 'what more or less unconsciously transpires between the accents' (Eisenstein in Law and Gordon 1996:117). Rhythm exists in the journey from one syllable/action to another. It is the spaces, and what occurs within them, that bring rhythm to life.[9]

Eisenstein's views on rhythm also drew strongly from those of Rudolf Bode.[10] Criticizing more formalist approaches to rhythm, Eisenstein warned against willing the body into a form, rhythmic or otherwise. Instead he proposed that the actor should focus on the goal at hand rather than mastery of aesthetic form. Understanding 'release' to be the fundamental principle of rhythm, he compared a flowing river to a constructed canal.

> Making the shores and bottom smooth destroys the rhythmical individuality for the sake of expediting of the process of movement. … The source of expressiveness is not the aesthetically perceived form, but the entire flexible system of expedient and goal orientated movements (Eisenstein in Law and Gordon 1996:177–8).

Eisenstein proposed that in expressive movement, the form is created not from the will but by the increase in rhythmical resistance provided by music. This was not the passive submission of movement to musical rhythm that Meyerhold attributed previously to Dalcroze and Duncan. Rather there is a sense in both Eisenstein and Meyerhold's writings that the actor and director's job involves an 'overcoming' and organizing of movements that have been aroused by music. These practitioners looked to exploit the tensions and dynamics of musical rhythm without being locked slavishly and blindly into its forms.

Tripartite rhythm

One of the means by which Meyerhold looked to empower actors in their rhythmic control and plasticity was through a structural device referred to as 'tripartite rhythm'. Pitches describes this as the 'central rhythm underpinning all Meyerhold's training' (Pitches 2003:55). Through this rhythmic formulation, each action or group of actions can be broken down into three phases, commonly referred to as *otkaz*, *posil'*, *tochka* or *i*, *ras*, *dva* (and, one, two).[11]

Otkaz is often understood as the preparation for an action or pre-action (i.e. crouching down before jumping or drawing the arm back before throwing a ball). This leads to the *posil'* – considered to be 'the physical expression of the intention, the releasing of the energy stored in the *otkaz*' (i.e. the jump or the throw). This is followed by *tochka*, described as a 'rest' (in the musical sense of the word). This is not a full stop, but rather a dynamic moment of 'fixity' (Pitches 2005:76). Breaking down their *etudes* and their individual actions into these component parts, Meyerhold's actors would at first work on each element independently and eventually bring these elements back together to form a continuous chain of actions.

EXERCISE 12: TRIPARTITE RHYTHMS IN BIOMECHANICS

This process is explained by Pitches through the following exercise:

1 Decide upon an action to perform – it might be picking up a glass.

2 Now divide this action up into three according to the *otkaz, posil'*, *tochka* structure. For example: (a) preparing to pick up the glass, (b) picking up the glass and (c) returning the glass. (Make sure this finish in some ways anticipates more action.)

3 Now perform the action again while counting 'and' (for the *otkaz*), 'one' (for the *posil'*) and 'two' (for *tochka*).

4 Try performing the separate actions in an exaggerated physical style.

5 Try performing them in a very understated style.

6 Have someone look at your action and suggest different rhythms for each part.

7 Pair up with someone else and perform a duet – either with the same action again or with something complimentary. (2003:56)

Here again, there is a clear dialogue between qualities of structure and spontaneity. It is the systematic and choreographic quality of these approaches that offers the performer a means of discovering a more flexible relationship between fixed points within a sequence.

These approaches provided the sense of freedom and spontaneity that Meyerhold insisted on through his emphasis on 'rhythm' over 'metre', while at the same time offering a quality of precision and structure.

Here rhythm is less defined by qualities of repetition or concepts of musical notation and is more closely linked to a sense of forward momentum and the innate tension, development and resolution of muscular actions. This sense of rhythm as a progression rather than repetition, is a theme discussed in detail by the philosopher and dance theorist Susanne Langer. In defining her understanding of rhythm, she explained:

> A person who moves rhythmically needs not repeat a single motion exactly. His [or her] movements, however, must be complete gestures, so that one can sense a beginning, intent, and consummation, and see in the last stage of one the condition and indeed the rise of another. Rhythm is the setting-up of a new tension by the resolution of the former ones. (1953:128)

There is a perpetual quality to such rhythms, each phase being the product of what has come before it and carrying with it a sense of intentionality for what is to come. In such a way, *otkaz, posil, tochka* establishes a quality of progression by which each moment is not an isolated event but rather provides the impetus for the next. 'The tochka is already the preparation for the next otkaz and thus the next cycle of activity begins. Each action links to the next in a chain of connected movements' (Pitches 2005:76).

While Meyerhold's earlier productions made clear use of these rhythmical structures and devices, as his career progressed, the aesthetic use of these forms became less dominant. Although he maintained the use of tripartite rhythms throughout his training, in his productions, he increasingly looked for ways in which these elements could be used to support his actors' movements without being obtrusive. As with his approach to metre, Meyerhold looked to draw on the structure of these tripartite rhythms without 'revealing' them to the audience: to 'overcome' the metrical framework supporting the actions, finding precision along with a sense of improvisation and freedom.

Reflections

While Meyerhold's concept of improvisation may not always correlate with common understandings of this term within acting practices, these approaches nevertheless highlight a number of key principles related to improvisation and performance. Here it might be more useful to think of fixed performance and improvisation as existing in parallel or dialogue, rather than as opposite ends of a scale. While some approaches may choose to emphasize one over the other, ultimately all improvisation (and all performance) involves a combination of these processes. Even when generating a performance 'from scratch', as it were, the performer and audience are to some extent complicit in drawing on preconceptions and techniques for producing and interpreting the material that is being created in the moment. Inversely when Meyerhold asked his performers to work within highly prescribed physical and temporal forms, spontaneity and the immediacy of rhythm still remained present and received significant emphasis. It is also worth considering that through the structuring of spontaneity and by restricting improvisation to a limited set of parameters, the sense of immediacy, vitality and liveness can be seen to receive more, rather than less, focus. Here we encounter improvisation at the level of micro-timings and rhythmic variations. A subtle breathing that fills the gaps and informs the 'sub-text' of the performance – the heartbeat, through which the actions and text flow.

In Meyerhold's training and directing practices we can observe a detailed and complex use of musical rhythm, working in support of, or in opposition to, the physical and vocal rhythms of his actors. Both sides of rhythm are revealed here: the ways in which it imposes a sense of a rule, a path, a pattern, a form to be followed or challenged; and the ways it suggests a quality of freedom, immediacy, a flowing forward that pushes against the restrictions and confinements of the very rules it generates. Inhabiting both of these roles, the rhythms of the actor can be seen to invite both structure and spontaneity into performance.

6

JOHN BRITTON
SMASHING THE ENSEMBLE GROOVE

My first encounter with John Britton's ensemble improvisation training was as part of a residential workshop just outside Melbourne, Australia, in 2000. What I recall most strongly from this initial work are the ways Britton was able to generate an inspired enthusiasm for working together as an ensemble and the importance given to discovering the qualities we valued in ourselves as performers and in others. Although these are aspects I have encountered in other practices, in Britton's work they were conveyed with a sense of significance that I have not come across elsewhere. This experience had a lasting impact on my work and left me pondering the interrelationship of the development of an ensemble and the creative growth of an individual performer. Since 2000, I have continued to work with Britton in numerous contexts and roles: as a collaborator and accompanist in performance improvisations, as a member of the Duende ensemble and as a co-facilitator/director on workshops and as part of his ensemble physical theatre school.

Despite the significant role played by rhythm within Britton's practices, he rarely speaks of it directly. Instead he uses words such as 'dynamics', 'energetic', 'flow', 'shape' and 'music'. The role of rhythm is perhaps most noticeable in the strong presence of musical accompaniment in training sessions, as well as in the use of game-like exercises and improvisations.

Musical accompaniment

Britton's training and workshop sessions invariably begin with a room full of people warming up individually while music plays in the background. Participants stretch out and move through the space, often with the playful sounds of jazz evoking a distinct atmosphere that is relaxed while also being energized. This choice of music seeks to immerse the performers in a new context; to excite and sharpen their senses and to establish the quality of a shared social environment; a basis for the formation of ensemble. Having set up this relationship from the outset, Britton then draws on music in various ways throughout his training sessions. It is used to support group movement exercises such as walking and running, as well as improvisations undertaken individually, in pairs, small groups and larger ensembles (sometimes with up to twenty participants). Explaining his preference for jazz music as an accompaniment for improvisation training, Britton suggests that it is the variability and unpredictability of its forms that attracts him:

> In the training I general work from a sort of small group jazz. Which is often not in particularly complex rhythms – it's in threes or fours – but it's seldom entirely regular. There's a swing in there, which is useful. It's much more useful than working to, for example, hip-hop, which might have a very regular rhythm. Although hip-hop might be a very interesting music, there is a rhythmic prison in there, which is generally not there in jazz. (Interview with author, April 2016)

In this context, jazz provides a musical backdrop with an accessible pulse while also offering fluid variation and at times a destabilizing rhythmicity. In Britton's selection of music, we find a complex interplay between the predictability of their forms (i.e. a fixed chord structure, repeated refrains and accessible rhythms) and the improvised search for novelty and nuance growing from their spontaneity, liveness and sense of risk.

For Britton, music is also more than simply a source of accompaniment. It also forms a key model for his approach to ensemble.[2] The term 'music' brings attention to the coherence of the ensemble rather than the roles played by individuals. Describing 'the overall effect of the relationship between individuals, rather than simply the individual "musician"' (Britton 2013:24), 'music' offers a metaphor or model for approaching and discussing ensemble. Notions of musicality also play an important role in Britton's approaches to performance. He discusses this in terms of both the use of musical forms/characteristics in his work and what he refers to as the 'internal phrasing of each moment':

> When does it hang and when does it drop? When does it push through and when does it disrupt? When is it lyrical and when is it discordant? When is what you are doing a counterpoint or an accompaniment, or when do you take the lead? (April 2016)

Music here provides a lens through which the performer can consider their actions and relationships within the ensemble. Britton's use of music reflects not only an aesthetic choice, but also a shared ethos in regard to ensemble and the sense of creativity, spontaneity and risk taking encouraged within this work. As a model of understanding, it informs the performers' attitudes to themselves and to each other.

Jazz as model for ensemble improvisation

Viewed as a model for improvisation, jazz presents a framework in which individuals interact both spontaneously and according to preconceived structures, simultaneously generating and responding to the immediacy of their shared performance. David Roesner suggests that in this regard, jazz has been highly influential in the evolution of contemporary theatre improvisation in general, establishing new models for thinking about relationships between ensemble and soloist, as well as increasing the focus placed on *how* rather than *what* is done in performance (2014:179–85). In jazz improvisation more attention is often given to 'how' the performer interprets and navigates a form, rather than the characteristics of the form itself. The qualities of a player's 'sound', their sense of spontaneity and responsiveness, their individual timing and 'swing' are the aspects that are given attention and often celebrated. Reflecting on this principle, Roesner observes that in theatrical improvisations there has been a strong movement away from narrative models (which he terms 'what' improvisation) and a shift towards an increased emphasis on the qualities of action, sound or text ('how' improvisation) (2014:179).

Highlighting the significance of 'how' something is performed over 'what' is being performed, Britton offers an example of his displeasure in watching a badly performed production of a Shakespeare play versus the delight in watching primary school children performing in a school play. In each of these instances it is not *what* is being performed but rather *how* it is done – the ways in which the material is encountered and brought to life – that is critical. Interestingly though, Britton will often begin a training session or exercise by intentionally drawing focus to 'what' is happening. He will ask the participant to notice details such as what parts of their bodies they are using, when they are moving or being still, or what they are looking at (themselves, others, the space). The work then gradually builds to a detailed awareness of the specifics of 'how' these actions are done or perceived. Britton suggests that in this training context: 'Paying attention to 'what' disciplines the use of the body, paying attention to 'how' opens up narrative, emotional associations, character and other expressive possibilities' (2013:347).

Perhaps the most obvious correlation between Britton's work and jazz is the focus placed on ensemble as a collection of unique voices. This is a principle that Daniel Belgrade identifies clearly in his description of bebop jazz:

> the antiphonal structure of bebop suggests an intersubjective dynamic, one in which the individual and the community empower one another. Each presence enlivens the other, creating a whole that is animated by the collective energy without which individual expression would not exist. There is no dichotomy. (2014:229)

In both cases, it is the mutual dependency of these aspects that is important. Britton highlights the significance of these inter-subjective relationships through the name he gives to his training – 'Self-With-Others'. Here, as with a jazz ensemble, the performers' cultivation of their own creative identities is seen to be linked directly with their abilities to interact and respond to 'others': 'Self-With-Others is a psychophysical approach to training performers in the context of ensemble. It trains each individual by facilitating encounters with him/herself in evolving and dynamic relationship with others' (Britton 2010b).

The focus of this type of ensemble training (as with jazz) is not on generating a unified mass of anonymous performers, but on simultaneously developing the uniqueness of each performer (self) and their ability to effectively be 'with-others' on stage. This notion of being 'with' is critical to Britton's approach. Building the capacity to maintain an awareness of one's own tasks, actions, intentions, rhythms, etc., while also sustaining an awareness of one's relationships to the 'others', is at the heart of this training. At times this can feel like an impossible task – the temptation being to either close off from the rest of the group or to forget about one's self and just pay attention to the others. Yet, what Britton is proposing is not so much a state of 'dual consciousness', in the sense of being aware of self and *at the same time* being aware of the other. Rather the suggestion here (at least as I understand it) is to pay attention to the *self as it exists in relationship to others*. Here, rather than ensemble being the product of a group of selves, we might view the self as a product of ensemble relationships; the self is formed (or informed) by the ways it relates to others.

Ensemble

As with rhythm, the notion of ensemble often resists definition. It is a term that can mean very different things to different people.[3] And as with rhythm, it is often most noticeable in its absence or when the performers are struggling to achieve it. In the context of music, there are a number of obvious give-aways that indicate when a performer is not playing as part of the ensemble. They might be out of tune, or out of time, or just not quite 'swinging' with the rest of the band. Yet often when they are truly playing together, we do not notice any of these things. All we experience is the music or the effect that it has on us. The same could be said for a theatrical or a dance ensemble. When they are really 'with' each other, it is often not the ensemble that we notice, but rather a heightened sense of the present moment, the significance of what is taking place.

In the context of theatre or dance, however, the parameters of what it means to be *with* others can be much broader and obscure than in music. Where in music we can sense the quality of ensemble by simply listening to how their sounds sit together, in theatre and dance our perception of ensemble involves the synthesis of a far broader range of elements (e.g. sound, image, language and movement). I am not suggesting that a musical ensemble is easier to form or that this is a purely technical phenomenon. It is just that there are clearer vocabularies and more obvious frameworks through which a musical ensemble can be approached (as noted by Meyerhold in Chapter 5). This in turn means that it is often easier to define, discuss and attend to the nature of ensemble through the use of musical terms or metaphors.

Smashing the groove

One of the key concepts that Britton associates with rhythm 'is the notion of establishing a normality and then disrupting it' (interview with author, April 2016). Discussing this he suggests that 'at the heart of all dramatic development ... something is established and then something changes. And that from that change, there comes a new rhythm – a new normality' (April 2016). His interest in these concepts came initially, not from music, but from Marxism and the progression of 'thesis, antithesis and synthesis'.[1] Although Britton no longer uses these terms within his practice, the process of 'establishing something', then 'creating something which breaks that' and then 'seeing what emerges' has remained a central 'rhythmic' principle within his work.

Britton comments on the jazz pianist Keith Jarrett, describing him as a bold, daring, exploratory artist, whose 'unwavering commitment to improvisation' is part of what fuels his fearlessness. He states that his own pedagogical approach is 'based in improvisation for exactly these reasons' (personal correspondents). Here Britton emphasizes the sense of risk involved in improvisation, a model that asks the performers to put themselves on the line and to be open to the possibility of failing, in front of either their peers or an audience. Although cohesion and flow are critical aspects of Britton's vision of ensemble, his training also seeks to cultivate dynamism and a capacity for individuals to break away from the ensemble's rhythm, becoming catalysts for change. He identifies the importance of performers recognizing when to stay within the flow of an improvisation, when to drive this flow onward and when to break away and establish something new – what Britton calls 'smashing the groove'. This notion of development through disruption – associated with the Marxist model of 'thesis, antithesis and synthesis' – can also be seen as tied closely to Britton's interest in jazz improvisation and its ethos of pushing at the edges of familiarity and comfort.

An example of how this model is applied in training can be observed clearly in the following exercise. Setting up the parameters for an ensemble improvisation Britton instructs:

> Pay attention to what you think the performance needs – initiation of new material or response to/development of existing material. Be willing to 'smash the groove' – to notice when the performance has become too comfortable, has entered into a dead zone of familiarity. You might find being 'in the groove' really comfortable, it requires no detailed attention. It's predictable. Resist the comfort! (Britton 2013:351)

We can observe the way a performer's own sense of comfort is used as a barometer indicating when change is needed. Through this work, Britton is looking to cultivate a quality of liveness, marked by a sense of immediacy, spontaneity and a strong capacity for change. There is a restless evolutionary quality here that seeks development rather than complacency and stagnation. As within a jazz ensemble, every member of the group is responsible for keeping this sense of progression, for not letting the improvisation go to sleep or rest too comfortably on a sense of familiarity. Describing the music of jazz saxophonist, John Coltrane, Eric Nisenson writes:

> [Coltrane's music] made one always vitally aware of being alive. It is not easy music and it does not make life easy. It does make us braver, stronger, and unlike so much of our mass culture, never accepting of a life of 'quiet desperation'. (Nisenson 2009:270)

As with Coltrane's music, Britton often encourages performers to avoid the 'easy route' and to work at 'the edge' of their comfort. This is more than a stylistic or aesthetic choice. It is about being aware of what is being created by the ensemble and taking responsibility for keeping this alive. This does not necessarily mean that the group is always changing rhythms or seeking to introduce new material. Sometimes, sustaining a rhythmic quality or letting it develop slowly over time can be the most provocative action taken by an ensemble. Similarly, the act of allowing a structured rhythm or a period of sustained silence/stillness to emerge within an improvisation can offer a clear form of disruption to what might otherwise be an intensely complex and busy ensemble dynamic. The main criteria here are that the performers are always looking and listening and are open to change in whatever form this might take.

The shape of an action

Britton's use of rhythm is generally less prescriptive than most of the approaches discussed in this book. He seldom instructs performers to work to specific rhythmic structures or qualities of timing. Instead he looks to encourage performers to develop an awareness and sensitivity to the shape and dynamics of their own actions, along with a sense of how these relate to those of the ensemble and the performance as a whole. He explains that '[e]very action has a form (or shape) and an internal dynamic (or energetic)' (2013:353). The performer's job is to learn to observe and use these as means of constructing their performance. Here, the use of the word 'shape' refers to both the spatial and the temporal trajectory of an action. In this sense Britton often asks performers to observe how their actions 'begin', 'develop', 'decay' and 'end'. This framework is applied to a wide range of actions, from single gestures and movement sequences to the 'shape' of an entire performance. A simple exercise in which this can be observed is one that Britton refers to as 'the ball game'. This is a core exercise used throughout Britton's workshops, training sessions and rehearsal processes with numerous variations and permutations.

EXERCISE 13: 'THE BALL GAME'

The premise of this exercise is a simple and familiar one. A group stands in a circle, throwing and catching balls. This is an activity used within numerous training approaches and has clear links to similar exercises referred to previously, in regard to the work of Bing and

Copeau (Chapter 4).[4] But where Bing and Copeau would often impose strict rhythms and work towards accelerating the speed of these exercises, the rhythms in Britton's 'ball game' emerge primarily from the participants' actions themselves and the flow of the group.

For Britton, the initial aim of this exercise is *not* that the performer becomes better at throwing and catching, rather that they encounter the ways in which they receive and respond to impulses. These processes are used to help the performers identify blockages or forms of habitual behaviour that may be preventing them from responding directly or 'genuinely' to the moment. As Britton points out, 'often we respond not to an impulse, but to our idea of what the impulse will or should be' (Britton 2013:318). The 'ball game' in this sense becomes a clear model or analogy for improvisation, reflecting the qualities of immediacy and responsiveness often sought in performance.

The simplicity of this game also means that it can easily be adapted to include various sub-tasks, or specific points of focus, according to the area of work that Britton is looking to develop. Often beginning with a single ball, over time more balls and tasks are added. Initially these might include having one foot of the ground when catching, or spinning after a throw, or clapping before a catch. Over time these tasks may also involve participants paying particular attention to 'how' they are working within these processes. An example of this can be seen in Britton's introduction of the concept of 'shape' within the 'ball game':

> Every time I move to catch a ball, transform the incoming energy into outgoing energy, return to rest, the shape of the action I experience is unique. Sometimes, if the incoming throw is wild or unexpected, responding to the ball entails a large physical response. Often, the response is more subtle. Recognizing this uniqueness emphasizes the live quality of each moment. (2013:353)

Considered as a form of rhythm training, 'the ball game' can be seen to provide a simple context in which performers train their attention to be able to track and comprehend the 'shape' that their own and other performers' actions form over time.

There is a noticeable change in quality as a group becomes more experienced in these exercises. It is not that they are necessarily dropping less or that their throws are more regular or predictable. Instead, there is an emergence of what might best be called 'flow' – a sense of continuity and fluidity passing between one action and another. With this sense of flow, we can observe that when drops do happen, or when a throw comes at an unexpected moment, the group's response is more integrated, with these variations easily incorporated into the rhythm of the ensemble as a whole.

There is a sense of an *ensemble rhythm* that is simultaneously being generated by and feeding back into the individual actions of the group. This sense of rhythm is a long way from the notion of a regular beat or repeatable phrase. It is something more elusive, yet equally tangible. We could describe this as a form of 'collective entrainment'.[5] Jessica Phillips-Silver suggests that this form of synchronization is responsible for facilitating many general forms of 'groupwise interaction, such as group conversation, or the coordination of any work that requires individuals to be sensitive to one another's movement and effort' (Phillips-Silver, Aktipis and Bryant 2010:9). A similarly interrelational form of synchronization can be observed in the 'ball game'. Here participants are involved in a process of continuously adapting and coordinating the timing of their own movements (the catching of balls) in response to the rhythmic actions of others (the throwing of balls). As more balls are added to this process, the complexity of this collective entrainment becomes increasingly sophisticated and subtle.

The energetic

One of the ways that Britton talks about this emergent aspect of his work is through the term 'energetic'. This term is used to describe the characteristics of an action's dynamics, intensity, trajectory and potential. Using the 'ball game' as a way of making performers aware of both their individual and the group's 'energetic', Britton explains:

I ask people to listen to the exercise. As the balls flow, some are dropped, some are caught. There are moments of crescendo, moments when everything seems to be falling towards stillness, moments of unchanging dynamic. We hear that the exercise itself has a life, a breath, a trajectory, independent of the individuals creating it. If we start to pay attention to the energetic of our own actions, while also listening to the 'music' of the exercise we notice that they are often different. ... As in an orchestra, there is the music of the whole, and the music of the individual instrument. They are not always doing the same thing. (2013:355)

This sense of 'listening' to the 'music' of the exercise is both literal and metaphorical. From within the flow of the exercise, there often emerges a fluid quality of musical composition formed by the gentle thud of balls landing in hands and on the floor. Like listening to rain falling on a roof, we begin to get a sense of an ebb and flow, patterns forming and passing away. It is also perhaps more in our listening than in our looking that our sense of the whole emerges. When I *look* at this exercise, what often strikes me is the actions of individuals – a skilful catch, a wild throw. My *listening*, however, more easily encompasses the whole. In listening, I perceive a single schema – an integrated sense of musical composition starts to form. But there is also another level to this sense of 'music'. There is an experience of something 'other' – a rising and falling, moments of tension and release, focus and dissipation – what Britton sometimes refers to as the 'intensity' or the 'it-ness' of the ensemble (Britton 2010a).

As a group becomes more experienced in listening to the 'music' of their own work, Britton gradually lessens the amount of recorded music used within his training exercises and improvisation. He comments: 'I work with music and gradually fade it out until the constituent elements are left dancing naked in the performer's awareness' (April 2016). Where musical accompaniment initially establishes the context or territory in which the performers meet one another, as the work progresses, they themselves learn to discover and create the 'musical' landscapes of their work. This rhythm (shape or energetic) eventually emerges from the qualities of listening and doing, rather than from an external musical stimulus or form.

Reflections

As with the other practitioners discussed here, Britton often looks to disrupt a habitual tendency towards working within a fixed rhythm or 'groove'. We can note how this dynamic improvisational aesthetic is also mirrored in many of his choices of musical accompaniment, with a large amount of jazz and contemporary musical compositions being used in his training exercises and extended improvisations. Similarities can also be found in the use of musical accompaniment in Meyerhold's training and Britton's own dominant use of music and, in particular, jazz. In both cases music serves as a tool for focusing performers and developing their sense of compositional flow and musicality. Yet where Meyerhold used music as means of organizing time and structuring the rhythms of his performers' actions – giving them a form to work with or against – Britton's approach to music is far less prescriptive, often adopting music as an energetic stimulus rather than a strict guideline or compositional framework. In contrast to Meyerhold's use of music as a means of maintaining discipline and clarity, Britton's immersive use of music is often intentionally disorienting and disruptive. In this context, performers are rarely instructed as to how they should relate to a musical composition. Instead music provides a backdrop over which other, more interpersonal and physical forms of relationship are played out.

While Britton's use of rhythm is often related to music, it also clearly encompasses other processes including the rhythmic dynamics that form from social and game-like interactions and the embodied sense of rhythm that emerges from the 'energetic' and 'shape' of bodies or objects moving through a space. Here, rhythm is not so much a compositional tool; rather, it forms a sense of relationship to the ensemble, to the moment, to a shared sense of listening and the performance being formed. Learning to listen and respond to these rhythms often takes precedence over responding to the rhythms of the music being played. In this way, Britton seeks to encourage the performers to discover the 'music' of what they are doing in relationship to one another and how their own actions (or choice not to take action) can contribute to keeping this music alive.

7

ANNE BOGART AND TINA LANDAU

A HORIZONTAL VIEWPOINT

Anne Bogart and Tina Landau describe 'Viewpoints' as a 'clear-cut procedure and attitude that is nonhierarchical, practical and collaborative in nature' (2005:15). Inspired by the practices of Mary Overlie (the original creator of 'Six Viewpoints'), Bogart and Landau developed Viewpoints as an approach for building a greater sense of physicality, spontaneity and ensemble openness in performers. Constructively applying these practices to their work as directors (Bogart with the Saratoga International Theatre Institute, SITI and Landau with Steppenwolf Theatre Company), Viewpoints has also come to be disseminated widely through international workshops and training programmes.[1]

Through practical exercises and a collection of terms, Viewpoints deconstructs performance into a number of individual elements listed as Shape, Gesture, Repetition, Architecture, Tempo, Duration, Topography, Spatial Relationship and Kinaesthetic Response. First approached as discrete elements, these Viewpoints are later combined and configured into various relationships through improvisations and simple game-like activities. These processes aim at cultivating a stronger awareness of creative choices within devising and performance, as well as looking to establish a shared vocabulary and set of understandings to be drawn on by performers and directors. It is interesting to note the absence of the word rhythm from this list of performance aspects (viewpoints). On the few occasions when rhythm is referred to by Bogart and Landau, its meaning is often tied to qualities of regularity or an overt sense of musical structure such as a 'waltz rhythm' or a driving musical beat.

Rather than discussing rhythm specifically, Viewpoints works with a collection of temporal and compositional elements grouped under the subcategory of 'Viewpoints of Time'. These include Tempo, Duration, Kinaesthetic response and Repetition. There is a technical nature to these terms, which primarily addresses a performer's physical relationship to time. Where Meyerhold and Stanislavski's approaches drew strongly on musical terminologies, models and metaphors, Viewpoints makes a concerted effort to break away from the formalist trappings associated with musical structure. In Overlie's own Viewpoints approach, she warned performers of the risks of 'adding exterior rhythm' or formalized qualities to their movements (Overlie 2006b). In regard to time, Overlie also commented on the tendencies that actors can develop in relationship to their timing and rhythm:

> Actors trained to entertain the audience by using excitement and high emotion become locked into a limited understanding of the use of time, and believe that the audience demands a certain kind of timing in order to be satisfied with their performance. Since, in Viewpoints work, there is no idea of entertainment, the focus of this primary practice exposes time as a solid and ever-present material, moving the actor past preconceived fears of audience judgment. (Overlie 2006a:325–6)

Here Overlie emphasizes the importance of approaching time, not as a means of entertaining an audience but as a material which 'communicates on its own terms'. She proposed that by establishing a new vocabulary of time, actors could find greater freedom and subtlety in their movement rhythms released from the limitations of 'common' understandings and terms (Overlie 2006a:326). Following this philosophy, Bogart and Landau have looked to establish a clear and direct vocabulary by which performers and directors can discuss time in performance – addressing this predominantly from the perspective of physical movement rather than applying existing musical or poetic models to their work.

A non-hierarchical ethos

Viewpoints identifies itself as growing out of a movement of artistic reform and experimentation that emerged in New York and San Francisco during the 1960s, in particular the work of the Judson Church Theatre. Bogart and Landau comment:

> One of the fundamental agreements that united this group was their belief in nonhierarchical art and the use of 'real time' activities which were arrived at through game-like structures ... Music, for example, would not dictate choices. An object could have the same importance as a human body. The spoken word could be on equal footing with gesture. One idea could hold the same importance as another on the same stage at the same time. (2005:4)

This non-hierarchical ethos strongly informs the principles adopted by Viewpoints, in terms of the relationship between performance elements, as well as through the ways it seeks to empower performers to make creative decisions from within the work itself. This second point presents an intentional challenge to the dominant model of an autonomous, all-seeing, all-knowing director/author, and looks to establish a more pluralist approach to performance making and improvisation. Commenting on the fact that some might view this 'release of hierarchy' as simply chaotic, Overlie stated:

> Far from being chaotic or passive, this new interpretation of creativity and art was based on the sound principle that the act of seeing or witnessing generates its own structures. These structures produce their own progress without a preconceived and definitive statement created by a singular person/artist. (2006a:189)

As with Britton's practices, there is an emergent nature to these processes, whereby form and composition grow out of the processes of doing and of the collective interactions of the ensemble.[2] Rather than attempting to layer preconception or impose external notions onto a creative process, Viewpoints seeks to locate understanding, decision making and compositional form within the realization and experiencing of the practice itself.

These artistic and political ideas spring from a wider American experimental performance movement tied to the work of the Judson Church Theatre as well as other companies such as the San Francisco Mime Troupe, the Second City, the Living Theatre and the Open Theatre, whose work emerged in the 1960s. The influence of this non-hierarchical ethos can also be traced into the work of other American practitioners and companies including Ruth Zaporah, Steve Paxton, Wooster Group, Goat Island and Elevator Repair Service. These practitioners, along with Bogart and Landau, have in their own ways established alternative models of creative practice, which have looked to challenge dominant frameworks within American theatre. Many of these companies have also drawn strongly on the use of improvisation as a training and performance approach and have also often engaged in sustained processes of collaboration between a core team of performers. Empowering actors to make creative decisions as members of an ensemble, these companies have sought to break away from 'conventional' systems of theatre in which creative control and artistic 'voice' have often been allocated to a single external author, director or 'star' actor. Here, the concept of ensemble becomes as much a political viewpoint as an aesthetic choice.

The performance philosopher Laura Cull describes collective processes such as these as a form of 'Immanent Authorship' (2012:22–56). But as Cull rightly points out, the distinction between 'immanent' and 'transcendent' authorship is not always so clear-cut (2012:55). While the use of ensemble improvisation may appear to be an ideal model for democratizing performance, such approaches can also be used to promote self-indulgence, cliché and group conformity.[3] Conversely, we can observe many instances in which an 'outside eye' and the use of imposed 'creative constraints' support plurality within a creative process. Rather than hampering individual creativity, a director can open new potentials by challenging a performer's more 'ego-driven' tendencies of wanting to dominate a performance or add unnecessary embellishments to his or her work. Discussing these aspects within the work of Goat Island, Cull explains:

In this instance, the director's 'outsideness' serves to question and challenge attempts by performers to 'hold on' to moments of performance that may serve individual needs, but do not serve those of the performance as a whole. (Cull 2012:45)

In their own ways, Viewpoints and the work of SITI also seek to balance the sense of individual freedom with the precision of technical tasks and constraints. The methodical nature of Viewpoints, and its almost coded use of terminology, could be seen as a way of mitigating against what might otherwise become a form of 'free-for-all' creative process. In a similar way, the controlled system of introducing one performance element (Viewpoint) at a time helps establish a more 'level playing field' in which these 'views' can potentially be better expressed and heard. At times deconstructing performance to an almost clinical level of precision, Viewpoints looks to avoid the trappings of aesthetic formulas, artistic clichés and habitual patterns of performance making.

Musical accompaniment

Distinct from many of the other practices described in this book, in Viewpoints, music is only introduced once the foundational principles have been well established. Bogart and Landau advise:

Music is a vastly powerful and seductive element in the theatre and to introduce it before the individual Viewpoints have been digested would be, in a sense, too great a temptation, too strong a stimulus. Introduced at the right moment, music becomes a portal: an inspiration, a boost and a challenge. (Bogart and Landau 2005:94)

If introduced too soon, music is seen to distract from the core elements of this work, with a group's initial response to music described as limiting their creativity. Performers are seen as being enslaved by the dominant effects of music – in particular its 'rhythms' – their work losing a quality of 'openness and unpredictability'. The suggestion here is that in music a performer is often 'imprisoned rather than freed' (Bogart and Landau 2005:96).

In contrast to Britton and Meyerhold's use of music as a foundational tool within their training, Viewpoints intentionally avoids the presence of musical structures early in the work. Where these practitioners saw music as encouraging precision and focus in their performers, Bogart and Landau identify it as being manipulative, 'domineering' and 'binding'. When music is eventually introduced into the Viewpoints process, it is done so in a way that gradually builds 'from the least intrusive to the most' (Bogart and Landau 2005:102). Yet despite these distinctions, the first exercises for working with music in Viewpoints bare many similarities to those used by Meyerhold (Chapter 5).

EXERCISE 14: 'TO' AND 'AGAINST'

Music is played with an obvious and consistent beat. The group are at first asked to walk 'to' the music. Having established a sense of the pulse, they are then instructed to move 'against' the 'tempo and/or rhythm', being told 'to move in counterpoint'. Working with the principle of moving in ways that are other than the dominant 'rhythm', participants are instructed to explore at least five or six ways of walking in relationship to one piece of music. Building on this exercise, performers are encouraged to find a more dialectic relationship to the music – to treat it as another 'partner' within their improvisations – a 'gift' that can lead to an expansion rather than a restriction of possibilities (Bogart and Landau 2005:97–8).

Rhythm in Suzuki work

In looking to understand the ways that rhythm, metre and music are being approached within Viewpoints, it is worth noting that these practices are seldom used in isolation. SITI's practices combine Viewpoints with other training and devising approaches, specifically: 'Suzuki work'[4] and 'Composition'. Providing a complimentary set of approaches, Composition encourages the performance makers to draw from other art forms including music, film and architecture, as inspiration for developing performance dramaturgies, while Suzuki work involves a highly disciplined approach to physical training.

In contrast to Viewpoints, many of Tadashi Suzuki's exercises require an almost total submission to the rhythms of the accompanying music. Suzuki describes a performer engaged in 'stomping' (one of Suzuki's core training elements) as moving 'like a puppet to the rhythm of the music' (Suzuki 1986:11). As an example, in the exercise 'Stamping Shakuhachi', the participants engage in the sustained action of stamping at a constant regulated tempo that is guided by the pulse of a recorded musical composition. As the music builds to a climax the group arrange themselves in a line at the back of the space, and when cued by a change in the music, they collapse to the floor. Throughout this work the performers are looking to not only maintain the precise rhythm and steady tempo of their leg movements but also to regulate and control their breath (Allain 2002:118).

Viewpoints and Suzuki work, each in their own way, look to 'break' a performer's habitual rhythms. But where Viewpoints works on deconstructing the relationship between performer and musical accompaniment, encouraging the performer to discover their own rhythms separated from the music, Suzuki uses music as means of deconstructing a performer's personal rhythms. This contrast of approaches suggests a possible reason for the strong association between rhythm and regularity within Viewpoints and its emphasis on the performer working outside of, or in contrast to, a metric notion of rhythm. In this way, we can observe a number of oppositional relationships to rhythm in these two practices, with Suzuki's dominant use of music and patterned movements (to some extent) informing the notion of rhythm within Viewpoints.

Viewpoints of time

Many of the introductory Viewpoints exercises take the form of simple game-like activities and structured improvisations. Seeking (at first) to isolate the individual Viewpoints, this work often involves tight parameters that limit the choices available to the performer. For example, many of the initial improvisations will involve participants only being able to travel in straight lines, up and down the space (referred to as 'lane work'). Improvising in this formation, performers begin by working from a simple pallet of choices, such as either walking or stopping. Over time these structures are opened up to include working within a 'grid' structure, with this eventually opening out to participants having freedom to move through the space, following any path they choose. With the introduction of each new Viewpoint the various combinations of these elements are also explored, eventually leading to what is known as Open Viewpoints. Bogart describes this through the metaphor of learning to juggle. Starting with one 'ball' and then gradually adding one more at a time, the performer eventually builds the capacity to keep all the 'balls' ('viewpoints') in motion simultaneously. This then becomes the main task of the performers, sustaining their awareness of this multitude of performance elements and languages, while remaining open and responsive to all that is happening inside and outside of them.

Tempo

Often the first Viewpoint to be worked with is Tempo, with Landau defining this as 'the rate of speed at which a movement occurs: how fast or slow something happens on stage' (Landau 1995:20).

EXERCISE 15: TEMPO: 'THE BASICS'

As an initial exercise performers are instructed to:

1 Choose one action, with a clear beginning and end.

2 Repeat it several times, making sure the form is exact and repeatable.

3 Perform the action in a medium tempo.

4 Perform the action in a fast tempo.

5 Perform the action in a slow tempo. (Bogart and Landau 2005:36)

Performing the same actions at varying tempos performers are given the opportunity to develop greater control and versatility as well as an awareness of how Tempo can affect the meaning and/or emotional association that one has with an action.[5]

Viewpoints establishes a spectrum of tempos. These range from 'the slowest you can go and still call it movement' to the opposite extreme, which is termed 'hyper-speed'. 'Medium tempo' suggests here a point somewhere in the middle of these two extreme ends of the scale. This way of talking about tempo is closer to a qualitative description than the quantitative definition often adopted in music theory. Bogart and Landau propose: 'Most actions, when initially performed without thought or context, will occur at a medium tempo' (2005:37).

Here, the guidelines for what is 'fast', 'slow' or 'medium' tempo are based more on a performer or audience member's relationship to an action rather than a set measurement of time.[6] David Roesner points out that while musical tempo is generally linked to the rate of a regular beat, in theatre, tempo often emerges from a 'sense of expectation and realization or surprise' (2014:84). In this sense, a gesture is often read as 'slow' or 'fast' relative to our expectations. This can come from having seen a similar gesture in the same performance or by comparing the speed that a gesture is performed to how it is normally executed in daily life.

Duration

Here Duration deals specifically with the length of time a performer or ensemble 'stays within' a section of movement or activity before it changes. The focus of this Viewpoint lies in cultivating an awareness of the length of time needed 'so that something occurs, … so that you exploit the moment of actual event, but not so long that it starts to fall asleep or die' (Bogart and Landau 2005:102).

As with Tempo, the exercises used for working on Duration aim at deconstructing habitual tendencies towards performance timing. The metaphors of 'death' and 'sleep' also suggest that one of the ensemble's main jobs is to keep the performance awake or at least alive. Here, I am reminded of the vitalist concept of rhythm as a living entity of its own (Chapter 2). Yet, where many of the early vitalist theories of rhythm referred to a set of natural 'laws' or 'rules' by which rhythmic/timing choices should be guided, Viewpoints emphasizes the performer's own sense of the duration needed 'so that something occurs'. Seeking to keep the performance awake and alive, the ensembles are engaged in an active enquiry based on sensing when change is needed or when something needs to be sustained. Instead of being based on an imposed notion of 'correct' or 'organic' timing, or a model drawn from musical composition, in Viewpoints performers are encouraged to work primarily from the perspective of seeking to interest and surprise themselves.

EXERCISE 16: DURATION AND TEMPO

Improvising with changes in tempo, performers are instructed to sustain the duration of each tempo for longer or shorter 'than feels comfortable', looking to 'surprise themselves' by varying their use of duration and not predetermining when a start or stop will take place. As with Tempo, Bogart and Landau propose that most performers will habitually fall into predictable patterns of durations in their work, often sustaining actions over short regular bursts. 'We tend to live in a medium area with Duration, a gray zone, in which things last a comfortable, average, seemingly coherent amount of time. We tend to shy away from things that last very long or change very quickly' (Bogart and Landau 2005:41).

Exploring the ways that sustaining (for example) a fast run over a long duration, or a slow walk that is broken by bursts of other tempos, allows the performers to begin to gage the effects these choices have on their interest and engagement with the improvisation.

Similar to Britton's notion of 'smashing the groove', here performers are instructed not to get stuck in patterns of behaviour. The performers are encouraged to become aware of feelings of familiarity and comfort. Their aim is not to surrender to these, but rather to use such feelings as a reference point, which they can intentionally move outside of (or 'smash'). At the same time performers are looking to subvert expectations and avoid demonstrating when something is about to stop, start or change. The liveness of the performance is tied here to its lack of predictability – the sense of immediacy with which each action is undertaken.

Kinaesthetic response

Bogart and Landau define Kinaesthetic Response as a 'spontaneous reaction to motion which occurs outside you; the time in which you respond to the external events of movement or sound; the impulsive movement that occurs from a stimulation of the senses' (Bogart and Landau 2005:8). Where Duration can be seen as rooted in the performers' feelings of 'interest' and 'surprise', Kinaesthetic Response is maybe best related to a less analytical approach, something closer to an instinctual reaction. The performer is instructed to relinquish choice (at least for the moment) and 'only receive and react' in a way that is 'immediate' and 'uncensored' (Bogart and Landau 2005:42). This Viewpoint shifts the focus from the performer making choices about the speed and duration of their actions to a sense that these decisions are determined by an external source.

EXERCISE 17: INTRODUCING KINAESTHETIC RESPONSE

Participants engage in an improvisation in which they can only move in straight lines through the space, following a 'grid pattern'. All of their choices as to when to take action are triggered by external stimuli. Bogart and Landau instruct: 'It is no longer for you to choose what is right or wrong, good or bad – but to use everything. If someone runs by you – use it! If the group suddenly shifts into slow motion – use it! Let everything change you' (2005:42). Here the performer's job is not to try and 'be interesting', or 'inventive', but to simply open themselves up to what is happening around them, listening (in a sense) with their 'whole body'.

The spontaneous, immediate and non-cerebral nature of these responses highlights the improvisational and somatic characteristics of this training. It also further emphasizes the 'immanent' qualities being fostered by Viewpoints. The performers relinquish control, not to a director, author, dramatic structure or narrative, but to the immediacy of what is happening in the space, in the moment.

From a rhythmic perspective, this Viewpoint also opens up some interesting areas of enquiry. What are the rhythmic qualities that emerge from working primarily with an immediate instinctual response, as distinct from the more considered analytical approaches of previous Viewpoints? By diminishing a sense of self agency, do we move closer to a quality of *ensemble rhythm,* or do the rhythms of the individuals become increasingly fractured by the unpredictable nature of their responsiveness?

Repetition

The last Viewpoint of Time to be discussed is Repetition. Two types of Repetition are defined: 'internal' and 'external'. Where 'internal repetition' involves 'repeating a movement within your own body', 'external repetition' refers to 'repeating the shape, tempo, gesture, etc., of something outside your own body' (Bogart and Landau 2005:9).

EXERCISE 18: INTRODUCING REPETITION

Improvising as an ensemble, the performers work with detailed awareness of each other's movements, looking to recycle the gestures, floor patterns and movement qualities that they see around them. This can happen simultaneously (i.e. I copy the actions, or floor patterns that one or more performers make, while they are making them). Or this response can be delayed (I perform an action that another performer did earlier in the improvisation) (Bogart and Landau 2005:43). As with Kinaesthetic Response, the performers' awareness is focused outwards, looking to draw material from others while establishing a sense of ensemble composition.

Through this intentional use of Repetition there comes a sense of motif and the emergence of structures and patterns forming within an improvisation. We can also see a potential for a stronger sense of rhythmicity, with material returning and being layered in various ways, creating developments and variations on established themes. However, this use of Repetition is not so much a metric device but is more focused on the ways performers generate and reincorporate material. In Viewpoints, Repetition generally does not mean to repeat actions again and again, as a kind of cyclic or metric pattern. It suggests rather that the same actions can crop up at different times and/or places within an improvisation. Intentionally drawing on each other's material can also add a stronger sense of composition to the group's work, encouraging performers to pay more attention to the ensemble, and draw on what has already taken place instead of looking to generate their own personal material.

Reflecting these principles in her work as a director, Bogart proposes that she is not an 'original thinker' or 'true creative artist'. Evoking a sense of Repetition, she refers to herself instead as a 'scavenger'.

Like a bird that goes and pulls different things and makes a nest … I take little bits of what I read and I put them together into thoughts and ideas. I juxtapose ideas. I like the satisfaction of putting things together like that. (Bogart cited in Mitter and Shevtsova 2004:221)

It is not the originality of the work that is important here but rather the ways the elements are brought together, arranged, related to one another. In 'scavenging' and Repetition, Bogart's practices could be compared to the creative processes of collage in visual art and 'sampling' in music. Similarly, in these examples we can see the ways that 'authorship' is challenged/fractured by the act of externally sourcing material and content. Working within a Viewpoints improvisation, the performers have no need for 'originality'. Instead we might label them as collaborative 'scavengers' – those who steal, pluck at, recycle and reinvent the material that they find around them.

Reflections

Ultimately what Viewpoints is seeking is choice. Here, 'choice' is not so much a form of rational decision making, as it is a freeing of the body from the limitations of habit, preconception and external authorship. This is done partly through a process of breaking down the hierarchical tendencies of 'conventional' approaches to performance. Introducing one element at a time, Viewpoints looks to inhibit any singular performance language from dominating the others. The focus that is given to the kinaesthetic sense of the performer's own body also offers a means of empowering performers by expanding their awareness and in turn their creative choices. In approaching each 'Viewpoint of Time', the performer is asked to listen to their body's response: to the feeling of comfort, familiarity, excitement, impulse and interest. These choices are shaped more by instinctual responses than by external or idealized notions of form or composition. Time and rhythm become bodily, kinaesthetic and responsive, rather than musical, textual or conceptual.

Instead of presenting a system or method for making performance, Viewpoints offers a means of enquiry. In this way, Viewpoints raises various questions about how rhythmic choices are made in performance. When should a performer challenge their instinctive response to rhythm and when should they follow them? When should a performer exercise their capacity to make individual choices and when should they give over this choice to the ensemble? Do concepts of 'right' or 'correct' rhythm, duration and tempo have any place in this work, or are these choices entirely subjective, based in each performer's sense of appropriateness in the moment? Viewpoints offers a framework in which the individual performer and ensemble are given the chance to make a practical enquiry within the context of ensemble improvisation.

Reflections on structure and spontaneity

This brings us back to the relationship between structure and spontaneity observed throughout this part of the book. Each approach discussed here has, in its own way, sought to challenge the habitual structures and rhythms of the individual performer. This has been done primarily through imposing new structures, as well as by encouraging spontaneity, immediacy and responsiveness. Yet, while all the practitioners discussed have sought a quality of spontaneous and integrated rhythmic expression in their performers, their approaches to this have been noticeably distinct. Each emphasizes a different characteristic of rhythm, and in doing so encourage a particular understanding and relationship to time in performance. At its most obvious, this is done by directly imposing an external rhythmic or metric structure onto an improvisation, as seen in the work of Meyerhold and Bing. However, at a subtler level, we can also witness the distinct ways each approach seeks to emphasize and promote certain aspects and relationships to rhythm over others – notions of play and continuity (as seen with Bing) or spontaneity within precise structure (as with Meyerhold). Further, we have observed notions of risk-taking and liveness within the context of a shared ensemble energetic/music (as with Britton) and the sense of a somatic temporal awareness (with Viewpoints). Another important rhythmic characteristic of these improvisational approaches is the role played by and the relationship established with music. In looking to further elucidate this aspect, we can consider:

- At what stage in these processes is music introduced?
- How prescriptive is the relationship between performer and music?
- What are the characteristics, styles, forms and genres of music used?
- Are these sourced from recordings or live accompaniment?

A further area of consideration is the ways that each approach asks performers to relate to their own sense of rhythm and time. In all these practices, we encounter instances when individualistic qualities of rhythm are emphasized (i.e. following one's personal sense of timing/ phrasing) and other instances in which the individual's rhythms are subjected to an external form or tempo or to the rhythm of the ensemble.

The rehearsing of these relationships to time and the embodiment of these rhythmic principles through training develop their own understandings of rhythm in each performer and ensemble. While these are to some extent conceptual, they are also largely experiential, forming a personal or shared sense of rhythm – of what is 'right' or 'appropriate' in each instance. Informing the ways performers express themselves and relate to each other, these understandings contribute to each performer's sense of identity and how they locate themselves within a body of work. Part of the creative process of performance making and training is exploring the extent to which we *work within* our understandings of rhythm and timing and to what degree we *challenge* and *redefine* these territories. As an effective model for negotiating structure and spontaneity, for building trust and taking risks, improvisation also provides a context in which performers can experiment with and encounter various rhythmicities, expressive territories and temporal domains. In the improvising of rhythm, we are given the opportunity to define (and undefine) rhythm through the meeting of our preconceived understandings and the doing/listening of our performances as they occur.

Viewing rhythm as an act of improvisation brings us in contact with both the immediacy of this phenomenon and its formal nature. We may choose to consign rhythm to either of these categories – viewing it as either a spontaneous act of expression or an imposed structural form. It is, however, the meeting of these aspects that is of concern here – the interfacing of structure and spontaneity – of knowing and not knowing.

PART FOUR

THE ECSTATIC PERFORMER

In his book *Shamanism: Archaic Techniques of Ecstasy*, Mercia Eliade presents a description of a shaman entering a state of ecstasy through the imitation of animal behaviours:

> He who, forgetting the limitations and false measurements of humanity, could rightly imitate the behaviour of animals – their gate, breathing, cries, and so on – found a new dimension of life: spontaneity, freedom, 'sympathy' with all the cosmic rhythms and, hence, bliss and immortality. (Eliade 1964:460)

While this example is related specifically to the use of choreographic animal dances undertaken in the context of sacred ritualistic practices, this description could easily be applied to the experience of a performer, who, in the act of performing, encounters a sense of personal transformation, freedom and 'sympathy'. Examining some of the common grounds shared by ritual and performance, in this part of the book I will discuss the roles played by rhythm in facilitating altered states of consciousness within performance and actor training practices. To open out this enquiry, I would like to begin by discussing the ways ecstasy can be viewed as a 'performance technique' (Schechner 1988:175) – a mode and approach to being in performance.

While the term ecstasy is most often associated with religious experiences as well as dance and drug-induced states of euphoria, this term can also be understood as a capacity or mode of experience that (like rhythm) can be cultivated and embodied by the performer. Ethnomusicologist Judith Becker identifies ecstasy as a form of trance, defining it as: '(a state of mind characterized by intense focus) the loss of the strong sense of self and access to types of knowledge and experience that are inaccessible in nontrance states' (1994:41). Becker's research reveals correlations between ecstatic trance within religious practice and what she terms 'deep listening' – the transformative experience of listening to music within a secular context. Her findings revealed that both religious 'ecstatics' and 'deep listeners' described a 'loss of boundaries' between self and other, as well as experiences of 'wholeness and unity' (Penman and Becker 2009:63). Becker's definition and descriptions of ecstatic experiences also translate clearly into the context of performance and training.

As observed throughout this book, performers are often encouraged to work with 'intense focus', while also developing a strong sense of relationship and unity to fellow performers and audience. Similarly, the processes of training performers often involve the cultivation of a particular state (or mode) of being in which the performers can access intuitive forms of creative knowledge, seen to be distinct from those encountered in daily life. Actor and pedagogue Michael Chekhov, described a shift of consciousness occurring in moments of inspiration – moments in which the performer's sense of self 'undergoes a metamorphosis', from that of 'everyday consciousness' to what Chekhov described as a 'higher self', a 'creative state' of a 'true artist'. Chekhov recounted:

> If you have ever known such moments, you will recall that, with the appearance of this new *I*, you felt first of all an influx of power never experienced in your routine life. This power permeated your whole being, radiated from you into your surroundings, filling the stage and flowing over the footlights into the audience. ... Thanks to this power, you are able to feel to a high degree ... your presence on stage. (2002:86–7)

Chekhov's description blurs the boundaries between a religious experience of ecstasy and the secular notion of 'performance presence' or a creative 'flow state'. In performance, this notion of a heightened 'presence' is understood in terms of both the performer's own experience of 'being present' and the ways an audience experiences or relates to a performer. Theatre director Nicolás Núñez refers to this moment of intensification as the 'actualized instant': an 'enlivening' of time through the use of attention and physical action. Such moments are also often characterized by a deep sense of connectedness and unification (Middleton 2001:47).

Linking ecstasy directly to the context of performance, Richard Schechner describes it as a state of 'transparency', in which obstacles that block the flow of impulses are eliminated (1988:175). The performers, in a sense, become 'open' to what is around them, with the barrier between self and others seeming to dissolve. To clarify this, Schechner makes a distinction between ecstasy and possession. Where possession is seen to be linked to the idea of 'character acting', this involving the performer relinquishing personal identity/agency and 'becoming another', in ecstasy, the performer, stripped down to his or her essence, remains present and conscious.[1] In pursuing such states of ecstasy, the intention is not that performers lose awareness of themselves, but rather that their sense of self is transformed or transgressed. As director Jerzy Grotowski explained:

> The point is not to renounce part of our nature – all should retain its natural place: the body, the heart, the head, something that is 'under our feet' and something that is 'over our head'. All like a vertical line, and this verticality should be held taut between organicity and the awareness. Awareness means the consciousness which is not linked to language (the machine or thinking), but to Presence. (1995:125)

An important aspect of ecstasy is highlighted here – the sustaining of conscious awareness tied to the 'Presence' of the body. On the surface this might seem contradictory, in the sense that the term 'ecstasy', from the Ancient Greek: *ekstasis* (ἔκστασις) refers to a state of going out from, or from out (*ek*) of one's position or standing (*stasis*). However, it is precisely this paradoxical tension, between a giving over of control (or understanding) and the sustaining of conscious awareness, which characterizes many examples of ecstasy found within acting practices.[2]

Building from these understandings, here ecstasy describes *a technique of transforming or transgressing the familiar parameters of the self, while simultaneously remaining consciously present within one's experiences and actions*. We can consider this form of ecstasy as either a transcendence or an encounter with immanence. Transcendent is understood in terms of going beyond or outside of the self and immanent in the sense of being 'equally present in all things' (Deleuze 1990:173). While historically philosophers have tended to view these as oppositional concepts (Cull 2012), here I would like to propose that the unifying nature of the ecstatic experience is a potential site for the dissolution of such dualist frameworks along with dichotomies of body and mind, action and experience, self and other. This opens the possibility of the ecstatic performer becoming both immanent and transcendent, of being both within and without a sense of self, time and space.

In the following four chapters, relationships between altered states of consciousness and rhythm will be examined in more detail. Chapter 8 will discuss this from a theoretical perspective, drawing on scientific and anthropological studies as means of drawing out some of the principles that underpin the use of rhythm as a tool for altering consciousness in ritual and performance practices. The three chapters that follow will address this topic in relation to the practices of Jerzy Grotowski (Chapter 9) and Nicolás Núñez (Chapter 10), as well as my own practices (Chapter 11).

8

RHYTHM AND ALTERED STATES OF CONSCIOUSNESS
ENTRAINMENT AND COMMUNITAS

The link between rhythm, ritual and altered states of consciousness is a topic of interdisciplinary significance. Over the past century, this subject has been given considerable attention within the sciences and humanities, as well as this being reflected within the discourses of many performance and ritual practitioners. Stanislavski's own research into the use of yogic breathing as a means of accessing internal energetic qualities points to the significance of rhythm within these processes (Chapter 3). As Phillip Zarrilli points out, over the twentieth century a number of theatre practitioners have 'drawn inspiration or specific techniques from ritual/shamanic practices in order to explore both alternative approaches to acting and/or processes of audience/ performer communion' (2011:314). These have included Antonin Artaud, Alexander Fersen, Jerzy Grotowski and Nicolás Núñez. Notably the use of meditation, sacred music, mask and other ritual elements within many contemporary training/performance forms suggests not only a continued but also a growing interest in this area of practice.[1]

Examining the correlations between ritual and performance we can note the ways that both are often sites of intensified rhythmicity. This can be observed in the patterning and repeating of actions and the alternative temporalities that these activities promote. Anthropological and neurological research in this field highlights the effect that rhythm in general, and more specifically repetitive rhythmic movement and music, has on an individual's psychophysical state. Here, a number of studies have focused on the significant role of sustained rhythmic drumming, chanting, and repetitive swaying or rocking. In reference to ritual practices, these processes are often described as monotonous, repetitive and driving, with gradual increases in speed and volume (Fachner 2011:370). The sustained nature of ritual activities is also seen to generate its own qualities of intensity. It has been suggested that the 'driving' effects of such behaviours act as a mechanism for 'tuning' and sensitizing specific aspects of the central nervous system. Describing the impact of rhythmic and repetitive actions on the human nervous system, Barbara Lex suggested that these processes encouraged a preferencing of the right hemisphere of the brain. And that the driving act of sustained and intense rhythmic behaviour could effectively overload the nervous system leading to states of 'equilibrium' characterized by both heightened awareness/responsiveness, alongside an experience of stability and calmness (1979:136).

Grotowski and Núñez have both linked this sustained quality of intensity to the notion of the 'warrior'. Viewing performance and ritual as sites of 'conquest', Grotowski wrote:

To conquer knowledge he fights, because the pulsation of life becomes stronger and more articulated in moments of great intensity, of great danger. Danger and chance go together. There is no real class if not in regard to real danger. In a moment of challenge appears the rhythmization of human impulses. The ritual is a moment of great intensity; provoked intensity; life then becomes rhythmic. Performer knows to link body impulses to sonority [or as in later translations 'the song'] (the stream of life should be articulated in forms). (1988:37)

This description offers a clear example of ecstasy viewed as a performance technique. Here the performer is one who has the ability to 'conquer' his or her own 'knowledge', to synchronize their body's impulses to those of the music, to access the 'stream of life' via the use of rhythmic and musical forms. Further, this intensification of the performer's 'presence' is seen by Grotowski as forming a bridge between the audience and 'this something' other (1988:37). Through the use of rhythm both the audience and the performer are brought into contact with something that is both, of them and beyond them. Ethnomusicologist John Blacking described how rhythmic movement qualities associated with altered states of consciousness are often characterized as following the basic mechanics of the body. These include simple actions based on the characteristic motions of muscles and limbs, as well as patterns that reflect those found in human neurophysiology, such as the rhythms of our brainwaves, respiration and heart rates. He also pointed out the ways that movement patterns within ritual practices are commonly associated with organic and natural rhythms of the environment, including the movements of animals and plants, as well as basic elements such as water and fire (Blacking 1989:66).[2]

An emphasis given to stepping patterns of the feet is another significant principle found across numerous ritual practices (Goodridge 1999). This includes the order of the steps (e.g. left-left-right-right or left-right-left-right), their direction (e.g. forwards, backwards or sideways), the weight given to each step (heavy or light), their metric nature (e.g. regular, syncopated, symmetric or asymmetric) and the formation of the group (e.g. in a circle, a line or spread throughout the space). A group stepping in unison, produces a rhythm through both its sounds and motion (often enhanced by ankle bells and rattles, as well as the coinciding of steps with spoken syllables and/or musical accents).[3]

The rhythmic nature of such movements also contributes strongly to a group's ability to coordinate themselves collectively within these processes. Observed previously in regard to Britton's ensemble training practices, we can note how as a group's movements begin to synchronize more deeply, a greater sense of unity is often established between participants and across the group as a whole (Chapter 6). The synchronization and entrainment of musical rhythms along with internal bodily processes (including breathing patterns, heart rate and brain activity), as well as the movements of a group of people, can also play an important role in the formation of altered states of consciousness.

Rhythmic entrainment

Entrainment is a principle that describes the way two or more independent rhythmic processes can interact with each other to gradually synchronize and lock into a common phase/periodicity.[4] This phenomenon has been observed over a wide range of contexts, including the swinging of pendulums, the movements of planets, the collective flashing of fireflies and the oscillation of molecules (Strogatz 2004). Entrainment has also been used to explain the processes of rhythmic perception, occurring through the synchronization of our attention with points of accent or intensification within our perceptual field (Jones 1986; London 2004). This capacity is also seen to be the basis for coordinating the communicative exchange of physical movements and sounds between parents and infants (Feldman 2007; Malloch and Trevarthen 2008) and the ability to move in relation to a musical beat or the actions of a group/partner within forms of social and ritual dance (Phillips-Silver, Aktipis and Bryant 2010). Stanislavski's likening of a performer to a 'clock', which, through its rhythmic actions brings the audience into 'unison and rhythm with their hours' (Stanislavski 1986a:230), presents an intuitive description of the principles of social entrainment that have been articulated within contemporary scientific studies. Yet, while some researchers continue to describe these processes in terms of neurological or bodily 'clocks', such analogies remain limited. The neurobiological rhythms located in the brain and other areas of the body are never entirely metric or constant. While they may have a preferred periodicity, 'unlike mechanical or electronic clocks, [they] are adaptable to circumstances of their actions in the body and in engagement with the world' (Schögler and Trevarthen 2007:284).

Growing from this field of research, a number of clinical and ethnomusical studies have looked to entrainment in order to explain the effect that external musical rhythms seem to have on internal neurophysiological processes. Of particular interest here is the use of sustained drumming, rhythmic movement and rhythmic breathing. Melinda Maxfield's research into the effects of rhythmic drumming on brain activity have revealed strong correlations between particular rhythmic drumming patterns and forms of neurological activity, as well as the types of conscious experiences that accompany these. Building on the earlier research on brainwave entrainment by Andrew Neher,[5] Maxfield has found evidence to support the notion that 'rhythmic drumming acts as an auditory drive mechanism, affecting the electrical activity of the brain by bringing it into resonance (at a particular frequency or set of frequencies) with the external stimuli' (Jovanov and Maxfield 2012:32).

A research experiment involving subjects being exposed to different forms of rhythmic drumming over twenty-minute intervals demonstrated a significant correspondence between listening to drums played at a rate of four to four-and-a-half beats per second and an increase in theta brainwave activity.[6] The majority of participants in these experiments also reported being consciously aware of shifts in their mental functions, including losing a sense of time, heightened energetic/arousal, vivid images and/or somatic experiences. In this research, Maxfield also compared the effects that slower syncopated rhythms (three to four beats per second) and 'free drumming' (no sustained rhythmic pattern) had on brain activity. The slower rhythm produced considerably less theta brain activity. And when exposed to 'free drumming' participants showed no increase in brain frequencies, with these readings either remaining constant or declining (Jovanov and Maxfield 2012:39).

In addition to the effect of listening to rhythmic music, it is also important to consider the role that rhythmic movement can have on an individual's state of consciousness. In studies examining the brain activities of *Salpuri* dancers (a Korean shamanic dance) and *Calonarang* (a Balinese ritual drama), a suppression of cortical and an enhancement of subcortical functions was observed,[7] as well as a slowing and increasing of alpha and theta brainwaves (Fachner 2011:364–5). Rhythmic body movements are also often accompanied by the increased movement of bodily fluids and with the synchronization of breath and heart patterns with the movements of limbs or bodily swaying. This form of cardiovascular synchronization can contribute to the slowing of heart rate and changes in blood pressure, with this seen to affect visual perception, muscular reflexes and the augmenting of pain thresholds (Vaitl et al. 2005:107). Chanting and the use of controlled breathing patterns have also been seen to bring about indirect stabilization of the limbic system. This form of stabilization has been associated with the experience of 'inner stillness' and access to 'deep insights and a variety of integrated experiences' (Jovanov and Maxfield 2012:45).

In these examples, the rhythming of the body's physiological process can be seen as corresponding with changes in consciousness, including the emergence of experiences of transcendence and experiences involving a reduction in emotional 'noise' and a settling of the mind. Other effects, including the suppression of cortical brain functions and the enhanced activity of subcortical functions, also suggest that rhythm plays an important role in processes of altering consciousness. However, it is important to observe that while there is a large body of research indicating the existence of strong links between rhythm and altered states of consciousness, such links should not be confused with a direct or causal relationship. In these examples it is not that an individual enters into a trance simply by being exposed to this or that rhythm. Instead, it is perhaps more useful to consider rhythm as establishing the context or basis from which an altered state can be approached.

Ethnomusicologist Gilbert Rouget argues: 'No rhythmic system is specifically related to trance' (1985:317). Instead Rouget suggests that trance states are context dependent and rooted in learned cultural symbolism; proposing further, these states do not result automatically, but must in some way be actively 'willed' by the shaman (1985:182). Rouget establishes his argument by citing examples in which trance states are triggered without the use of music, where the same use of music produces vastly different results and where different forms of music and instrumentation produce the same results. He argues that if trance was simply caused by rhythmic drumming, then 'half of Africa would be in a trance from the beginning of the year to the end' (1985:175). Rouget does not dismiss the significance of rhythm and music in ritual practices. Rather he proposes 'that music, words, and dance create at the same time a great physical effervescence and a state of "monoideism" that, in combination, create psychophysical conditions apparently very favourable to the occurrence of trance' (1985:317). Building from these 'collective' emotional experiences, Rouget suggests that it is symbolic structures and belief systems, which are the main contributing force in the emergence of trance.

Group/ensemble rhythm

While many studies have focused on the effect that rhythmic activities have on individuals, it is important to note that most ritual and performative processes involve the collaboration and interaction of groups of participants and/or observers. It is also worth noting the significant role played by a shared social context and set of intentions. Even though entrainment can and does occur without these elements being present, an awareness of being a group and a collective sense of occasion are seen in many circumstances as being crucial elements in establishing a strong interpersonal entrainment.[8]

Synchronized group activities such as collective chanting and dancing appear to be universal phenomena, taking place within a vast range of cultures and contexts, both historically and geographically. For this reason, it is suggested that these capacities have played an important role in human evolution, 'engaging biological competences that create empathy and group solidarity and cohesion' (Fachner 2011:362). While there are many aspects and intentions underpinning ritual behaviour, the process of unifying the individual and the group can be seen as a significant objective within many of these practices. Anthropologist Eugene D'Aquili points directly to this when he defines ritual as:

> a sequence of behaviour which is structured or patterned; which is rhythmic and repetitive (to some degree at least), that is, it tends to recur in the same or nearly the same form with some regularity; which acts to synchronize affective, perceptual-cognitive and motor processes with the central nervous system of individual participants; and which, most particularly, synchronizes these processes among the various individual participants tending to eliminate aggression and to facilitate cohesion among the participants. (D'Aquili 1985:22)

In addition to generating group cohesion and camaraderie, the rhythmic entrainment of a group is also seen by Becker as a *prime catalyst for musical ecstasy* (2012:49, italics in original). Clear examples of this can be found in many rituals and other social activities where groups move together in simple stepping patterns and/or chant repeated rhythmic phrases as a means of encouraging states of trance and a sense of union. Describing the use of a shared rhythmic stepping pattern (known as *Tloque Nahuaque*[9]) in the training practices of Nicolás Núñez, Deborah Middleton explains how 'participants move in repeating rhythmic patterns of coming together and moving apart, in such a way as ultimately to blur one's sense of boundaries and separateness from the other' (2008:53). Building in intensity, these actions often lead to a sense of being energized and supported by the momentum and sustained commitment of the group.

While the simplicity and focus of a single rhythm is often an effective means of unifying a group, Becker also points out that rhythmic entrainment can, and often does, involve the interaction of multiple rhythms, these contributing to the emergence of a more complex polyrhythmic environment. She offers this insightful description of the way different rhythms can come together and entrain within a ritual or performative context:

> the phenomenon of rhythmic entrainment is transpersonal, [it] does not take place in one particular mind alone, although it also takes place there. The dancing and musicking are ways in which a group of people may be-in-the-world. And by their being-in-the-world they communally bring forth the world in which rhythmic entrainment is a natural, expected, un-sensational occurrence. ... The world brought forth by all the participants makes possible the extraordinary moves of the ritual practitioner, or the endurance of the dancers, or the inspiration of the musicians; what may on another day seem strange, is coherent, reasonable, truthful, and authentic within the situation itself. (2012:63–4)

Rhythm establishes not only a temporal structure but also an emotional/cultural framework of expectations and ways of 'being-in-the-world'. In this example, we can note how a shared rhythm is seen to result in the normalization of what might otherwise be considered abnormal experiences. This collective sense of 'appropriateness' can be seen here as a form of *communitas* – a quality of union or camaraderie that often emerges within the context of shared ritual activity. As in many of the examples throughout this book, here the sense of group rhythm is not the result of an externally imposed structure or subordination to an established social norm. Instead this quality of rhythmic togetherness is something that emerges from the activities of the participants themselves and a sense of what fills the gaps between them. As Victor Turner points out, 'communitas emerges where social structure is not' (Turner 1969:126). As in Becker's example, it is not that the individuals conform to an existing norm, but that through their actions they generate a norm of their own. They transform what would otherwise 'seem strange' into something coherent and authentic.

It is worth comparing these experiences to those found within performance ensembles, where a sense of a shared rhythmic territory can also be seen to facilitate the normalization of behaviours that would otherwise be seen as transgressive or extreme. Common to these experiences is a sense of belonging and a quality of sustained energy and focus. In both performance and ritual, we can also note the ways that a shared rhythm within a group can establish an ambiguity in the relationship between self and other – the boundaries between performer, group and observer, blurred or dissolved by the commonality of their rhythms.

Reflections

While most studies agree on the fact that rhythm plays a critical role in inducing, sustaining and navigating altered states of consciousness, they generally propose that it is misleading to reduce this relationship down to a simple causal trigger. The ways by which an individual or a group is affected by rhythm can be seen to depend as much on the rhythms themselves as on the setting, intentions, associations, beliefs and previous experiences of participants. Becker points to the fact that in instances where music is seen to trigger ecstatic states, an individual's relationship to this music is often critical to how they respond. This is not to imply that musical content is irrelevant or arbitrary but that the effects of music and rhythm are not simply deterministic (Penman and Becker 2009:2009). Rather, these emerge through a relational and adaptive process in which rhythm can be seen to engender a strong sense of connection and build effective associative links. Rhythm in this sense provides the scaffolding on which these experiences are hung and the context in which collective and communicative processes are given space to function. In metaphoric terms, rhythm is not so much a 'trigger', but rather 'a series of pathways and banisters' (Rios and Katz 1975:68) by which the participants negotiate their experience, or a 'territory' within which community can be (trans)formed or transgressed.

9
JERZY GROTOWSKI
SEEKING PULSE,
MOVEMENT AND RHYTHM

In a rehearsal diary from the early 1960s, Grotowski sketched the following notes:

> If I had to define our theatrical quest in one sentence, with one term, I would refer to the myth about the dance of Shiva. I would say: 'We are playing at being Shiva. We are acting out Shiva'....
>
> Shiva says ... I am without name, without form, and without action ... I am pulse, movement, rhythm. (Shiva-Gita)
>
> The essence of the theatre we are seeking is 'pulse, rhythm and movement'. (Grotowski cited in Osiński 1986:50)

The initial research into rhythm, undertaken by Grotowski and the Laboratory Theatre in the early 1960s, built strongly on foundational approaches laid out by the European theatre practitioners who preceded them. In addition to these, Grotowski also marks the important influence that Asian performance techniques,[1] including Peaking Opera, Kathakali and Noh theatre, had in stimulating his enquiry and search for the essential qualities of theatre. Where many of his European predecessors had based their use of rhythm in musical paradigms and terminologies taken from 'classical' and jazz music, Grotowski's research led him away from these (in some ways) more conventional frameworks, opening out his enquiry into areas of ritual practices, including the use of sacred dances and songs drawn from Indian, Afro-Caribbean and Central American traditions. In this sense, Grotowski's use and understanding of rhythm can be seen as a synthesis of a wide range of approaches and principles. Yet more than anything, Grotowski's work with rhythm reveals a search. This was not a quest for a particular style, or for the reproduction of traditional forms, but rather a sense of what might be considered an essential rhythmicity located deep within the performers themselves.

Influences and sources

Many of the initial training practices explored by Grotowski and the members of the Laboratory Theatre in their early period (1959–69) were based directly on rhythm exercises and principles drawn from the work of many of the early twentieth-century practitioners already discussed in this book. Writing in 1965, Grotowski made clear reference to these formative influences, stating:

> Most important for my purposes are: Dullin's rhythm exercises, Delsarte's investigations of extroversive and introversive reactions, Stanislavski's work on 'physical actions', Meyerhold's bio-mechanical training, Vakhtangov's synthesis. (Grotowski [1965] 1969:16)

Grotowski directly references Charles Dullin's[2] use of improvisation, mask, animal and plant exercises as an early source of inspiration, explaining that these provided a useful 'preparation for the actor. They stimulate not only his imagination, but also the development of his natural reactions' (Grotowski 1969:207). Strong references to Delsarte's formalist and spiritualist principles can also be found throughout Grotowski's early writings. Zbigniew Osiński indicates that an important reference point for the initial training exercises used by Grotowski and the Laboratory Theatre was the textbook by Sergei Volkonski, *Expressive Man: Shaping Stage Gesture (Following Delsarte)* (1913). Translated into Polish by the actor Mieczysław Szpakiewicz, a member of the Reduta Theatre Company, this instructional text provided the basis for many of the initial training practices use by Grotowski and his company (Osiński 2009:47).[3] In *Expressive Man*, Volkonski wrote: 'Art is the knowledge of those external methods by which life, the soul and the mind are opened up for the person – the ability to possess them and to direct them freely. Art is finding a sign corresponding to the essence' (Volkonski cited in Whyman 2008:125).

The inheritance of these concepts is clearly laid out within Grotowski's theoretical writings, particularly in his earlier work. Echoing these sentiments in *Towards a Poor Theatre*, Grotowski wrote:

> The form is like a baited trap, to which the spiritual process responds spontaneously and against which it struggles. The forms of common 'natural' behaviour obscure the truth; we compose a role as a system of signs which demonstrate what is behind the mask of common vision ... A sign, not a common gesture, is the elementary integer of expression for us. (Grotowski 1969:17)

Also linked to the work of Volkonski, the influence of Stanislavski's 'outer tempo-rhythm' exercises can also be seen clearly in the rhythm exercises adopted by the Laboratory Theatre between 1959 and 1962. A series of exercises first documented by Eugenio Barba during his time with the company offers a clear example of the ways the 'Laboratory' initially drew on basic rhythm approaches previously developed by Stanislavski, Meyerhold and Bing.[4]

EXERCISE 19: MOVEMENT SCORE (GROTOWSKI)

The actor devises a movement sequence based on the action of lighting a cigarette, the first stage being to reduce this action down to its composite parts:

1 I want to light a cigarette: thinking, then stillness
2 I look to where the cigarettes are
3 I reach out my hand
4 I take the packet by lifting it up
5 I bring the packet up towards myself
6 I choose a cigarette, etc.

Having established a 'kinetic sequence' (made up of twenty actions)
the participant then explores these actions in relationship to a
rhythmic score based on 'standard notation' starting with a simple
structure in which each *crochet*[5] note represents a single action
from the sequence:

Later the actor applies a more complex pattern containing long and
short durations made up of *crochets* and *minims* such as:

Or:

And later with a combination of *quavers*, *crochets* and *minims*:

With each change in rhythm the performer maintains the same detail
of their actions. The only difference in each sequence is the speed
and duration of each movement.

Figure 9.1 Scored notation of physical actions, based on transcriptions by Barba (1965:132–3).

Working on these scores, the actor was instructed to find a 'logical
justification' for each change in rhythm, with Barba offering the following
example:

a man thinking feverishly makes fast and frantic gestures. Suddenly he finds the solution to the problem that plagued him; slows down his movements and then speeds up again. (1965:133)

As with earlier examples from Stanislavski and Vakhtangov, the actor constructs an inner narrative or 'given circumstance', in order to avoid a purely mechanical enactment of these 'external' rhythms. Further, Barba describes how other similar rhythm exercises were used by the company including synchronizing physical actions and spoken text to the rhythms of the heartbeat and breathing patterns (1965:134). These exercises were intended as a way of developing the actor's awareness of rhythm, gesture and movement, with the primary role of revealing to the actor any 'tendencies towards distraction' (Barba 1965:131). Curiously, Barba specifies that this work was *not* aimed at bringing about any profound changes in consciousness or trance states but were rather (as with Meyerhold's practices) seen as a way of disciplining the focus of the performer.

Reflecting on the approaches of Stanislavski, Meyerhold and Bing, we can see how these models of training are applied here almost directly, with participants breaking down movements into technical sequences and then performing these through the structures of musical rhythm, working with and without accompaniment.

From these and other source materials, the Laboratory Theatre experimented to develop their own practices and understandings of rhythm, gradually moving beyond what Grotowski described as 'stereotyped' movements. As the focus of their training became more concerned with the relational aspects of their work, and drew increasingly on the use of personal associations, their practices also shifted away from the mechanical uniformity of their early training. Exercises that started off as 'purely physical' – described on one occasion as 'beautiful gestures with the emotions of a fairy dance' (Grotowski [1968] 2001b:45) – evolved over time into more dynamically embodied movement sequences, which existed as part of a body of work known as *exercises plastiques*. Building from their initial work with exercises drawn predominantly from Delsarte and Dalcroze,[6] the *plastiques* provided the foundations for the actor training of the Laboratory Theatre, as well as the basis for many investigations in the later period of Grotowski's research from Theatre of Sources to his final work on Art as vehicle.

Exercises plastiques

These practices offered a clear means of negotiating the relationship between the 'mechanical' and 'organic' notions of rhythm (Chapter 2), the former being characterized here by terms such as 'artificial', 'structural' and 'objective' and the latter relating to the 'living', 'spontaneous' and 'subjective' aspects of their practice. Through this dichotomy, actors were able to research ways of maintaining the 'objective' elements of their performance, such as a physical movement score or rhythmic structure, while also going 'beyond them', moving towards what Grotowski identified as 'purely subjective work' ([1968] 2001b:45).

Grotowski perhaps best explained this relationship through the use of analogy, describing a performance as being like 'two banks of a river', the 'water flowing between those banks' representing the process of the actor (Schechner 1988:52). We can see here a dialectic relationship established between the two key notions of rhythm – one being fluid and dynamic and the other being static and structural. Ryszard Cieślak, a member of the Laboratory Theatre, elaborated on this in his description of the performer's score and his or her inner experience, this time through the simile of a candle and the glass that protects it:

> The score is like the glass inside which the candle is burning. The glass is solid, it is there, you can depend on it. It contains and guides the flame. But it is not the flame. The flame is my inner process each night. The flame is what illuminates the score, what the spectators see through the score. The flame is alive. Just as the flame in the candleglass moves, flutters, rises, falls, almost goes out, suddenly glows brightly, responds to each breath of wind – so my inner life varies from night to night, from moment to moment. (Cieślak 1970 cited in Schechner 1988:51)

It is mutual dependency, rather than exclusivity, that is integral to both these analogies, with each aspect seen to complement the other, and the relationship between the two forming a third aspect – the living score. This concept is framed by Grotowski's term *Conjunctio Oppositorum*, defined as 'the necessity of bringing together opposite forces in order to create a unified whole' (Lavy 2005:177). We find this concept present throughout many of the practices discussed in this book, revealing itself clearly in Stanislavski's work with tempo-rhythm and in Meyerhold's discussion of metre and rhythm. For Grotowski, *Conjunctio Oppositorum* was far more than a conceptual model. It constituted a 'basic aspect of an actor's work' requiring a practical and methodical approach, by which these actors could encounter and cultivate their use of these principles (Grotowski 1969:217).

EXERCISE 20: PLASTIQUES

This process began with the performer making a score – fixing a certain quantity of details and making them precise. The next step was to rediscover the personal impulses within these details – to begin to embody and allow some of these details to change. Grotowski explained:

> Change them but not to the point of destroying them. How at the beginning to improvise solely the order of the details, improvise the rhythm of the fixed details and then change the order and the rhythm and even the composition of the details, not in a premeditated way but in the sense of a flow dictated by our own body. How to discover that 'spontaneous' line of the body which is incarnate in the details, which encircles them, which surpasses them but which, at the same time, preserves their precision. (Grotowski cited in Kumiega 1985:119)

These descriptions present an approach to rhythm that is clearly distinct from the formal musical systems described previously. These more improvised methods suggest a way of working with rhythm that was more intuitive and corporeal in nature. In this regard, Grotowski insisted that within these exercises all actions and rhythms come from the 'line of the body' rather than the intellect or analytical thoughts. Grotowski explained that while the performer should preserve the details of their actions, if they try to premeditate their choices and give themselves commands such as 'now I must change the rhythm, now I must change the order of the details then the "body memory" will not be liberated' (Kumiega 1985:120). Instead the performer needs to preserve specific details, while at the same time letting 'the body dictate different rhythms, all the time changing the rhythm and the order'.

> at that moment who gives the command? It is not thought, but neither is it chance, it is related to our life. We do not even know how, but it is the 'body memory' which is in command, related to certain experiences and certain cycles of experience in our life. (Grotowski cited in Kumiega 1985:120)

Here, like in Britton and Bogart's practices, we encounter a sense of rhythm emerging through the physical and kinaesthetic experience of an action – the 'doing' rather than the 'conceptualization' of rhythm. But where Britton and Bogart's approaches tie this 'doing' primarily to the performer's relationship with the group, Grotowski links it to a bodily sense of 'memory'. And where, in Grotowski's earlier exercises, rhythm was 'justified' through an intellectual form of analysis, here it took on a kinaesthetic logic of its own, rooted in the impulses and the memories of the body's own rhythmic and cyclic nature. In this, we approach a more 'essential' understanding of rhythm – a sense of rhythm as archetype or *ur-rhythm*. Although these exercises demonstrate a strong element of improvisation, there remains a deep interest in working with form. But rather than imposing external forms (taken from music or existing imagery) the *exercises plastiques* worked from an internal sense of rhythmicity, with the suggestion that there are fundamental rhythmic forms embedded deep within us.

Reflecting on some of the phases of work within Grotowski's career, we can observe how the dual sense of rhythm, being both objective and subjective, continued to inform many aspects of his practice. This is perhaps most notable in his later periods of work known as Theatre of Sources, Objective Drama and Art as vehicle. Throughout these, Grotowski gave considerable attention to the use of traditional and sacred dance and song forms applied as 'tools', facilitating the performer's personal encounter with a sense of memory, a personal association or an archaic or primal mode of being.

Techniques of sources

Theatre of Sources took place from 1976 to 1982, across a range of countries including Poland, Haiti, Mexico, Nigeria and India. Explaining the aims of this project in 1978, Grotowski stated:

The participants of the Theatre of Sources would be people from various continents, with different backgrounds and traditions. The Theatre of Sources will deal with the phenomenon of source techniques, archaic or nascent, that bring us back to the sources of life, to direct, so we say, primeval perception, to organic primary experience of life. Existence-presence. (Grotowski 1978:9–11)

Grotowski made clear that this was not an attempt to recreate or reproduce traditional practices, but rather a search for a 'precultural sense of beginning' (Grimes 2001:272). This was as much about returning to an 'untamed' condition of 'childhood' as it was about the rediscovery of 'archaic techniques'. Through this period, a body of international practitioners were involved in exploring and developing practical techniques. These were aimed primarily at finding means of shifting an individual out of a habitual mode of being, or tapping into a fundamental quality of 'organic' or primal 'existence-presence'. As part of this process, individual participants were given the freedom to explore and propose their own practices. Some were drawn from their own cultural backgrounds and others were based on observations or experimentation. Polish performer Teo Spychalski describes a ritualistic dance practice that he introduced to the group as part of his involvement in Theatre of Sources:

I proposed a circling, marching-dance in a regular rhythm that was kept by somebody playing on a tree stump placed at the centre of the circle – this was reminiscent of what I'd seen in 1977, among the indigenous Canadians in a reservation on the island of Manitoulin. (Spychalski and Ziółkowski 2015)

Here we can observe one of ways these practitioners drew on traditional forms and models taken from sacred practices, and investigated the potency of these forms outside of their cultural frameworks.

Rhythmically, what was striking about many of the practices used within Theatre of Sources was their extended durational nature and their lack of expressive quality. Describing his participation in the previously mentioned 'Manitoulin' circle dance, Roland Grimes stated 'the sense of monotony was profound ... The sameness and repetitiveness of the steps, like the simple monotony of the drums, provided meditative potentialities once the technique had been learned' (Grimes 2001:273). Again, we can note the use of repetition and sustained rhythmic movements enacted by a group, these aspects being seen as instrumental in facilitating a shift in conscious awareness. Yet as Grimes points out, while some found this work 'grounding', others experienced it as 'boring', lacking in variation or personal freedom.

EXERCISE 21: SLOW WALKING (GROTOWSKI)

'Slow walking'[7] is another example of a simple 'technique' that was explored during this period. Describing this practice, Grotowski explained:

> in Theatre of Sources, one of the most ordinary actions is just a way of walking which, through rhythms different from the rhythms of habitual life, breaks the kind of walk which is directed towards an aim. Normally, you are never there where you are because in your mind you are already in the place where you are going, like in the train seeing only the consecutive station, but if you change the rhythm (this is a very difficult thing to describe but it can be practiced), if for instance you change to an extremely slow rhythm, so slow that you are virtually standing still ... then in the beginning you can be very irritated, questioning, vomiting the thoughts, but after a few moments, if you are really attentive, something does change. You begin to be where you are. (Grotowski 2001a:263)

In these descriptions we observe clearly the effect that a change in rhythm (or tempo) can have on consciousness, with an experience of daily consciousness being linked to the habitual rhythms of walking.

Relating these practices back to the principle of *Conjunctio Oppositorum*, Grotowski observed that in many of these 'techniques' there existed a bringing together of what might otherwise be seen as separate or oppositional qualities. One of these is 'movement which is repose'. Explaining the application of this concept, he identified the ways that many traditional techniques (including slow walking, running or yoga) were used as ways to 'break through the techniques of the body of everyday life', and approach a condition in which a physical action could become a 'movement of perception'. Entering this state: 'One can say that our movement is seeing, hearing, sensing, our movement is perception' (Grotowski 2001a:263). Where, in our 'daily' activities, perception and action are often experienced as separate (I speak then I listen, I move then I feel), we can note the ways that many traditional 'techniques' as well as approaches to performance seek to unify these aspects.

Another area of Grotowski's research involved the use of sacred dances and 'vibratory songs'. Grotowski observed that certain dance or song forms could be utilized as 'tools' (or vehicles) by which a performer/participant could access what he referred to as a 'primary energy' or a quality of 'verticality'.[8] Reflecting on his participation in the Theatre of Sources project, Núñez states: 'In these ancient songs what was important was the rhythm. And through the rhythm [we] catch the flight'. Núñez goes on to explain that in approaching these ancient songs and dances the intention was

> first to develop the skills in the singing and in the stepping and so forth, and then really to contact the big spirit through this. This also became a tool of ecstasies, so the rhythm is a means to put you there. (Author's interview with Núñez and Guardia, October 2010)

Núñez elaborates on this, identifying that for him, connecting with a spirit or deity is a connection with a 'state of consciousness' (interview, October 2010).

A central element of Theatre of Sources was the work undertaken with traditional Haitian songs and dances led by Maud Robart and Tiga Garoute. These practices formed the basis for much of Grotowski's 'post-theatrical' research, with Robart playing a critical role in the development of work with traditional song and dance forms in Objective

Drama and Art as vehicle. One of the traditional forms that was explored as part of this research was the Haitian 'reptile' dance known as *yanvalou*. Grotowski describes the process of working with *yanvalou* as part of Objective Drama, explaining:

> there are precise steps – a tempo-rhythm – involving waves of the body, and not only of the backbone. If this is done with the songs which are, to be precise, those of the snake-divinity Dambhala, the manner of singing and of emitting the vibrations of the songs helps the movement of the body. (Grotowski 1987:35)

As with Núñez's description, this work began by focusing specifically on technical details and artistic competence. Grotowski insisted that before they looked to encounter the 'archaic', the participant must first achieve the ability to 'dance and sing in an organic and structured manner' (1987:35). This involved finding the right 'tempo-rhythms' and qualities of contact with the ground, as well as locating the specific resonances of voice. It was only once these technical and aesthetic aspects had been 'resolved', that the performer could approach a more intuitive relationship to the form, Grotowski proposing that at this point they could 'begin to work on what rhythm really is'. Grotowski described this as 'the waves of the old body in the new body' (1987:36) or as later translated 'the actual body'.[9]

Through the 're-actualization' of these traditional forms, the performers were given a means of accessing an archaic aspect, located within themselves. Described as 'reptilian' or 'animal', this 'primary energy' was characterized as an intuitive and instinctual mode of being. The performers sought to access this primal animal aspect within themselves, while all the time remaining vigilantly attentive and consciously present within their experience. Highlighting the tension created through this simultaneous task of accessing instinct while remaining present, Grotowski insisted: 'See what is happening! Look after yourself! Then, something exists as the presence of the two extremities of the same register, two different poles: that of instinct and that of consciousness' (Grotowski 2001a:300).

As referred to previously, the capacity to simultaneously sustain two oppositional poles of being is a central principle found across Grotowski's work as well as many of the other practices described in this book. This can also be identified as one of the 'traditional techniques' being investigated within this body of work. These techniques were often as much about the forms themselves as they were about the attitudes being adopted by participants within these. This included the capacity to access childlike qualities of innocence and naivety, along with the ability to maintain vigilant watchfulness and attention to the details of one's actions. Despite the predominant absence of religious beliefs or cultural associations within these practices, there remained a clear set of intentions that often guided the participant's engagement with the work. Throughout these descriptions, we encounter the dynamic potential resulting from a meeting of opposites: structure and spontaneity, stability and flux, conscious and intuitive, shared and personal, objective and subjective states. Far from a state of abandon, these examples point to a rigorously technical approach to rhythm and ecstasy.

Reflections

In tracing the use of rhythm from Grotowski's initial work with the Laboratory Theatre in Poland to his later research projects working with traditional and sacred techniques, we can observe the evolution and sustaining of a number of key principles drawn from early twentieth-century approaches to rhythm. We can take note of Grotowski's references to terms such as 'tempo-rhythm' and 'score'. These provide clear examples of how Grotowski adapted highly technical aspects of European actor training to the task of approaching sacred ritual practices. His description of rhythm as 'organic' and 'bodily' and his references to performance as a 'system of signs' also tie this work closely to the vitalist philosophies of the late nineteenth and early twentieth centuries. In both Grotowski's work and these earlier theories, rhythm was viewed primarily not as a musical system but as a 'living' process whose origins were rooted in biology and spiritual experience.

In looking through Grotowski's work with rhythm, we are also reminded that it is both the specific qualities of a rhythm and one's attitude towards it that are critical in realizing a shift in consciousness. The re-actualization of such forms is not simply the result of listening to, playing or dancing a rhythm. These practices relied on a process of embodiment, involving the participants' sensitization as well as detailed and sustained use of attention. As with Stanislavski's insistence that his performers engage their imaginations and attention while working with rhythm, Grotowski also insisted that individuals take on a particular attitude to their work, 'watching', being attentive and always remaining open.

10
NICOLÁS NÚÑEZ
BECOMING PRESENT

The work of Nicolás Núñez and the *Taller de Investigación Teatral* (Theatre Research Workshop or TRW) is focused on the application of sacred practices within the secular context of theatre and acting. Founded in 1975 by Núñez and a group of Mexican practitioners (the 'gang') including his main collaborator Helena Guardia, the TRW has developed its own approaches to what it has named 'Anthropocosmic Theatre'. This work has involved extended research into the indigenous Nahuatl traditions of Mexico, while also drawing from other cultures including 'Western theatre' practices taken from Núñez's training at the Old Vic Theatre School (England, 1973–74) as well as Guardia and Núñez's training with Lee Strasberg (America, 1978–79), and their research with Grotowski (Poland and Mexico, 1978–85). As part of their enquiry into sacred performance practices, members of the TRW have also travelled to the Tibetan Institute of Performing Arts (India, 1986), where they studied traditional forms of Tibetan theatre and monastic dance.

My first experience of Anthropocosmic Theatre was in 2004 at a workshop run in Wales by Núñez and Guardia. This encounter was both challenging and revealing. The work confronted many of my understandings of performance and acting, as well as the philosophical and spiritual ideas I had regarding how I related to the world and to myself within it. We were repeatedly asked to let go of preconceptions and expectations, to break out of our automatic patterns of behaviour and to surrender control while also attempting to master our physical and mental behaviours. While at the time, I struggled to grasp many of these propositions intellectually, my practical encounters – the ways in which I was directed to perceive and engage with myself and my environment – had a profound impact on my embodied understanding of myself as a performer and a person. What remains most vivid in my memory is the deep sense of liberation I encountered through the long durations of running and the sense that I had on a number of occasions of somehow 'arriving' in the present moment. This experience is difficult to capture in words; in these instances, I felt both deeply rooted in the present moment and also somehow outside of it.

There are numerous aspects of Núñez's work in which the theme of rhythm features strongly. These include his frequent use of live drumming as a means of focusing and directing the energetics of the group, along with the application of traditional dance forms within many of his training practices. While I have discussed these in previous writings (Morris 2009, 2013), for the purposes of this chapter, I will focus primarily on Núñez's use of 'slow walking' and 'contemplative running' and the roles played by rhythm in these practices.

In these practices, rhythm can be seen as both emerging from and acting upon the performer and the group. As they move through the space (sometimes slowly, sometimes fast) each participant generates their own rhythms and begins to tune into the rhythms of the others. This attunement (an entrainment of sorts) is one of the tools by which the performers become 'present', existing in the flow of the moment – what Núñez refers to as the 'actualized instant'.

Slow walking

A key technique used by Núñez and the TRW is that of 'slow walking'. Núñez began exploring the use of 'slow walking' as a psychophysical technique, while working in the forests of Poland with Grotowski as part of Theatre of Sources in 1980. Núñez had encountered this practice previously through his contact with the work of Carlos Castaneda. During his time with Grotowski in Poland, Núñez further explored the use of this technique and developed ways of leading it. Elements of this research were continued within Grotowski's later projects, with Núñez also continuing to draw on 'slow walking' as a key technique within his work with the TRW and in public workshops.

As previously described in regard to Grotowski's practices (Chapter 9), reducing one's walking pace down to an extremely slow tempo can have an effect of disrupting established forms of conscious behaviour (Grotowski

2001a:263). Rather than focusing on a future destination or outcome, awareness is brought into the present moment. Synchronizing attention with the slowness of the body, a new relationship is established between movement, awareness and time. Walking, an act which in daily life is often unconscious and habitual, here becomes uncanny and immediate.

EXERCISE 22: SLOW WALKING (NÚÑEZ)

This work often begins with participants walking through the space travelling in an anticlockwise direction. Núñez instructs the group to gradually slow their pace bringing their movements towards a quality of 'slow motion'. As Deborah Middleton, a practitioner and scholar with a long history of engagement with Núñez's practices, explains:

> The participant aims to move as slowly and smoothly as possible, taking exaggerated steps so that there is maximum activity in the muscles of the supporting leg. The participant's attention is quickly drawn to balance, and to her shifting centre of gravity as she moves slowly forward in space. The pace of the walk has a calming effect and breathing is slowed and harmonized accordingly. Throughout the walk the participant must ensure that her attention is not allowed to wander but instead is fluidly fixed upon the sensation of the body in motion. (Middleton 2001:51)

Here the calming effect of slow movement and breathing is placed alongside an intensified use of mental and physical energies, with the participants seeking to raise their energy levels from a daily mode of being, to what Núñez refers to as 'heroic' or 'epic' qualities. Middleton also highlights the specific use of attention required by this practice. Attention must remain present while also being fluid – fixed but free to follow the motions of the body.

As with many of the approaches described in this book, rhythm is used here as a means of disturbing or altering habitual modes of doing and perceiving. Núñez describes this as a 'deprogramming' of daily behavioural patterns (Middleton 2001:47). Simple tasks such as walking backwards, suddenly stopping or closing eyes are also used to further disrupt expectations and intensify the participant's commitment to the physical and mental requirements of the activity.

From within my own experience of this practice, I observe a sense of time slowing. A sharper quality of focus comes into each moment to the point that these almost crystalize into a sense of time being suspended. There are times when I feel like I am falling into each moment, like a drop of water passing through me. Momentarily, I catch glimpses of how I am, where I am, what I am doing; my sensations, thoughts and inner experiences – a series of instances in which I feel myself to be present. Although there are times when my mind wanders, Núñez's ongoing instructions aid my attention in returning again and again to the task at hand.

Contemplative running

Another important technique used throughout the TRW's practices is 'contemplative running'.[1] As with the 'slow walking', Núñez developed this practice during his research with Grotowski in Poland in 1980. As part of his research in Theatre of Sources, Jacek Zmysłowski had begun work on a form of running in circles over long periods of time, with a sustained regular rhythm. When Zmysłowski fell ill suddenly, Grotowski requested that Núñez carry on this research himself, with the aim of developing a running 'technique' and a means of leading it (Dunkelberg 2008:648–9). This sustained form of running has become a key aspect of Núñez's practice forming the basis for many processes used in his regular training and workshop sessions.[2]

EXERCISE 23: CONTEMPLATIVE RUNNING

The group moves in a continuous and flowing running motion, travelling in an anticlockwise direction around the space. The participants' main tasks are to release any unnecessary tensions from their bodies and to maintain an open awareness of their experience within the 'here and now'. Middleton explains: 'the contemplative run is not contemplative in the sense that one contemplates ideas while running. Rather it is contemplation in the sense of meditation, a total focus of the mind on the body, on the *experience* of the run' (2001:52, italics in original).

Lasting for extended periods of time (from twenty minutes to up to three hours), the sustained nature of this work is important both in terms of breaking through the barrier of durational effort and in terms of the collective energy that is generated as the group relaxes into the flow of the exercise:

> we trot floating through the area, relaxing at every step, avoiding the tension in the arms which one gets in a running race, and do not try to advance, since there is nowhere to reach and nobody to beat. We keep our look open, i.e. without focusing, and the same goes for our active internal chant; we must feel that we are hanging by a thread which comes from the crown of our head and is tied to the stars, and flow at our own pace in a constant here and now. (Núñez 1996:88–9)

In contrast with other, more individually orientated contemplative practices (such as seated meditation or yoga) in which the focus lies primarily on perceiving one's own body, in contemplative running the individual's movement/perception is opened out to encapsulate the movements and rhythms of the people around them and the group as a whole. From within the running Núñez instructs:

> I hear the stepping of the group, I see the group, I taste the group, I smell the group, I have spatial consciousness of the group. And I put myself into the flow – I don't isolate myself. ... I put myself into the flow of the river of the group. ... Relaxing *in* movement. I don't move myself – the body of the group is moving me.
>
> When I reach with my mental intention that level, that's when I make a jump. I get the feeling that something else is happening. I go out of 'mechanics' or our 'automatism'. And reach a pleasant point, where I fly, where I relax through movement.

Who am I? I am with the others, I am with my partners, I am in the instant, where I am with the people around me. I am a river of energy, and I get into the river. It is not my will that is moving me. (Transcribed from personal recordings of workshop with Núñez in 2016)

The distinction between self and others, individual and group begins to dissolve here. If we understand rhythm as a form of territory (Chapter 1), then these practices can be seen as a process of merging the territories of self and others into one – a form of 'boundary loss'. In Núñez's metaphor of a river, there is also an evocation of being swept along by a force that is more than just a collection of bodies moving through space. From the continuity and synchronized quality of both movement and attention, there comes a sense of something other emerging and supporting the motion of the group. At times this leads to sustained phases of effortlessness and waves of energy that seem to carry us along as we run.[3]

Whereas in the 'slow walking' I experience a sense of time crystalizing, within 'contemplative running', I often have the experience of each moment merging into the next. To develop this analogy, time feels less like raindrops and more like a rolling stream. I recall the experiences of my awareness slipping through time with almost no traction, being unable to locate myself in a specific moment or place. While both the 'slow walk' and the 'contemplative run' aim towards an encounter with the present, my experience in each of these is distinct, both in terms of the ways I experience time passing and in terms of my sense of self in relationship to the group and the environment. There are moments, however, in each of these practices, in which I also have the opposite experience. In the 'slow walk' there are instances in which time seems to flow through my actions, where the stillness has a sense of continuity which breaks from the static crystallization of each moment. Conversely, within the flow of 'contemplative running', I can recall a suspension of time. In these moments I seem to be outside of the familiar flow of time and encounter a sense of temporal expansiveness, time taking on a thicker, more solid consistency. Time seems to become denser, uncanny, unfamiliar, changed by my relationship to it.

Cosmic verticality

Within these processes the performer/participant often seeks to raise their energy from that of everyday 'life' to a 'heroic' or 'epic' level of being. Núñez locates these qualities along a vertical spectrum, the pinnacle of which is 'pure undifferentiated energy'. At the bottom he places the 'theatre of life': the 'psychological, philosophical, political even pornographic' (2016).

Following a similar model, Grotowski described the search for a 'passage' from a coarse 'everyday' level of energy, located 'in the density of the body', to 'a level of energy much more subtle' (1997:88–9). Discussing his work on Art as vehicle, he made an analogy to 'a kind of elevator as in ancient times': 'a big basket with a rope by means of which the person who is inside, by his own effort, has to move himself from one level to another' (1997:88).

This is a process of transformation resulting from personal effort. In both Núñez and Grotowski's practices, the individuals seek to 'pull' themselves up, raising their quality of energy through action and attention. As with the 'slow walk' or 'contemplative run', the critical point is not whether I am *doing* more or less (travelling faster or slower), but rather that my relationship to what I do is altered, heightened in a sense. This transformation of energy can be understood as a qualitative transformation, in the sense of moving from 'coarse to subtle', as

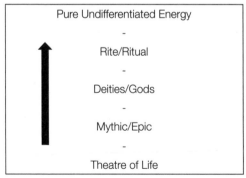

Figure 10.1 Energetic levels of cosmic verticality.

distinct from a quantitative change, which would involve becoming 'more or less energetic' (Allain 2009:228).

In both these examples, it is through the intentional engagement with the task – through the sustained use of attention to one's own body as well as the others and through the combination of 'movement and repose' that a change takes place. This is achieved through the use of 'concrete actions' and through a focused awareness of what *is* happening in the moment.

'Here and now'

Núñez states that the intention of 'being present' is a central concern of both the actor and the ritual practitioner. This common 'mechanism' forms a bridge, uniting the profane and sacred territories of theatre and ritual. As Middleton explains:

> [Núñez] sees the relationship between the two as centred upon an essential axis, a common dependency on the actualized instant; that is, at the centre of each is 'the moment'. Both theatre and ritual are activities which take place in a spatial and temporal terrain which requires the 'enlivening' of time through focus and action, full psychophysical presence in what Stanislavsky called the 'here and now'. (2001:47)

Bringing attention to the reality of the moment can be seen here as a transformative tool, described by Núñez as an 'archaic mechanism' through which consciousness can be altered (1996:36).

It could be argued that no matter what we pay attention to (memories, anticipations or distractions) we remain 'here and now'. For me though, the distinction between simply *occupying* the moment and *being present* in it is an issue of intention and the ways I choose to use my attention in regard to both space and time – the ways I relate my own rhythm to the rhythms around me. Within the context of Núñez's practices this is an active process in which, through the use of mental and physical efforts, the performers come into contact with themselves within the moment. Through this encounter, time takes on a different quality. It is 'enlivened', 'actualized' through the use of attention and intention.

We can reflect here on the ways that Núñez's practices look to alter a performer's relationship with time, generating heightened moments of intensification in which time can seem to be suspended or stretch out expansively. In other instances, time appears to flow rapidly, an entire sequence of actions seeming to pass in an instant. In each of these experiences time is shaped, to some extent, by the ways I direct my attention and actions: the ways I inhabit and relate to the rhythms taking place 'here and now'.[4]

As a central principle of Stanislavski's system, the actor's ability to experience and act in response to the present moment on stage (and all that this contains) is a key aspect of many forms of actor training. This is a principle I have already touched on briefly in John Britton's use of ball games as a means of focusing attention onto responding to what *is* happening in the moment rather than pre-existing ideas of what we think *will* or *should be* happening (see Chapter 6 and Britton 2013:318). Similarly, the use of 'Kinaesthetic response' within Viewpoints training can be seen as a means of bringing the performer into an immediate relationship with impulses emerging from within an improvisation as it is occurring, rather than making decisions based on established expectations or artistic preconceptions (Chapter 7). The premise behind these approaches is that by maintaining an awareness of events as they unfold in the 'present', the performer's work becomes more focused, immediate and responsive. Britton, commenting on the effects that focused attention has on his own students, explains: 'In the face of a simple task experienced "in the present moment", the distortion of the body and the distractions of the mind can become clear' (2013:337). Through the 'simple' act of directing attention, performers are made aware of their own capacities and tendencies towards manipulating and distorting their experiences of reality.

In his own practice, Núñez also emphasizes the performer's active relationship to reality, relating the role of the actor to that of the shaman. Here, it is the actor/shaman's encounter with reality, which constitutes an altering of consciousness:

> we have to make clear that the shaman or the actor is someone who, at will, can go into an altered state of consciousness, go in and out at will ... [T]he mind has two main functions; the first one ... is to intellectualize or rationalize ... the second one is to perceive reality

directly with no interference of any kind of thinking, to intuitively catch the reality – not what we think it is – see what it is. (Núñez 1993 cited in Middleton 2008:45)

This state of consciousness is described as an intuitive rather than intellectual relationship with reality, with the present moment experienced directly, without interference or rationalization. In a similar way, psychologist and theatre practitioner Etzel Cardeña describes the experience of the intellect being separated from our physical actions as a form of 'dual consciousness'. He explains that, where consciousness is often experienced as being distinct or separate from the body, the other or the environment, in working with Núñez and other similar practitioners.

this separate dual consciousness starts breaking down at times. [...A]t one point there will be no observing self that is separate from the action that is occurring. [...I]f there is a movement that has to happen [...,] instead of a thought preceding the action there is a consciousness in action, or an action in consciousness. (Cardeña 1998 cited in Middleton 2001:53)

From a rhythmic perspective, we could say that in 'dual consciousness', action and perception appear to occupy their own pockets or trajectories of time; I do, then I experience; I think, then I act; I speak, then I listen. In contrast, 'non-dual consciousness' can be seen as a form of synchronization or entrainment between these processes. As noted in Grotowski's Theatre of Sources (Chapter 9), where in daily life, perception and action often have qualities of separateness or independence, in ritual/performance the actor/shaman often seeks to synchronize the various aspects of their being and their environment into a unified experience/act, a sense of being or becoming 'present' in one's totality.

Becoming present, in this sense, is more than simply being aware of what one is doing as one does it. Rather, this involves a more integrated quality of 'rhythmic' relationship both within the individual and amongst those present. This integrated (rather than isolated) experience of self is a central aim of the TRW's practices. Núñez describes these relationships through analogies, such as viewing the body as an 'echo box of the cosmos' (1996:xvii) or the act of becoming a 'perforated mirror' through which we can read both our own body and the stars within a single vision (1996:69). Here the individual seeks to realize an integrated relationship not just with the other but with the universe as whole. Hence the name given to these practices is Anthropocosmic Theatre.

Continuity of effort and the sustaining of rhythm

Where many of the approaches described in this book have involved relatively short durations of activities each directed at a different skill or technique, the focus throughout much of the TRW's work lies in the sustaining of attention and action over extended periods of time. Often, a session lasting from around fifty to ninety minutes will comprise a single process undertaken without any breaks or interruptions. The continuous nature of these practices, in itself, generates a distinct relationship to time. Here our familiar temporal markers and goal-orientated attitudes are challenged and disrupted. There are times when Núñez explains to the participants that they are to have no expectations – no sense of how long this activity might continue. As the group runs through the space, he suggests (half-jokingly), *this may last all day*. For me, instructions such as these help discourage me from fixing my mind on an end goal – a task to be achieved at some point in the future – and bring my focus to the continuous task of attending to my experience of the present moment.

There is also an accumulative effect, resulting from the continuity of these processes, with the repetition of actions and rhythms generating an increasing sense of integration and resonance. In reference to this, Núñez describes a kind of 'reverberation', which emerges from the group's movements and rhythms:

> When you reach some level of vibration through movement or rhythm, if you keep it, like a 'Jericho trumpet', you can really affect the energy around you. And when you do this for several hours, you can see that this totally affects you to 'enroot' yourself deep into the earth, and your meaning of being. (Author's interview with Núñez and Guardia, 2010) ·

It is interesting to observe the ways that sustaining, rather than intentionally (or unintentionally) changing an action, can generate a distinct quality or 'energetic' within a group (Chapter 6). In some moments, I have a sense that 'something else' has emerged from the activity, the space feels enlivened by the group's sustained presence within it.

In terms of repetition, it is also worth considering the ways these practices (in Mexico at least) are often repeated on a weekly or semi-regular basis. In returning to the same forms again and again, we have a chance to observe the changing or stable qualities of experience that arise within the work. The repeating of specific forms becomes a mirror in which I can encounter myself 'here, now, today', placed up against the familiarity of the activity. To some extent this describes a paradoxical relationship present within many forms of ritual and performance. There exists a dual process of working through existing forms or techniques, with the intention of being engaged with and available to the immediacy of the occasion – the improvisation. As with the relationships described previously (between metre and rhythm, structure and spontaneity, form and flow) we can see here how these aspects (repetition and the present moment) can be seen to support and inform one another.

Reflections

While altered states of consciousness, trance, ecstasy, ritual and performance are often characterized as departures from reality, here it might be more useful to consider these as shifts in perspective or quality. In the practices of Núñez, we can observe a disruption or dissolving of habitual and dualistic modes of relating to one's self, in relationship to others and to one's environment, time and space. Where these elements are often viewed as being separated, these practices look to bring about a quality of deeper integration. Rhythm's capacity to both disrupt and unify contributes strongly to the transformative nature of these processes. At times it is seen to challenge habitualized behaviours including the durations and tempo of attention and action – the sustaining of an action over a long duration or the act of moving at an unfamiliar speed. Rhythm is equally seen to be supportive and unifying with in this work – experienced as carrying and sustaining the group as they run and encouraging qualities of 'boundary loss' and *communitas*.

Reflecting on the process of *becoming present* within Núñez's practices as well as in ritual and performance in general, we can consider some of the ways that rhythm is applied as a *tool*. Here rhythm often takes on a role of both disrupting habitual forms of behaviour/perception and offering a means of generating unity between aspects that may otherwise be seen to be separate (see Table 10.1). This table is in many ways an oversimplification of what in reality are complex processes involving multiple elements, not least of which is the subjective experience of the participants, performers and audience members. However, viewed as a framework, this does help to identify some of the ways that rhythm can be (and is being) used as a tool for affecting/altering consciousness. This can also help us to consider some of the ways these principles may be applied within performance and training practices.

Table 10.1 Rhythmic dramaturgies of attention in ritual and performance

Rhythmic Descriptions	Psychophysical Qualities
Demarcation of stages (marking the beginnings/ends of an entire process and its sections)	Shifts focus and establishes temporal framework, pattern or flow
Alternation and repetition of actions/sounds by an individual or a group	Anchoring and synchronizing physical actions and attention, blurring boundaries between individual and group
Sustaining of a single image/action/sound over prolonged durations	Breaking habitual modes of attention, heightening focus
Development from simple-complex, slow-fast, quiet-loud, and back	Increasing energy/commitment of attention and the intensification of time/space
Layering of multiple rhythms (polyrhythm or cacophony)	Disorientating and bewildering or alternatively establishing a greater sense of integration and intensification
Non-daily rhythms and rhythms with specific associations, symbolic meaning, cultural significance	Disrupting habitual rhythmic patterns and establishing distinct energetic/perceptual qualities

11
EILON MORRIS
ORBITS – CULTIVATING SIMULTANEITY

Rhythm always involves a relationship: between two or more events in time; the relationship between what precedes an action, its beginning, middle, end and what follows it; the relationship between a rhythmic phrase and the 'canvas of metre' over which it is enacted and perceived; the relationships between multiple rhythms which share a moment in time; the relationship between our expectations and what actually happens. As a trainer of performers, a large part of what interests me are the ways we explore and inhabit these relationships. Central to this is the search for ways of cultivating performers' capacities to sense, not only their own rhythms but the ways these relate to those emerging within an ensemble and a performance as a whole. This was the starting point for the development of a collection of polyrhythmic training approaches for actors, which I began working on in 2010. Part of this training involves a collection of choreographic forms that I have named Orbits. This work was largely inspired by research that I undertook in Mexico City with Nicolas Núñez and the Taller de Investigación Teatrale (TRW) at the end of 2010. Over the past six years I have gone on to develop and refine Orbits through research workshops in the UK and France, as well as drawing from other areas of my training, including working with Afro-Cuban music, TaKeTiNa (a polyrhythmic movement and voice practices developed by Reinhard Flatischler) as well as movement improvisation exercises stemming from Britton's Self-With-Others practice.

By way of introduction to Orbits, I will begin this chapter by examining the notions of polyrhythm and simultaneity in performance.

Vertical time

Grotowski and Núñez both described their practices as a process of 'verticality' (Chapters 9 and 10). While these practitioners made reference to an 'energetic' verticality (shifting from coarse to subtle and back again), it may be useful to briefly reflect on the notion of *temporal verticality* and its relationship to rhythm. Within Western culture, time has often been represented as a horizontal linear (time) line, a journey from one moment to another or a trajectory reaching infinitely into the future and/or past. Where this *horizontal time* can be described in terms of durations and sequences of events occurring along a single timeline (one event after another), we might also consider the presence of a *vertical time*, one that describes the simultaneous relationships between events (one or more events occurring during one another; see Figures 11.1 and 11.2). Otherwise referred to as 'simultaneity',[1] this vertical dimension encompasses all things occurring at the same time. As artist and theoretician Peter Weibel puts it: 'Simultaneity describes the world as the nucleus of the Now' (2008:vii).

Stanislavski famously established the model of a 'through-line', by which a performance or an individual character's trajectory could be mapped from the start to the end of a scene or an entire play. This has been characteristically represented by a horizontal line with arrows pointing from left to right (Stanislavski 2008:316). This image

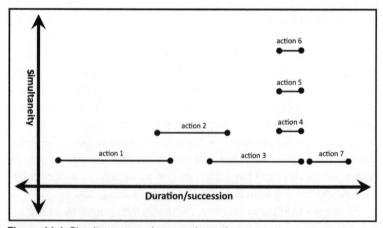

Figure 11.1 Simultaneous and successive actions.

gives the impression of a highly linear understanding of time and performance. Yet, in his own notes (made in the 1930s) Stanislavski insisted that while people often think that 'the through-line is a single line, like a cable, that extends through the whole play ... this is not so. There are many lines, not one, which are woven together' (Stanislavski 1986b:300 as translated by Carnicke 2008:2). Listing these he included: 'the line of events'; 'the line of a scenes bits' (otherwise referred to as 'beats'), 'tasks and desires'; 'the line of inner and outer actions', the imaginative line of the 'given circumstances'; 'objects of attention'; 'truths and beliefs'; 'physical' and 'spiritual communication'; lines of 'energy' (*prana*); conceptualization of the role; 'tempo-rhythm'; 'sound speech and voice'; 'characterization'; 'self-control' (Stanislavski 1986b:300; Carnicke 2008:2). Far from existing along a single trajectory, the actor here is seen to inhabit a multiplicity of through-lines, which are simultaneously realized and woven together to form their performance.

Lee Worley offers another model for considering the cultivation of simultaneity in the performer. In her workshops she describes a process of 'flickering' between sense modalities. As part of her 'sense perception work' she instructs participants to direct their conscious attention: beginning with attending to their bodily and visceral sensations, then adding to this an awareness of taste/smell, then hearing, and then sight, gradually building up to a process of alternating through a multitude of sense experiences including an awareness of breath and the space extending in all directions. Worley comments that she learned this technique from 'Mudra Space Awareness where, as the intense space is meeting the body, the mind has to move quickly around to check on all aspects of the body/space meeting' (personal correspondence).

This metaphor of 'flickering' offers a way of considering a more dynamic and manifold use of attention. Where many approaches to meditation and acting encourage a sustaining of focus on a single objective or area of attention, 'flickering' presents a model for how attention can be trained to shift between multiple elements taking place simultaneously inside and outside the body. Rather than being fixed on a single line of thought or sensation, rapidly shifting between these aspects begins to open up a complex, yet potentially more integrated experience. Worley explains that from her experience it 'takes some training in slowing down, [through] meditating or something like it, to recognize the aspects of mind and harness them to this task' (personal correspondence).

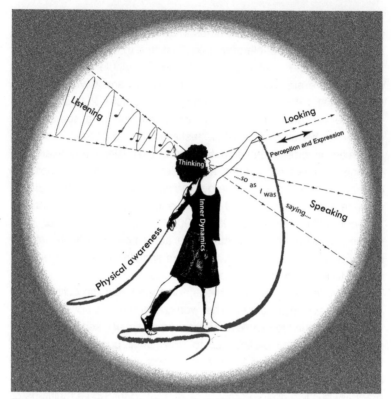

Figure 11.2 Simultaneous tasks of an individual performer.

Although 'now' is often considered as a single event, it is worth reflecting that to some extent all experiences of time involve the correlation of multiple elements, the bringing together of events occurring both inside and outside of ourselves.[2] Patrice Pavis opens this notion out to examine the ways an audience perceives performance, suggesting that the nature of this experience is always 'vertical and synthetic'. The audience member is always engaged in a creative process of bringing together all the elements of the performance to form 'temporal totalities': 'In short, the spectator does not break up a performance into pieces, but employs broad spatiotemporal cross-sections within which meaning forms a coherent ensemble' (Pavis 2003:307).

An 'ensemble' of experiences is formed by each audience member and performer as they bring together the range of perceptual, philosophical, associative and visceral experiences which arise from and direct their performance. What is of particular interest, regarding rhythm in performance and training, is the way that multiple rhythmic elements can come together within the performers' and audience members' experiences of 'now'. In this sense, I am not attempting to describe an 'absolute' notion of simultaneity in time, being somehow objectively viewed from the outside (if such a thing is possible). Rather, what is being discussed here is the individual's encounter with the present moment – time as it is *experienced* from what Otto Rössler has named the *endo-perspective* (1998). Considering time from this point of view opens the way for discussing our relationship to time as 'observer-participants' (Vrobel 2008). From this perspective, our experience of time can be understood as both a product of our embodied perceptual capacities (i.e. the neurophysiological constraints that shape the ways we perceive and combine visual, auditory and tactile senses) and the metaphors that arise from our encounters with the world (how we conceptualize and understand time) (Vrobel 2008:4). Our experience of the present is a process that we both observe and participate in. For the performer, this also means that time can be considered as something that is engaged with creatively, shaped by their use of action, sound, attention and imagination. We come back to Aristoxenus' principle of rhythm as an active process (Chapter 1), something done to a movement, sound or time, rather than an object that is simply perceived. Here I am as much interested in the performers' creative capacities to be active in these relationship, as I am in their abilities to perceive and sense these, finding different ways of locating themselves within and relating to time.

Orbits

Approaching rhythm as a means of engaging with time and simultaneity, the central aim of Orbits is to train performers in how to perceive and enact multiple rhythms, cultivating the dexterity of shifting and directing their attention while in motion. This is by no means an original concept. Work on polyrhythmic awareness and action has been a part of many approaches to performance, including those of Dalcroze, Stanislavski and Meyerhold (Chapters 3 and 5). Yet, arguably this capacity is one that seldom receives direct attention in actor training. While the actor/

performer is often asked to engage with multiple tasks simultaneously, the process of cultivating this ability or exploring its potentials is rarely supported beyond a basic level of instruction, or direction.[3] The question remains as to how performers can develop this capacity and further explore its potentials within performance.

What follows is a brief description of a 'thirty-beat orbit form' and the process by which I often teach this. Training with these forms generally begins with a number of initial movement exercises that introduce the basic principles of this practice, including awareness of a shared pulse, a sense of rhythm as movement through space and the ability to enact one rhythm while perceiving others. In approaching these principles, a sense of playfulness and personal curiosity is essential. Rather than emphasizing the need for technical perfection, at this stage it is more important that the performers develop an awareness of rhythm as something that they are making and *participating* in, rather than a form to be learned and adhered to. Many performers are initially anxious and stressed about getting a rhythm 'right' or not being seen to get things 'wrong'. As such, they tend to focus mostly on what they *think* they *should* be doing, rather than on what they are *actually* doing and observing. Instead of aiming for perfection, at this stage it is more important to discover an open and responsive relationship to rhythm.

EXERCISE 24: DEPARTURES, ARRIVALS AND JOURNEYS

Starting with exercises that sensitize the performers to a sense of pulsation in their own movements and those of the group, we explore ways of directing attention to simple actions, such as walking, breathing and clapping, being aware of the movements and spaces/silences between them. Here the performers are encouraged to shift their attention between moments of 'accent' or intensity (a footfall, a clap) and the journeys/intervals between these moments. What leads us from one step to another? What happens between one clap and the next? Building on this work, we explore ways of walking through the space, stopping and starting at will, and observing a sense of *arrival* and *departure*. Where/When do we begin and end our journeys? What is the passage from one point in space/time to another? We play with different lengths of journeys, from one step up to thirty-two (or sometimes more). We explore different ways of arriving and departing (fast, slow, sudden, gradual, increasing or decreasing in intensity). The participants are encouraged to be aware not only of their rhythm but also to pay attention to where they are in the space and their relationships with each other. Working with these key points of attention, the participants become aware of the correlations and differences between their movements through space and the length of time that these take. How can we travel a short journey over a short duration, a long journey over a long duration, or invert these and travel a long distance quickly or a short distance slowly?

Once this sense of rhythm as physical experience is established, the participants work on devising a fixed movement through space: they set a start point, a journey and an end point. This can be long or short in duration; I can travel a big distance through the space or be almost stationary. What is important is that the performers are clear and precise about how/where/when their movement begins, travels and ends. And that they can repeat these details. As they start developing a sense of their personal journey, becoming clear about the duration as well as the spatial trajectory of their movements, they can begin to observe the ways their journey intersects and relates to the other bodies moving throughout the space.

With time, these exercises can also be applied to devising more complex physical scores as well as to compositions of sound and spoken or sung language. Working with the basic principles of observing points of departure, journeys and arrivals, performers learn to pay attention to the compositional nature of their actions and sounds, gaining an embodied sense of what Langer described as 'complete gestures', containing a 'beginning, intent and consummation' (1953:128). Having established a clear journey through the space and the physicality of their bodies, the performers can also explore ways of maintaining the integrity of their journeys while changing dynamics, tempo, qualities of accentuation, weight and other characteristics.

Working in pairs, the participants can combine their journeys as a way of encountering a number of compositional relationships and forms of simultaneity:

- A and B both start at the same time
- A and B both end at the same time
- B begins at the moment that A ends (and vice versa)
- B begins at a point half way through A (and vice versa)
- A and B alter the tempo of their journeys so that they both fit into the same duration
- A and B alter their tempo so that A can take place two or three times within a single duration of B (vice versa).

Through these processes, performers have a chance to explore notions of musicality, composition and relationships between structure and spontaneity.

As part of this initial work, the participants are also introduced to the practice of 'contemplative running' (Chapter 10), which is later used as part of the Orbits sequence.

While there are clear applications of these exercises in the devising of ensemble performance material, the central aim of this 'journeying' work is to develop an awareness of relationships between space and time and a capacity to do/move/speak while also perceiving/sensing/listening. Cultivating the performers' abilities to track the journey of their own actions, they encounter a set of tools for observing the rhythms of others and ultimately a way of experiencing the simultaneity of their own rhythms and those taking place around them.

Building on these principles, I introduce the group to the forms of the Orbits we will work with. In the case of the thirty-beat orbit, the forms are cycles of two, three and five beats (i.e. accenting the first of every two, three or five pulses/steps in a sequence). This is one of the simpler forms of Orbits that I use within workshops and ensemble training processes. It is referred to as a thirty-beat orbit because it takes thirty beats for all the cycles to coincide on their first beat.

The participants are often first introduced to these forms by standing in a circle and clapping these out, using simple stepping patterns to mark their durations. This eventually leads to walking and running these patterns freely through the space. Accents are marked with the voice through spoken syllables and/or with claps and rattles. Although these patterns are described here in numbers, I intentionally avoid using counting or musical notation in teaching these patterns.[4] Instead the use of simple syllables and physical movements are used as a way of dropping these cycles into the body so as to become an intuitive sense rather than conceptual framework. Drawing on the previous exercises exploring ways of 'journeying', the participants are encouraged to find a sense of how each of these cycles feels as a motion through space and through their bodies and to use this (rather than counting) as their primary point of reference. For many performers trained in music or dance, this can be a challenging experience. At first it might feel difficult keeping track of a duration without counting. With time, this capacity becomes extremely useful, particularly when they come to combining and shifting between multiple patterns. Having an embodied sense of the rhythm, the performers free up their capacity to direct their attention to others and to be able to improvise within these forms. While at times counting can be useful as a way of analysing a pattern, in the process of training and performing (from my experience) it often gets in the way.

Once participants have embodied these cycles (to the point at which they can comfortably move these through the space), we begin to combine and layer these sequences. One group sustains a two-beat stepping pattern while another group marks out a three-beat or five-beat cycle. We slowly build to the point where we can comfortably layer all three patterns. Having begun to develop a deeper awareness of these cycles and their relationships, we mark out the forms that will be used within the Orbits[5] (see Figure 11.3). For this sequence it would be:

- a central circle travelling counter-clockwise accenting a two beat rhythm;
- a second circle around that, going in the opposite direction marking the first of every three steps; and
- a third outer circle travelling in the opposite direction again, marking the first of every five steps.

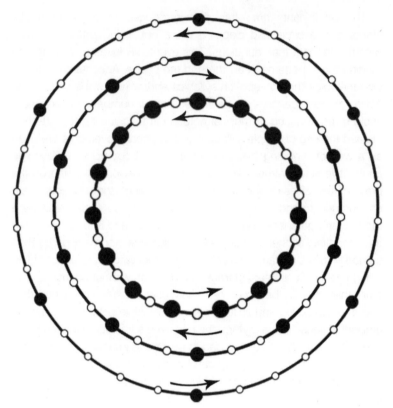

Figure 11.3 Thirty-beat orbit form consisting of two-, three- and five-beat cycles.

These exercises introduce the basic ingredients of Orbits: an awareness/understanding of working with a pulse, accents, durations/ journeys, polyrhythmic cycles and the practice of contemplative running. Underlying this work is the development of an ability to embody a rhythmic cycle, not as a set of numbers or notes, but as a physical experience of moving through space in relationship to others.

Running Orbits

The sequence and duration of events within Orbits are closely related to the structure of a training 'dynamic' developed by Núñez called *Huracán.*[6]

As with *Huracán*, Orbits begins with a period of 'contemplative running'. During this time, the participants are given the opportunity to tune into their own sense of motion and rhythm as they move through the space opening out their awareness and connection to the ensemble as a whole. Drawing on the principles of TRW's practices, the participants are working throughout this time to maintain their attention on the 'here and now' of their experiences. They are instructed to observe when their focus drifts and continuously bring their attention back to the sense of their body moving through space and an awareness of their relationship with the others moving around them.

After around fifteen minutes of running, I give a signal and we divide into three subgroups, which have been set before commencing. These smaller groups form the three concentric floor patterns (see layout in Figure 11.3). Starting by establishing the central circle, the other circles form one by one until all three rhythms are orbiting simultaneously. Sharing a basic pulse, the participants look to maintain an open awareness of their own rhythm in relationship to their subgroup, as well as a sense of the collective rhythm of the ensemble.

Once the patterns are established, participants begin to explore the process of shifting from one circle to another. In these moments participants are free to break away from their subgroups and to move independently between the three circles. This aspect of the work emerged from my discussions with Núñez in 2010. We talked about finding a way for the participants to experience a sense of shifting from one 'orbit' to another, of moving out of their rhythm, sensing the 'gravitational pull' of the other cycles, resisting or following this pull. With participants cycling and weaving between one another, the process becomes more dynamic. Each participant needs to sense their relationship to the composition as a whole, seeking to find a balance between keeping the patterns stable, and the fluidity and potential chaos that emerges as they transition between these patterns.

There are multiple tasks and points of focus that the participants are encouraged to shift between as they continue to move within these concentric forms. They are encouraged to shift (or 'flicker') between these, encountering moments in which multiple tasks come together simultaneously or overlap:

- tap into the underlying pulse shared by the entire group;
- be aware of your own rhythm;
- tap into the rhythmic cycle of your subgroup;
- be aware of the accents and the spaces between these;
- open out your awareness to the rhythms of the other groups;
- experience the pull of the rhythms and your relationship to them;
- open out to the emergent rhythm of the group as a whole;
- allow yourself to shift rhythms, moving from one circle to another; and
- be aware of the bodies moving around you and the spaces between these.

After around ten minutes the groups are signalled to break out of their orbit patterns and return to 'contemplative running'. The remainder of the process consists of an alternation between phases of running and phases of 'orbiting', finishing with a run that gradually slows to a walk, then a slow walk, and finally a duration of stillness. The entire Orbits sequence lasts between forty-five and sixty minutes. For this duration the participants are encouraged to remain present in the work, not taking breaks or leaving the room. There is always an option to stand still in the middle of the space and observe the orbits from a point of stillness, before finding their way back into the flow of the exercise, or to walk around the outside of the space, experiencing the process from another perspective.

Reflections

While some initial training is required, this 'thirty-beat orbit' form is relatively accessible to performers with little or no previous rhythm training. These introductory practices present performers with a direct means of encountering themselves within a complex yet accessible polyrhythmic experience. Although this practice involves learning certain techniques and forms, the focus throughout is directed primarily towards developing a greater awareness and sensitivity to rhythm and simultaneity. As with Britton's use of the 'ball game', Orbits acts as a 'mirror', reflecting instantaneously the relationship between the individual performer and the emergent phenomenon of the ensemble. From within this work, performers can easily observe when their attention is withdrawing into their own personal actions, or when their focus becomes lost or distracted by the actions of others. Looking to balance both an awareness of self and others, the rhythms of Orbits establish clear reference points for directing and developing new ways of attending.

As highlighted by Stanislavski (Chapter 3), there is always a risk that such exercises become purely technical, with performers becoming tense, frustrated or simply bored by the repetitions of their actions. While there are times when it is useful to push through the challenge of the work, if the performers start to stress too much about 'getting the rhythms', 'doing it right' or conceptually understanding these patterns, then the experiential and creative aspects of the process usually close down. Here, chasing after the rhythm or trying to perfect it, is generally counterproductive. This often leads to the work becoming uninteresting and meaningless, becoming a purely technical exercise in counting or choreography. Instead these practices seek to encourage the performers to inhabit and experience themselves within these rhythmic relationships, remaining present and attentive without trying to control or be critical of their experiences within the work. For many, this can be challenging having been taught to always strive for perfection and understanding of what they are doing. From within Orbits the performers encounter a lucid sense of this paradox as they negotiate their ways through their learning experience. The harder they try, often the more difficult the work becomes. The more they learn to simply listen and observe, the easier it is to engage with and navigate this process.

Providing a simple means of shifting from one rhythmic pattern to another, Orbits cultivates a more fluid and malleable relationship to time and rhythm. With each shift in rhythm comes a change of perspective and an opportunity to perceive this polyrhythmic composition from a different angle. To begin with, the participants often experience the others' movements through the framework of their own cycle (i.e. hearing a two- or five-beat cycle as layered over the metre of their three-beat pattern). There are also instances when one's own movements can be experienced from the perspective of another subgroup's cycle (i.e. hearing my own three-beat pattern, through the metre of the five- or two-beat cycles). There are further instances where a composite sense of all three cycles is formed, with one's own rhythm seen to weave throughout this. Here, as with many forms of West African polyrhythm, there is no definitive way of experiencing these patterns. The repetitive and multi-layered nature of these forms allows the listener/performer to move between a number of distinct experiences of the same composition. The plurality of these forms offers a means of shifting the perceptual 'ground' from which the performers view their own rhythms, the rhythms of others and the composition as a whole, encountering multiple rhythmic experiences from within the same form.[7]

At times these shifts in perception can lead to a sense of immersion or even 'boundary loss', with the perception of self being strongly tied to how we locate ourselves within these rhythms. Sometimes participants describe transformative moments of experiencing themselves as merging with the group or their sense of presence being expanded to encompass the ensemble as a whole. A participant in one of my workshops commented:

> When we had to experience our own pattern in relation with the other people's pattern, I felt somehow integrated. I was part of a bigger thing. Pretty much the same as being alive in relation to all organisms in/at/around the world. You exist, but it doesn't matter whether you do or not, it matters that: if you are, you are part of what is going on. (personal correspondence with Orbits participant in 2012)

Participants have also described feeling disconnected from or 'at odds with' the 'core rhythm' of the group. They refer to an experience of being 'fractured' or 'disjointed', in some way, of an emerging sense of 'chaos' or 'bewilderment'. Through working with Orbits over extended periods of time, the participants develop a capacity to move between these states with greater ease and confidence, defining and redefining the rhythmic 'territories' they inhabit. That which at first provokes degrees of anxiety and physical stress over time is met with a quality of presence and adaptable responsiveness. Participants describe finding a greater sense of 'flow' and 'inner stillness', both within the process and following it.

In Orbits, polyrhythm and entrainment are adopted as a means of both destabilizing one's sense of self and establishing a tangible sense of being deeply connected to something that extends beyond the self. Inhabiting an experience of simultaneity, a participant may experience themselves 'flickering' through varying experiences of selfhood and moments of feeling isolated, of finding a connection with others, of experiencing a sense of unity or a loss of boundaries, a sense of the immediacy and of the expansiveness of time, of unity and plurality. The structured and formal nature of this work also provides a framework by which the performer can negotiate these relationships and perspectives, at times approaching states that could be described as ecstatic. In this way Orbits shares many of the intentions of TRW's practices, in that it seeks a secular context in which the performer can explore forms of self-transformation and *communitas* (Middleton 2008). While many of these experiences are highly personal, they also provide an invaluable basis for approaching work on performance. Drawing on these tools, the performer can explore the transformative potentials of rhythm as both an experiential and expressive device.

Reflections on polyrhythm and simultaneity

In the notions of polyrhythm and simultaneity, we encounter models and means of approaching time, not as an objectively singular line of events, but as a plurality of experiences and perspectives. Laura Cull evokes this beautifully when she states: 'Presence is a *plurality* of presents, or a multiplicity of inhuman as well as human ways of being in time' (2012:191, italics in original). The act of performing and training through rhythm opens up distinct ways of inhabiting time. Rather than viewing time, or the present moment, as something fixed or singular in nature, many of the practices described in this part of the book offer models and approaches for experiencing alternative and differing modes of being/becoming in/through time.

As we have observed throughout this book, performance often involves the realization of multiple rhythmic elements interacting to form either a sense of harmonious agreement or qualities of counterpoint, oppositional tension and complexity. This layering of rhythms takes place both across the ensemble/production as a whole and within individual performers engaged in simultaneous tasks. In Stanislavski's rehearsals and training sessions, we can note the ways that actors were encouraged to generate and work in relation to multiple tempo-rhythms while building a character or staging a scene. We can reflect on the ways distinct physical rhythms have been layered or contrasted with musical rhythms and metres, as noted in both Meyerhold's practices and in the Viewpoints work of Bogart and Landau. In Britton and Bing's practices we can note the importance of developing an ensemble awareness and the simultaneity involved in training 'self-with-others'. Reflecting on the role of rhythm in altered states of consciousness, we have looked at the ways in which multiple rhythms entrain both within the body and in relationship to a group's rhythmic territory or sense of *communitas*. In regard to the practices of Grotowski and Núñez, we have identified some of the ways rhythm can encourage the simultaneous sustaining of oppositional qualities (movement-repose, tension-release, watching-surrendering) and the unification of perception and action. What encompasses all of these processes is that they each, in their own way, ask performers to engage with and bring together multiple experiences and intentions within the present moment, be that within performance or in training, in structured works or within improvisations, within the relationships of the ensemble or within the individual. Rhythm in all these instances is a relational process. It is not an isolated form or pattern, but rather a way in which two or more elements relate to one another in time and space – their meaning or sense forming from the ways they correspond, conform, inform, shape and relate.

PART FIVE

A PLURALITY OF VOICES

While much of the discussion throughout this book has focused on physical aspects and approaches to rhythm, in this part, I will open out this enquiry to look at some of the ways rhythm is applied to and understood in regard to voice and language in performance. This is a vast field of enquiry, potentially encompassing poetry, linguistics, semiotics, translation, voice practices, script writing and analysis, including topics ranging from metre and rhythm in ancient Greek rhetoric and poetry to the semiotics and deconstruction of language in postmodern and postdramatic works. A comprehensive study of this field is clearly beyond the scope of this book. Where analysis of the rhythm and metre of performance texts has been given attention in a number of other books and studies,[1] the following chapters will focus on some of the ways that rhythm is approached by performance makers and performers themselves. In keeping with the ethos of this book, here attention is directed towards the ways rhythm is approached and considered in relationship to language and voice. In these chapters I will also look to open out this enquiry, bringing in more 'voices' and perspectives. Beginning with a general discussion of rhythm in relationship to spoken language in performance, the remaining chapters will present a collection of conversations and interviews with practitioners discussing the ways they use and understand rhythm in their own work.

12
RHYTHMING WORDS
WHERE, HOW AND WHY

Patrice Pavis points out that a number of contrasting perspectives exist as to where and how rhythm is applied to language in performance. He suggests that traditionally rhythm has been seen as something added to a script by the actor – a sort of 'ornamentation'. Here rhythm is understood to be, what actors bring to the script, a life they inject into the work through their 'delivery'. Pavis terms this the 'ornamental theory of rhythm'. Alternatively, we might consider rhythm as something created by the playwright – an aspect embedded in their work, which the performer and director must uncover. We might talk about the rhythms set out by the forms and structures that the author chooses to use. Here we could consider the extent to which a work conforms to an established model, or a form of verse, made up of strong and weak beats, such as an *iambic pentameter* or a particular form of comic/ dramatic timing. This is what Pavis defines as the 'versification theory' (1999:313).

Yet, while these two models can still be found within many current acting and performance practices, Pavis suggests that as a general trend, contemporary performance has moved on from these more formal notions of rhythm and language (ornamental and versification) and has come to focus on the ways that rhythm produces 'meaning' in a performance. Linked to theories set out by Bertolt Brecht, the emphasis here lies in the 'gestural' musicality of language and the ways that this encapsulates relationships and meanings. Referred to as a 'Brechtian theory', we can reflect on the ways Brecht himself intentionally sought to disrupt previously established models of performance tempo, as well as seeking to explore more 'irregular' approaches to metric form, seeing these as a way of opening up new interpretations and meanings within spoken language. This is seen as a shift away from rhythm as a means of stirring emotions or establishing a 'mood' on stage (see Stanislavski in Chapter 3) towards a sense that the rhythm of the language can change (and potentially challenge) the meaning of a text.

Brecht was far from dismissive of the role of form and metre. Comparing two versions of a line of text from the Bible, he pointed to the potency of the first over that of the second: 'If thine eye offend thee, pluck it out' / 'Pluck out the eye that offends thee' (Brecht 1964:117). While the second may be more 'logical', it is the 'gestural' quality of the first that appealed to Brecht, the way that it called on one to take action. In this regard, Brecht's approaches to the rhythms of language demonstrate a high level of precision and exactitude. Where his approach differed from those of Stanislavski or Copeau was in his willingness to experiment and distort rhythms, not simply as means of achieving a 'mood' or aesthetic, but as a way of generating further and varied meanings.

Brecht's use of the term *gestus*, and its adjective *gestisch*, relates to both 'gist' and gesture: 'an attitude or a single aspect of an attitude, expressible in words or actions' (Willett in Brecht 1964:42). This is perhaps clarified by Brecht's collaborator Kurt Weill, whose use of this term precedes that of Brecht's. In 1929 Weill proposed that music has a particular importance for theatre because 'it can reproduce the *gestus* that illustrates the incident on the stage; it can even create a kind of basic *gestus* (*grundgestus*), forcing the action into a particular attitude that excludes all doubt and misunderstanding about the incident in question' (Weill 1929 cited in Brecht 1964:42).

In looking to develop new modes of performance, Brecht stated that 'our ideas of tempo have to be revised', claiming: 'Mental processes ... demand quite a different tempo from emotional ones' (1964:55). Brecht saw the rhythm and tempo of a performance as an effective means of bringing the audience into a more critical relationship with its content. Discussing the structuring of language in Peter Lorre's performance of *Mann ist Mann*, Brecht insisted: 'the actor had not to make the spectator identify himself with individual sentences and so get caught up in contradictions, but to keep him out of them' (1964:54). This marked a clear shift in acting styles. Where previously the actor may have aspired to find 'carrying power' or 'a gift for making his [or her] meaning clear', here Brecht saw the rhythms of the actor as a means of engaging the audience's critical thinking. Rather than seducing an audience with the rhythmic flow of a performance, he looked to use irregular rhythms and distinct tempos as a way of disrupting expectations and sharpening perceptions.

The capacity of the voice and language to create meaning, through its music and gestural qualities, is an aspect that connects Brecht's ideas about language to those found in more contemporary forms of performance. Seeking to manipulate and diversify the comprehension of meanings taken from a text, these approaches challenge the existence of an inherent, objective or authentic rhythmic interpretation of a work. This has opened the way for more complex readings of the rhythms of spoken language, where rhythm is not simply added to an existing text as a form of 'ornament', nor is it a prescribed structural device applied by the playwright. In this Brechtian model, rhythm becomes a basis for creative and political expression, a means of generating more individual and distinct voices in performance.[1]

This sense of plurality also extends to an audience's interpretation and reading of performance. As Pavis identifies: 'The utterance is always intended for an audience, with the result that *mise en scène* can no longer ignore the spectators and must even include them as the receptive pole in the circuit' (Pavis 1991:37). Many early twentieth-century practitioners and theorists have spoken of rhythm's 'universal' capacity to communicate directly with their audience, establishing a unified understanding amongst them (Volkonski 1913; Laban 1980; Meyerhold 1991). In approaching the rhythm of language as something open to creative and individual (re)interpretation, we must also take into consideration the plurality of perspectives, associations, memories and understandings that the audience brings to the experience of the sounds, words and rhythms of a performance. In these ways, the existence of natural, organic, essential and universal 'rhythmic laws' as epitomized by Delsarte, Dalcroze, Laban, Duncan and Volkonski (Chapter 2) has come under serious questioning. Instead of a search for a 'true', 'organic' or 'essential' encounter with rhythm, what we find in many contemporary approaches is a growing emphasis on the 'difference' rather than the 'unity' of cultural and individual perspectives.[2]

Previous chapters have already referenced some of the ways this multiplicity of perspectives has informed the aesthetics of performance. Notably, Robert Wilson's use of isolated rhythms as a means of generating performance compositions (Chapter 1) can be seen as clear examples of this. Erica Fischer-Lichte also points to ways that rhythms in contemporary performance have been placed not only side by side but also in direct opposition to each other. Comparing the work of dramatist Einar Schleef to that of Wilson, she describes the ways Schleef juxtaposed the rhythms of speech with the performers' physicalities:

> The constant rhythmic shifts in movement and speech marked the chorus as a battleground. It emphasized the struggle between individual and community and between body and language. The rhythm of the spoken sentences tried to impose itself on the bodies by forcing them to move accordingly and subordinate physicality to the symbolic order of language. In response, the bodies not only defended themselves against such attempts but sought to transmit their rhythm to the language through the voice: their rhythm shattered the syntactical order of language and distorted it so much that the sentences lost their meaning and became unintelligible. (2008:134)

Here, the voice is not simply separated from the other elements of the performance (as noted in Wilson's work in Chapter 1). It takes the form of a 'battle'. The rhythms of the voice attack the very bodies that utter them. This takes Stanislavski's model of conflicting inner and outer tempo-rhythms to its extreme – pitting one against the other in a quest to express destruction, not simply oppositional tension. Even where Stanislavski and Meyerhold proposed the use of contrasts and counterpoint as a means of generating complexity and tension, there remained a search for compositional unity within both of their approaches.

Meaning and rhythm

The work of voice practitioner Cicely Berry offers us further insight into some of the practical means by which rhythm has been (and is) approached in regard to language in performance. As one of the leading advocates of an embodied understanding of metre and rhythm in spoken language on stage, Berry insists on the primacy of rhythm in all forms of language in performance. She explains: 'the rhythm of prose is just as important as the rhythm of verse; that's how primal language is – it changes all the time, but we have a reaction to the very rhythm and sound of the vowels and consonants' (Ellis 2010:121).

Berry's practices emphasize the 'muscularity' and motion of language realized through the performer's own physicality and breath, while also insisting that the performer understands the meaning of every word he or she speaks. Addressing the psychophysical nature of her practices, Berry explains that the performer needs to 'work from both ends ... The voice cannot open out and be responsive unless the muscles are ready. At the same time, it is no good the muscles being ready unless your thoughts and sensibilities are alive' (1973:36).

Berry points to the fact that many actors are frightened of speaking poetry, 'feeling that there is some sort of mystique about it, some way of doing it' (1973:101). For this reason, they are often either overly reverential in their delivery of poetry (emphasizing the metric accents in a mechanical or superficial manner), or alternatively they rebel against the metre of the poetry and ignore the form of the text entirely (just following the logic of the words, treating the poetry as if it were prose). Berry proposes that neither of these extremes are necessary and that ultimately a balance can be found 'between the formal and informal, the colloquial and the heightened language' (1973:101).

These approaches seek a dialogue between the formal structure of the metre (setting up the expectation of a certain number of stressed and unstressed syllables in each line) and the actual flow and sense of the words themselves. Berry insists that in the end there is no one 'correct' way in which a poetic text can be spoken. A well-written text, like a well-written piece of music, will often offer many possibilities and interpretations. The job of the performer starts from listening, 'for it is through listening for what the text contains that you will hear its possibilities' (Berry 1973:102). Here the performer is engaged in an active enquiry into the meaning and musicality of the language, with both these aspects emerging through the process of speaking and listening to words and rhythms themselves. Berry reminds us of the significance of rhythm as a link, both between performer and writer, and between fellow performers:

I believe strongly that we need to put time aside during rehearsal to heighten our sensibility to the sound and rhythm of language, to each other and to how we respond. For we all speak differently, we all hear differently, and that is as it should be, yet there is a rhythm, a music, however, which is intrinsic to the writing and which we have to carry through together. (Berry 2013:17)

While acknowledging the intrinsic rhythmicity of language, Berry also asks the performer to be open and responsive to the 'music' that emerges from the ensemble's expression of a text.

Comprehending the musicality of language is an important skill not only for the performer but also for the playwright. In line with Berry's claim 'Meaning is rhythm, rhythm is meaning' (Berry 2013:17), playwright and film director David Mamet proposes: 'If you break the rhythm, you break the meaning' (Sauer and Sauer 2003:225). In Mamet's work rhythm is responsible not only for generating meaning but also for providing a way of disrupting it, and at times, a way of bringing our attention to the lack of it. Discussing Mamet's use of rhythm Toby Zinman explains:

Content is never at issue; *what* Mamet has to say has been said before (American society is corrupt, Hollywood is more corrupt, life is lonely, loveless sex is empty, men treat women badly), but it is the *way* he says it that is so appealing…. Rhetoric has never been so destitute nor rhythm so triumphant. (1992:208)

Following in the tradition of absurdist playwrights including Samuel Beckett and Harold Pinter, Mamet often uses rhythm to highlight the absence of meaning, a sense of 'Nothing' taking place (Zinman 1992). Through, often fragmented rhythms, meaning at times eludes both the characters and the audience. The elusive nature of these rhythms often extends beyond just language, also playing a dominant role in the dramaturgy of Mamet's plays. Describing a production of Mamet's *Edmond*, Alain Piette suggests that it is the fragmented and fleeting nature of the scenes which prevent the audience from establishing 'any empathy or identification with the character' (1997:47). While at the same time, an association with the powerlessness of the protagonist is 'forced upon the spectator by the very structure of the play' (1997:48). Here the rhythmic form of Mamet's play has the paradoxical effect of both isolating the audience from the content and bringing them in direct contact with it. Interestingly, Mamet identifies Stanislavski as his main source of inspiration regarding his interest in 'the correlation between language and action'. Discussing this in an interview in 1976, he credited Stanislavski with the notion that 'words *create* behaviour' and went on to explain:

> my main emphasis is on the rhythm of language – the way action and rhythm are identical. Our rhythms describe – no, our rhythms *prescribe* our actions. I became fascinated – I still am – by the way, the way the language we use, its rhythm, actually determines the way we behave, more than the other way around. Everything I am as a playwright I feel I owe to Stanislavski – I mean, Jesus every playwright should be forced to read him just on consonants and vowels alone! (Wetzsteon 2001:11)

Stanislavski's approach to rhythm in language is a subject which in itself is worth considerable examination. Yet, for now, I will just touch briefly on this, as already considerable attention has been given to Stanislavski's use of tempo-rhythm (Chapter 3). As set out in his writings on 'Tempo-rhythm in Speech', originally published within *Building a Character*, Stanislavski's approach to speech rhythms (as with his work on movement) drew strongly on musical models and terminologies.[3] 'Letters, syllables, words replace notes. Pauses, breaths and counting fill in those rhythmical moments in which there is no spoken text in a speech bar' (Stanislavski 2008:398). Many of the approaches outlined in his text might appear excessively formal from the perspective of contemporary actor training practices. Yet it is worth understanding these approaches as a means of sensitizing performers to the structures of rhythm in language – affording them a set of tools with which to approach language, rather than being seen as a guide to performing text in rhythm.

Tying this back to the theories of language put forward by Pavis at the start of this chapter, we can see how Stanislavski considered the actor's role as one of mediating between an approach that overly emphasized 'versification' and that which focused on personal 'ornamentation'.

He explained that some actors are mostly attracted by the 'external' aspects of speech, approaching these with a 'pedantic precision' (2008:504). Conversely there are those actors who weigh down a text 'with psychological pauses, lumbering inner Tasks and complex, tangled psychology'. These performers overload a text with 'confused Subtexts' that are 'difficult to marry with the words ... themselves'. The ideal in Stanislavski's eyes was for the actor to find a medium between these two approaches – 'to enter into the waves of the Tempo-rhythm' while still making 'free use of pauses' and bringing a 'human warmth' to their expression. 'It is only then that the verse ceases to be a straitjacket and gives the actor total freedom for experiencing and for inner and outer action' (2008:504).

Reflections

In the descriptions offered within this chapter, we encounter some of the ways that rhythm is applied and understood in relationship to language in performance. This includes the sense of where the rhythm is located, be that in the work of the performer, the director or the author; how rhythm is approached and interpreted within performance, and the sense of why certain rhythms are used as well as the meanings (or lack of meaning) these generate. This is clearly a vast field, of which this chapter barely scratches the surface. Rather than attempt a summary, it seems fitting at this point to open out this discussion. As this book approaches its end, I would like to offer a further set of perspectives – to promote as it were a 'plurality of voices' on the subject of rhythm. The three brief chapters that follow will consist of a series of conversations, reflections and insights from practitioners who I have met, each describing their encounters with rhythm within their own practices. These are not intended to be the voices of authority, nor are they necessarily representative of the field as a whole. They are rather (as is the rest of this book) a glimpse into the ways rhythm is and can be understood, embodied and applied in acting and performance.

13

CREATING SPACES

CONVERSATIONS WITH JUDITH ADAMS AND KAREN CHRISTOPHER

Judith Adams

Talking with the playwright Judith Adams about her approaches to writing a script she explains:

> I like to be working with a group of people with different skills, different performance skills, and seeing if we can make an idea grow into something between us and nurture it to become what it is. Because I find that every project I work on comes with its own entity, its own structure and its own voice, and I'm not really very often able to find out what these are on my own. Either I write a script and then I need it to be explored physically, or in an ideal world I would – within one space – work with all the people who I think are bringing the things that it possibly needs, and see what comes out of it. (Interview with author, March 2016)

Adams describes here a process of uncovering the 'voice' of a script. Yet where previously Stanislavski, Copeau and Meyerhold spoke about this as the job of the director and actor in relation to an existing rhythmic form, Adams sees this as a collective endeavour, something that emerges through collaboration. Having previously been a performer (both an actor and musician), Adams comments on the dynamic sense of exploration that can exist within a rehearsal process: 'I loved the play of rehearsals and discovery, and uncovering and finding out things – because it had to be in an interactive way'.

While not all Adam's work involves collaborative processes, she highlights the importance for her, as a writer, of finding the 'body' and 'physicality' of the language she is writing. Reflecting on how her work has developed over her career, she comments:

> I become more conscious of how important my body is, in terms of being in the right 'frame' of mind.... And it's no accident that I've come to live out in the country, because that gives me an opportunity to go out instantly up onto the Moors, and then immediately I leave my house and I'm climbing a hill.

Living and working for the most part on the Moors in West Yorkshire, walking and nature are central to Adam's writing process:

> And I've become more and more aware of this thing about *crossing a line*[1] – where I walk out there and my brain is so busy that I am literally counting my steps because it won't shut up. I get from that stage to a point at which I ... stop thinking.
>
> And it's very curious because, I suppose I have assumed that we're trying to bring something out from the inside when we create. But the older I get – the more I walk – I wonder whether we're not just trying to shut the inside up so that something can pour in. It feels more like – *from the outside in*, than *from the inside out*.
>
> I am silenced by the rhythm of walking. And I've not found anything else that stills my conscious mind except possibly being on a sailing ship for a very long time, which is very hypnotic. But it [walking] seems to give something a chance to kick in. And I suddenly find myself solving things and creating things effortlessly, at that point.

Adam's process of looking outwardly and making space for creativity is a concept reflected both in the ways she collaborates and her use of walking as a stimulus for her writing. This principle of 'making space' also extends to her approach to structuring the rhythms of language in her scripts. Discussing a current adaptation she is writing for BBC radio, based on Ursula Le Guin's *Earthsea* series, she observes:

> There are far fewer words in these scripts than there should (normally) be (for the air-space given). The producer is confused, because he normally asks for five or six thousand words per half-hour episode. And sometimes these are coming in at three thousand six hundred or four thousand six hundred, and still they have to be cut down. And so I have been observant of [this in] writing the current scripts. And I write in the word 'beat' – quite regularly...
>
> [I]n all my live shows I've put 'beats' in where it's felt right to put something that's not a word, but needs to occupy space. And I'm doing it freely with my current project and no one's complained. And I presume and assume that's what's making everything take longer – even though it sounds manic fitting everything in. And having discussed it and thought about it, I think that it's an essential part of the meaning of what I'm transcribing. I feel there needs to be that space for – whatever. Space for thought; space for breath; space just for space. The importance of space – which can easily get lost.

I ask Adams if she can define what she means by the word 'beat'.

> It might be a breath as in music, if you're playing an instrument. Also I did play a wind instrument, which is interesting – I've only just remembered. I came to the recorder late – I thought it meant tape recorder so was very confused. I was quite good at it and I moved on to the clarinet. So again, as with acting, I am used to performing music. And it [the beat] feels like where you take a breath. For whatever emotion or whatever reason, it's just – it feels as natural as if I was writing music and [I] put a rest in. You might as well ask where does a rest come and why. Well for a huge (I imagine) variety of reasons.

Enquiring about whether there are particular times when she notices the presence of rhythm more strongly in her work, Adams replies:

> I just don't feel there's ever a time when I don't, because if it's not working – if a sentence isn't working rhythmically for me – then I don't keep it. I fiddle with it until it rhythmically works for me.

What is it then that is 'working' or 'not working'? 'It's actually the beat of the sentences. It is actually the rhythm of the sentences. It's actually – as with reading Shakespeare – it actually *should happen to be the right length and not any longer.*' Is there some kind of 'proper' form then that you are searching for?

> There isn't a proper form. It's endlessly, endlessly alterable, but I don't know. There is something about ... I read out loud what I write each day, and it has to sound rhythmic to me. ... Of course it's good to choose the right words and it's good to be saying the thing you want to say – but it has to have rhythm.
>
> Words come from the tongue – the gut – the body and they go to the body: the actor's – the audience's senses – the listener's ears are all accessing new and complex information. If that flows, if it sinks in like song, it can alter the colours of the mind.

Adams relates this process of finding the rhythmic flow of the language to a quote from Virginia Woolf. She quotes:

> this is very profound, what rhythm is, and goes far deeper than words. A sight, an emotion, creates this wave in the mind, long before it makes words to fit it; and in writing ... one has to recapture this, and set this working ... and then, as it breaks and tumbles in the mind it makes words to fit. (Woolf 1980:247)

Woolf observed that without 'the right rhythm', her mind may be full of visions and ideas but she had no means of 'dislodging' them, whereas having found the rhythm, everything starts to flow and 'you can't use the wrong words'. The form is seen to facilitate the content, to not only generate meaning but to provide a passage or vehicle by which that meaning can travel. Adams comments: 'It's always rhythm that offends me if it doesn't work'.

Karen Christopher

Similar to Adams, it is when the rhythm is not working that Karen Christopher is most acutely aware of it. Christopher states that 'for me rhythm is everything in the performance, but I just don't think of it until I have to sit and remember something or until something goes wrong'. She describes working on a tightly choreographed performance with the company Goat Island. The piece involved sequences in which the performers lifted and threw one another, as well as running in tight configurations through the space. Having devised their movements to be performed in the round within a very specific set of stage dimensions, on one occasion they arrived at a venue and discovered that the space had been enlarged by a few feet on all four sides to accommodate a fire exit. They insisted that the space had to be changed, but the venue refused to negotiate. Christopher explains:

> So we had to do it. And we were crashing into each other because the rhythms were off and the distances were off ... The spaces were different, and so the rhythms were different. (Interview with author, February 2016)

She recalls that although they had never consciously mapped out the rhythms of the performance, never counted out the steps, there was a sense that they had created 'a sort of rhythmic grid, that just happened [through] rehearsing it over and over again'. It was not until they were faced with the challenge of adjusting their movements to a new space that they became aware of how integral these rhythms were to the realization of the piece.

The ways that meaning is generated through the use of temporal structures is another subject that Christopher describes in detail as we discuss her work as a performance maker. She talks about her use of duration as a means of engaging an audience's capacity to form their own meanings within a performance. Explaining this she comments:

> depending on the material, it's either a long stretch of too much [material], that breaks down the usual volume of information a person would get at the beginning of the show. [This] breaks down meaning – it's not what they expect. So this is too long and they can't watch it anymore. Because something happens where they give up. ... [N]ot enough of anything and too much of things that you're not getting enough of, does a similar thing, because people aren't getting the usual dose and the usual pause and the usual *ok I*

see how this is gonna work. And I guess what that does is, when it creates a little bit more suspense, or a little bit more openness to the other possibilities - possibilities other than the one you are about to do.

Christopher comments that often in a rehearsal or workshop situation it can be useful to play with varying durations of activities as a way to get people to 'let go' of their personal issues and focus on making the work. Limiting or expanding the time that participants have to complete their tasks is one of the ways she does this. Similarly, the duration of a piece of performance material can also facilitate a letting go of – or giving up on – expectations.

They give up on expecting or assuming they know what this is going to be like. And there's a bit of a breakdown. And sometimes you lose an audience that way, but more often than not you get them back … Or you don't quite lose them and you manage to change and diverge just before you have lost them. So it's a little bit of a dicey thing and requires a bit of testing…

Not enough of anything and too much of things that you're not getting enough of, does a similar thing, because people aren't getting the usual dose and the usual pause and the usual *ok I see how this is gonna work.* And I guess what that does is create a little bit more suspense, or a little bit more openness to the other possibilities – [revealing] possibilities other than the one you are about to do. Which means that it's coloured by that and has a context that includes the constructions that are going on in the audience's own mind…

Christopher recounts the response from a student who saw one of her performances:

He said he didn't know what was going on: 'you were doing this, there was a little bit of that, it wasn't enough to understand what it was, and then you did another thing, and there was … Then I recognized something, then I recognized another thing, then all of a sudden I understood everything!'

But then his question was, 'did you do that on purpose?' … And the answer is complicated because, you could just say yes.

But of course actually I didn't do any of that. He did all of that....
But the hope is that, having supplied people with these kinds of
directions and these bits – that they do it. And if they do it, then it's
more important to them. And also it's like a memory. Like when you
need to remember something or if you have a traumatic memory, it's
easier to go back to it – it's more memorable – the more information
gloms onto it. If it's just really quick and there's not a lot of detail, it's
harder for you to remember....

There's a sense that you are giving more density to their experience
somehow by opening up all these possibilities.

[L]ike these guys who remember sequences of numbers, they're
creating associations with every single number. That's how they
remember the numbers, because they remember the associations.
They're still doing a hell of a lot of work. But doing more work makes
it easier in that regard, somehow. And I think this is about how the
inside of the mind works, you know. If there's just a bit more impact,
we're prone to be able to remember something more.

So by making the audience work harder to engage with the material,
then are they generating denser memories and associations?

Exactly, exactly. Because it leaves a bit of room for them to do some
work, and they do that work within the environment of their own brain,
their own thought-scape. So their associations, their experiences
kind of blend in there and it becomes a kind of aggregate ... Now
some people don't think you're meant to do that in performance.
You're meant to see a nice story. I love nice stories. I think nice
stories are fantastic. But my work just isn't doing that.

Reflections

In Christopher's descriptions we can see the audience becomes more
than simply a 'receptive pole' for the *mise en scène*, as proposed by
Pavis (Chapter 12). Generating their own stories and meanings, they
are actively engaging in their own process of creation, by which they

project their stories onto her performances. We might describe them as 'observer-participants', to use Vrobel's term.[2] As with Vrobel's theory of simultaneity, the observer-participant is always actively taking part in the outcome of a measurement – in the shaping of their own reality (see Chapter 11). The observer/audience member participates by generating their own version of the performance through what they bring to it, their interpretations, associations, their curiosities, the stories they themselves are searching for. In this case, Christopher's role is to create the structures and the potential for intensification through her use of durations and layering of material. Both Christopher and Adam's work relies as much (if not more so) on what is not done and said, as on the actions and words themselves. In these examples, rhythm creates spaces in which meaning can arise. It offers room to breathe, to remember, to imagine.

14

THE POETRY OF THE BREATH

CONVERSATIONS WITH BRUCE MYERS AND KATE PAPI

Bruce Myers

Discussing the associations he has with rhythm in his work as an actor,
Bruce Myers responds by reciting a poem by Osip Mandelstam:

> What shall I do with the body I've been given,
> So much at one with me, so much my own?
> For the quiet happiness of breathing, being able
> To be alive, tell me to whom I should be grateful?
> I am gardener, flower too, and not alone
> In the world's dungeon.
> My warmth, my exhalation, one can already see
> On the window-pane of eternity.
> The pattern printed in my breathing here
> Has not been seen before.
> Let the moment's condensation vanish without trace:
> The cherished pattern no one can efface.
>
> ('What shall I do with the body I've been given', 1909)[1]

In March 2016, Myers presented a series of performances in which he read forty of Mandelştam's poems alongside the work of dancers Elana Giannoti, Ioannis Mandafounis and Roberta Mosca. This project focused on a collection of Mandelstam's work titled *The Noise of Time*.[2] Reflecting on the experience of reading these poems in performance, Myers explains: 'I don't have any theories on reading poetry. I just read them' (interview with author, May 2016).

Myers observes that while reading, he is mostly aware of hearing his own voice and looks to keep it 'sober and resonant and true'. What is most striking in his memory of reading these poems is a feeling of it 'being right'. I ask about this feeling of rightness; how does he experience it. Myers explains: there is no direct 'focus' or 'work done on uncovering or bringing out the rhythms of these poems'. He comments that 'the rhythms just seem to come'.

While Myers makes no attempt to describe or define his sense of rhythm, it seems to have an undeniable presence in the way he articulates these poems. I reflect on the idea that while some performers approach rhythm through rigorous study and practice, there are others for whom this sense seems to come more from a process of listening and being available to the sounds and the breath of the language. Hearing Myers speak poetry, I cannot help feel a strong sense of flow and space. His words have weight and form to them. But rather than attempting to structure the rhythms of his speaking, Myers intentionally seeks a quality of improvisation, an immediacy between himself, the language and the moment of performance. There is an elegant simplicity to this – a grace, a sense of openness and honesty in the expression of these words as they hang in the air. The words appear (like in Mandelstam's poem) as a pattern *printed in breath*, condensing and then *vanishing without a trace*.

Another aspect of Myers' work with poetic language has involved explorations of poetic texts in languages other than English. This includes working with texts in ancient Greek and Yiddish, as well as being part of the development of the invented language of Orghast[3] through his work with Peter Brook and Ted Hughes. As Myers speak these texts, their meanings appear at first, unintelligible. I hear sounds and have a sense of an emotional current and an evocation of otherness. Without a direct understanding of these words, what becomes stronger is my sense of their musicality, of their physicality, of the body and the intensity of these sounds. Myers comments that in working with Brook and Hughes on texts in Orghast as well as in English: 'The ones we did not understand were easier, because the words just came'. Describing his approach to working on a text from Medea in ancient Greek, Myers explains:

> At first I did not understand very much. But I had to do it, to feel anything of what the sense is. Even the strong emotion, which comes from these vowels. And I'd begin with just going to the vowels. So:

Myers speaks some of the text at first, speaking both the vowels and consonants:

> 'Eh leh le ou eh le le ou, ou po maos sfakelos kai ... [sic]'

And then goes on to speak just the vowel sounds:

> 'eh eh eh eh oo oo oo...'

He gradually reintroduces the consonants while still emphasizing the vowels. Myers goes on to explain:

> I noticed from the beginning that there was something in these texts which silenced people or gave them an idea of something different, perhaps sacred, perhaps wild...
>
> Sometimes I have this feeling with speaking Shakespeare... It's possible to find something really new in the sound. It does have an effect over the years, doing these exercises. It is not necessarily to do with the words only. It's sort of making the words work for you. And that won't necessarily be comprehensible to me [when I am doing it].

Myers points towards another sense of meaning contained within language, something rooted in the sounds of the words themselves. As an actor, he seeks the resonance of these sounds as a means of communicating their meaning to an audience. I am reminded of the importance of speaking a text as a way of understanding or making meaning from it. As with Brook's descriptions of rhythm earlier in this book – where he stated: 'something in me was disturbed' (2009:15) – I have sense in Myers speaking of these texts that something is shifting at a visceral level, a quality of pulsation. The language moves like a muscle, and there is a quality of immediacy and mystery that draws me in.

Kate Papi

Over the past five years I have been working in collaboration with OBRA Theatre Co. as a musician, actor and teacher. OBRA's practices are focused on the relationships between language and physicality on stage. Its two main works to date have been *Fragments* – a bilingual production (English and French) based on a socio-philosophical discourse by Roland Barthes, titled *A Lover's Discourse* – and a production performed by an international ensemble adapted from a poetic work, *Gaudete*, written by Ted Hughes. Discussing these projects, Kate Papi, the director of the company, comments: 'one of the things that excites us is working with different texts, using the different qualities and the different voices of each author as a way to develop new creative practices and specifically new ways of approaching language' (interview with author, June 2016). With each production, the company looks to generate not only a dramaturgical approach to the text but also approaches to training that support the requirements of each piece. Here, the 'different voice of each author' initiates a distinct approach to language: 'each language has its own innate quality and its own innate rhythm. And that was a way for us to open up our practice and to develop new approaches to making material'.

In these processes, the performer's work on a text generally begins with encountering the language and the rhythms set out by the author. This is done through physical and imaginative processes rather than an intellectual form of textual analysis. Initially we approach the text by walking the rhythms of the language (the length and journey of each thought) through the space, working in relation to the punctuation.[4] Standing on the spot, we breathe in the full length of our sentence and then walk while speaking. When we get to a comma we change direction, and when we reach the end of the sentence we stop – change direction and continue the process working through the rest of the text. Papi explains:

> This gives you a sense of its innate rhythmic structure, directly relatable to the length of thought and progression of meaning or the idea employed by the author. What happens when an extended thought is placed alongside a shorter thought? How can a comma shift you in a new direction?

As with Berry and Mamet, here language is considered as an action in itself, with sentences taking space and having their own movement. Papi emphasizes the importance of the actor being able to continue 'to the end of a thought and then see where the next moment bounces off from it'. Papi explains:

> Work on the technical level does many things; one can experience and become aware of a certain innate tempo. When moving to the creative level, when it becomes about developing performative material, you can stretch and play with the text and explore its possibilities. But the performer needs to have a sense of the uninterrupted thoughts and not impose decisions in terms of emphasis from the outset.... The first stage is to get the language into the body. And this process is like taking on the language's own heartbeat or pulse somehow, and this you can jam with.

Having embodied the 'innate' rhythmic qualities of the text and begun to access imaginative associations arising from this language, we then begin to explore ways of playing with and disrupting these elements through generating and layering physical scores. These physical rhythms are then placed in relationship to those of the text. Papi insists that throughout this process the performers should remain open and flexible about their understanding of the text. It is important that from the outset they do not start making decisions about the meaning and the delivery of the text.

> In the learning process you need to put yourself to one side whilst at the same time almost carving the language into the breath and body, so that when more elements are layered on to the making process

and more tasks are added in the performance context, the performer does not 'get in the way' of the text by trying to overtly control it or imposing certain emotions or ideas on to it. This allows for new, unexpected possibilities to arrive, new meanings to be revealed and space for the public to experience the language for themselves. ...

One of the things ... we're trying to do in the performance moment – is always and consistently to facilitate the possibility of a revelation of meaning. That's what all of this highly technical and often very complex process of montaging is for.

The task, then, for Papi as a director is how to 'capture that moment when something new has arrived', to identify the moments when something is revealed by the actor and to begin to shape this into a piece of performance material.

What are the words that resonate? What are the sentences or the phrases or the ideas that make something open up inside of me, and open something up inside of the actor...? How can I capture that quality, moment or sensation and allow it to exist within the performance?... This must then be refined and rehearsed in order for this moment or moments to still exist and create openings for the audience, to allow new meanings to be revealed. How can we take these wonderful words and make them more accessible, not through a process of dumbing down but via an intricate process that should render these poems and/or discourses more accessible?

In working on *Gaudete*, the company continues to explore relationships between text and physical actions, investigating the ways these speak to and inform one another. Interpreting the narrative style of this text, we have been exploring ways of describing actions from within a scene:

We talk a lot about where language sits in relation to action. Are you going through an experience and narrating ... from inside of that experience? Are you narrating something and then it happens? We can take a sentence from *Gaudete,* like 'he begins to run'. If it was the person who is running – he could say 'he begins to run' as he begins to run. Or he could say 'he begins to run' and then he starts running. Or, he could stop and say he begins to run afterwards, as an afterthought. Or someone else could narrate the action for the doer, with the same possibilities applied.

These approaches establish a skewed sense of temporality and agency: at some points grounding the language firmly within the physicality of the performance and at other times creating a schism between these elements as they function alongside one another, often coexisting within a single performer. Having begun with the performer looking to 'completely embody the language, so it sits as part of their musculature', we can then begin to develop 'physical actions that could be a response to language or to something completely arbitrary'. Papi explains:

> you're constantly juggling the tension between the elements, and it's ... definitely a difficult task. It is a process of total chaos for a while. Things then, bit by bit start to click and sit alongside one another. It is then my job as the director to help set a new structure and [for the performer to] embody that, so that [they] can actually breathe through it. ...

As the work progresses, Papi insists on us being able to repeat our material while also continuing to find more details within our scores. She explains that it is important that even on occasions where the performer is 'not feeling it, ... that the construct you create – the piece of music that you create – is still engaging, as the performer, in the act of managing simultaneous task ensures that the work remains present whilst still delivering the "story"'. This approach involves a complex balance: on the one hand refining, honing and fixing material, while at the same time the performer must remain open, flexible and responsive.

Reflections

OBRA's approach involves an active enquiry into the 'innate' rhythms of the text, as realized through the performer's own physicality. This neither suggests the existence of an 'objective reading' of the text nor does it propose a purely subjective interpretation based on chance or even the whim of the performer. Rather, this work seeks to establish a creative discourse between the rhythms encountered within the language and those emerging from the physicality of the performer and the layering of dramaturgy. Where Myers approach seeks 'truth' and 'resonance' through the spontaneity of his spoken rhythms and the immediacy of his listening, in OBRA's performances, such 'resonance' arises through a detailed creative enquiry. In both cases, the poetry of the language finds meaning through the flow and dynamism of their performance. And while both approaches to rhythm are clearly distinct, each relies strongly on the embodied experience of the performer as they encounter the rhythms of the language itself, either spontaneously or through detailed study.

15

THE TUNE IS A FRAMEWORK

A CONVERSATION WITH CHRIS COE AND FRANKIE ARMSTRONG

Talking with Chris Coe and Frankie Armstrong about their rich experiences and understandings of rhythm in singing and voice work, we reflect on the relationships between melody, phrasing, movement and imagination. Coe begins by explaining the way that an image or a view can sometimes inspire her to compose musical phrases:

> A friend said to me one night 'I am killing time flies'. There was flies everywhere. I asked 'what are you doing?' He said 'killing time flies'. Ahhh…
>
> Years later, I am sitting in the kitchen looking at, as it happens, shelves of bottles. And they're on the side and they're making a pattern. And I start singing '1 2 3, 1 2 3 4, 1 2 3 4 1 2 3, 1 2 1 2 1'. Which is the way the bottle where lined up on the shelf. And then in the same night I came up with 'Killing flies, killing time flies, time lies heavy on my hands, killing killing time'. [*Coe sings the phrase to the same rhythm and melody as the counting of the bottles.*]
>
> I do that continuously. I see things in a different way…. I sing the valley – sing the repeats and the patterns in the valley etc. It's wonderful. (Interview with author April 2016)

Coe talks about how, at a certain point in her career, she decided to stop singing and focused on fine art. 'I wanted to find out how it worked without words ... The idea of communicating by objects, materials'. Coe explains: 'If I look I get one sense of information, if I sing it, it's a completely different quality of information – takes me somewhere else, adds a bit on.' These elements seem to speak with and inform one another. 'By describing it in other terms, I get more information'.

For both these singers, there is a strong sense of the interconnected relationship between the voice, imagination and movement. Armstrong reflects on her formative experiences of first encountering the solo voices of folk singers:

> I remember listening to the traditional singer, Phil Tanner. And he didn't sing with any kind of regular rhythm. But the way he pulls phrases around to heighten the visual imagery and the potency of the story. I'd been singing since I was sixteen ... and listening to Pete Seeger and the Weavers and getting all excited. Starting to really listen and hear what these consummate traditional singers were doing with their timing; call it phrasing, call it rhythm, call it timing.
>
> But it was quite different from the way I'd thought of singing before. It brought in a visceral, a kinaesthetic and a visual [image]. Somehow in the simplicity of this one voice... it was like a window opening onto another world. (Interview with author April 2016)

Armstrong talks about how this moment marked a shift for her in the way she listened and engaged with music. A vital component of this was learning to hear the way phrases were formed and came together, as well as being able to sense the way 'complexity was built on simplicity'.

Much of Armstrong and Coe's initial learning about voice came from listening and being around other singers. Coe explains that she learned by 'listening to the ones who knew how to do it'. She remembers the singer Bert Lloyd saying: 'Having a good voice is not the same as being a good singer'. For Coe, it is as much (if not more) about how the singer conveys meaning and tells a story, as it is about the quality of their voice. Describing her work with traditional folk ballads, she explains:

I think there's the idea of the tune being a framework only. It's only a framework. So if the words are such that they need you to elongate the tune, or curtail the tune – it's only a framework – the rest is how its best expressed for people to understand it. Or your version of it.

Armstrong points out an example of hearing people singing a Scottish ballad that they had learned from a manuscript:

It was so fascinating, because they made each verse's words fit to this 'manuscript tune'. So one syllable words had three notes to them ... The tune never changed and this meant that words were being pulled in inappropriate relationships, because they weren't using ... 'the tune as the framework' – as the skeleton.

Armstrong and Coe comment on the ways that the language of a song often asks for its own rhythms and that often it is more important to follow these than try making the words conform to the structure of the 'tune'. Coe explains:

Sometimes if I'm singing, I'll decide that I am going to use the language only as it is spoke – with the accents, the emphases. And the stuff that happens when you do that is glorious – because you have to dodge the tune – you have to dodge how many notes etc. But just in order to make it work as per the language.

Armstrong adds:

When I'm teaching someone who is performing a solo song, I just say [to them]: 'how would you say that line?' and then 'how would you find a way of putting the accent, the emphasis in exactly the same way? What do you have to do to the tune to make that possible?'. And it's always possible. ... It's just a different way of thinking about the relationship between melody and words.

In a similar way to the relationship between metre and rhythm in poetry, in Coe's singing, I get a sense of the tune and words sometimes pulling against one another, or breaking free or following each other. If the structure is followed too strictly then the meaning and the life of the song falls away. But having a tune or a metre to work off or against is also what seems to draw you into these ballads – what carries you along with them. Attempting to make a distinction between what she sees as rhythm and the underlying beat or pulse of song, Coe states:

> There's rhythm and there's pulse. You don't have to sing in rhythm, to sing to the pulse of the song. Sometimes I will sing the song with John [the fiddle player], and then I'll keep-ish to the rhythm. But I think the pulse is far more important.

For Coe, the rhythm means the basic set structure of a tune – the musical notes as it were. Instead of sticking to these, Coe focuses on working in relationship to the pulse of the music, letting the phrasing of her singing find its own logic and pathways. As Armstrong points out:

> For certain improvisations you definitely want the underlying pulse to be collective and disciplined. And then that allows for syncopation and playing across rhythms. … But once the pulse is lost … you just have anarchy.

For both Coe and Armstrong, the need to tap into the sense of the pulse is crucial. But where previously in this book, Meyerhold, Britton and Bogart have described the regularity of the beat as being restrictive (Part Three), here it is seen as a way of connecting to the group and liberating oneself from the restrictions of a set form of rhythmic phrasings or notation.

This emphasis on listening to and feeling the pulse of the music is explored further in both Armstrong and Coe's teaching work. A common exercise used by both these practitioners involves a group marking a pulse with their feet while singing call-and-response. Armstrong developed this body of work while running voice workshops in the 1970s. Having started by teaching in pub rooms that always had chairs, she moved to a dance studio with nothing to sit on. As a way to keep people active, she began using simple movements based on 'working in the fields', which she named 'Hoeing' (Armstrong 1992:106–11). Armstrong explains that often at first, people find it quite challenging to sing and move at the same time (especially in Britain). She states that although many people find this experience awkward at first, this is by no means a new concept: 'The idea of standing still and singing didn't come about until the late fifteen hundreds – early sixteen hundreds, in Northern Italy [with] tableaux opera.' Getting people moving (walking on the spot or around the space) while they are singing is used by Armstrong and Coe as a way to bring people in touch with their internal impulses and connect with each other. They clarify that it is not necessary for people to always move while they sing, but what is most important is that 'still does not equal stiff' (Armstrong). They explain that keeping the body in motion, with soft knees, helps keep people from becoming tense and rigid. It keeps them aware of each other and often helps them relax and open out their breathing without thinking about it.

Armstrong has observed that the simple act of standing in a circle and moving and singing as a group through call and response with short improvised phrases has a profound impact on people: 'particularly those who thought they could not sing'. She relates this to a combination of the regularity of the pulse, and the manageable durations of the phrases, along with the imaginative stimulus of the simulated work activity, which evokes a sense of 'who we might be'. To return to Stanislavski, we can consider the sense of 'as if' and 'given circumstances' that supports an imaginative engagement with these movements (Chapter 3). These practices are also strongly rooted in the collective and sustaining nature of 'work songs' and to what Armstrong sees as the first 'call and response' – the exchange that exists between parent and infant.

Reflections

While neither Coe nor Armstrong sets out to teach rhythm in their voice classes, both of them tap into a deep quality of collective pulsation as well as an evocative freedom of expression through their work with the voice, imagination and movement. The simple and accessible format of many of their practices, taps into something essential about being together sharing in sound and movement, that is both supportive and enlivening. Rhythm here is supported by a sense of a shared pulse and a desire to express meaning – to allow the words themselves to shape the phrases rather than imposing a rigid structure onto them. The 'tune' provides a 'framework' on which the words hang – a form in which their voices are free to play.

PART SIX

REFLECTIONS

Where we speak of rhythm, we might instead talk about the dynamic or energetic of a performance, the sense of composition, dramaturgy or musicality. We could use other terms such as tone, beat, groove, harmony, shape, structure, impression, phrasing or flow. In an attempt to avoid the confusion and the specialized associations with music and poetry, we might look to more general terms such as timing or form as a way of bringing clarity and a sense of neutrality to our descriptions. We might choose to apply other metaphors taken from painting, architecture, literature, science or nature as way of expressing the forms or qualities we perceive and aspire to in performance. While we may choose other words to describe this, acting and performance are inherently rhythmic activities, taking place in time, being developed, expressed and encountered through numerous rhythmic processes and understandings.

There remains (at least for me) a certain appeal in the word rhythm. Perhaps it is its complexity of meanings and richness of history or its poetic suggestiveness of something felt but not quite understood. The recent resurgence of interest and use of the term 'rhythm' across a broad range of fields and applications reassures me that I am not alone in feeling this way. Curiously though, as research into rhythm booms within many fields, ranging from molecular science to urban sociology, there seems to be some reluctance to examine and apply this term openly and creatively within acting and performance.

For some, there may be a sense of trepidation or stigma associated with rhythm particularly in the context of training. Speaking about this with a director of an international workshop series, he commented that the programme that received the worst attendance out of any that he had run was one on the theme of rhythm. When I asked why, he suggested that it was because many performers have a certain fear or negative association with rhythm, relating it to counting out beats in dance or music lessons. In almost every class or workshop I have run, I encounter at least one participant who will openly declare that they have 'no rhythm' or an intense fear of rhythm. In many cases this anxiety or ambivalence is less to do with the participant having a lack of rhythm (if such a state exists), but rather it is more related to some sort of miscomprehension about what it means to 'have rhythm' in the first place.

Critiquing what he saw as a poor use of rhythm in the work of other directors working in Russia at the beginning of the twentieth century, Stanislavski stated: 'Rhythm is a great thing, but to build up a whole production of a play entirely upon rhythm one must first understand why it is so important and what its real meaning is' (1967:107).

In looking for its 'real meaning', I do not think Stanislavski intended that we decipher some technical or formulaic definition of rhythm to be applied universally. Nor would it be right to assume that Stanislavski was advocating for all performances to be overtly rhythmic in their aesthetics. Instead we can see this as a response by Stanislavski to a growing use of the term 'rhythm' within his field. What he insisted on was that before broadly applying the word rhythm to the making (and analysis) of performance, actors and directors need to acquire an experiential understanding of rhythm as an active process. What his statements and practices advocated was that performance makers explore, play and experiment with rhythm for themselves, and then apply it to their work, not just as a collection of terms or forms but as a collection of embodied understandings.

Reflecting on his work with Stanislavski during the last phase of his career, the actor Vasili Toporkov talked about how 'in olden times there existed the universal word "tone"'. Each role had its own 'tone', as did the play in general. Directors would talk about 'lifting the tone' or finding the 'right tone'. But as Toporkov pointed out, 'No one knew exactly how this could be done', and if by some act of chance an actor or a performance found the 'right tone', 'no one, in reality understood what had happened' (1998:60). Toporkov suggested that it was through Stanislavski's persistent searching and 'mastery' of the practical aspects of 'stage rhythm' that the ambiguity of such terminology was avoided and resolved. As such, Stanislavski looked to replace the vague randomness of 'tone' with the actor's embodied understanding of 'rhythm' and 'tempo'.

We might ask today, whether the terms 'rhythm', 'tempo', 'metre' and 'tempo-rhythm' (like the word 'tone') have lost their ability to communicate practical meaning to actors and directors. When an actor is instructed to work on the rhythm of a scene, to break up the rhythm of their actions or text, to find the right inner rhythm or is told they are working in the wrong rhythm, on what basis are they to understand these terms? In this regard Stanislavski and Toporkov were both clear, stating that only through personal investigation and the training of techniques could actors establish effective working relationships with rhythm. Technique in this sense is not some mastery of a form or an ability to reproduce what is seen to be good timing or a masterful delivery. As a technique (viewed from a sociological rather than artistic perspective), we might best describe rhythm as an embodied form of understanding, a capacity to sense, engage with and shape the rhythms of one's performance.

Approached in this way, perhaps we can move away from our fears of failing to be *in* rhythm, of stepping or clapping *out* of time, and approach a more immediate and playful relationship with rhythm. It is in this capacity to play and discover ways of being and relating to rhythm, both inside and around us, that performance can potentially contribute most to the growing field of rhythm research. Embodied by the actor/performer rhythm becomes a dynamic process, rather than a set of concepts or philosophical propositions. It merges, adapts and transposes itself from one domain to another. From stage design, to movement, to lighting, to sound, to music, to text, to the ensemble, to the inner worlds of perception, awareness, emotion and consciousness, and out into the spatial domains of proximity and the designing of performance spaces, the creative and research potentials of rhythm abound.

Here as in so many aspects of performance, it is ultimately in the doing and observing that we come to understand. Faced with the vast and disparate range of definitions attributed to rhythm by scholars working in the fields of acting and performance alone, we find ourselves struggling to grasp any understanding only through words. Without a strong point of reference or shared practical understanding, it is questionable if any 'real meaning' can be communicated by the term 'rhythm' in the context of training and directing actors, let alone in the fields of academic discourse. While these terms continue to be used by directors, actors and theorists, there is a need for greater engagement with the nature of these aspects within this field, not just theoretically, but practically through training and creative acts of research.

In my work as a director and trainer of actors, I often find that it is useful to link these terms directly to the practices being undertaken. In the processes of training, devising and rehearsing performance, we often develop and apply terms to things as they arise. This is a fluid and mostly intuitive process. These labels act as reference points, meaning we have something to come back to later or something we can remember when we encounter difficulties in the work. In this sense, I find it is important to acknowledge when I am talking about a more general sense of rhythm and timing or when I mean something specifically related to what the students or ensemble are working on. I might talk about the performers using rhythm to extend or shorten their movement, stillness, sound or silence; the need to sensitize themselves to the 'ensemble rhythm', an underlying pulse or the dynamic of a scene or dialogue; the layering of a counterpoint over a beat or existing pattern; a sense of the rhythmic development of an action or spoken phrase from its inception through to its consummation. Or we might choose to name a particular rhythmic quality that arises in the work – one that we are seeking to repeat, develop or avoid. Rather than being theoretical notions or concepts, most of these understandings are derived from the experiences of training or a shared practice. These exist primarily as tacit forms of knowledge, which are often more flexible and adaptable than conceptual frameworks or definitions.

Despite much of the confusion surrounding this term, rhythm has continued to be seen by many as a central aspect of performance training and making. In looking back at many of the key practitioners and reformers of theatre, acting and performance over the past century, we can observe the ways that they have attributed significant importance to rhythm, both in their practices and writings. While it is impossible to list all of these, it is worth mentioning at least some of those who have explored in detail the practical application of rhythm in performance: Stanislavski, Meyerhold, Eisenstein, Appia, Bing, Copeau, Dullin, Decroux, Michael Chekhov, Brecht, Artaud, Grotowski, Kantor, Lecoq, Gaulier, Peter Brook, Robert Wilson, Tadashi Suzuki, Christopher Marthaler, Sebastian Nübling and Ang Gey Pin, as well as companies including Living Theatre, Odin Teatret, Théâtre du Soleil, Gardzienice,

Wooster Group, Complicite, Goat Island and SITI. Other contemporary companies and practitioners whose work places a strong emphasis on rhythm include Pieśń Kozła, Teatr Chorea, U Theatre, Duende, ZU-UK, Bread in the Bone, Elevator Repair Services, Jonathan Burrows, OBRA Theatre Co and the list could go on.

Far from reflecting a singular model, definition or framework, this field has and continues to offer up a plurality of understandings and approaches to rhythm that resist categorization and definition. While from a theoretical perspective, such ambiguity might be problematic, in the practical contexts of training, rehearsing and performing, this diverse fluidity of understanding is inevitable and often necessary. For although rhythm is commonly identified as an innate and universal human capacity, each individual, each ensemble, each production and each environment bring with them a distict set of tacit understandings and associations.

One of the strengths inherent in rhythm is its capacity to integrate multiple (and at times conflicting) aspects into a single system or instance of simultaneity. Each of these – an orchestra, an organism, a solar system, an ecosystem – finds unity through rhythmic relationships, enabling them to co-inhabit a shared timeframe, to be perceived as a temporal totality. In the same way, this book has looked to open out the plurality of rhythm and to gain a glimpse of its varied applications, within a range of settings and contexts. Rather than narrowing this term down, it seems more beneficial to at least begin by opening and stretching things out. It is only in this way that we can take a good look into the cracks and get some sense of what rhythm can do and mean within this field. As open as this book has attempted to be, it has also limited the scope of its discussion. Looking to find both a breadth and depth of understanding, this enquiry has for the most part focused on practices that exist within and have grown out of the context of 'western theatre'. While the term 'rhythm' has clear roots in European culture, the notion of rhythm in acting and performance is by no means limited to this frame of understandings and practices. In looking to open this discussion out to address cross-disciplinary, multi-, inter- and trans-cultural perspectives on rhythm, a great deal more research and dialogue is needed within this field. Rather than a final word, I would hope that this book provides stimulus for further conversation, practical exploration and reflections of rhythm in acting and performance.

Coda

When improvising as an ensemble within a training or workshop context, a director will often bring the improvisation to a close by asking the group to 'find an ending'. This simple instruction reflects a fundamental principle of compositional awareness and ensemble relationship: how do we know (collectively) when something has ended? How do we find agreement within a multitude of performance trajectories and experiences? Sometimes an ensemble will struggle to decide or commit to the endpoint of the improvisation. Each performer will have a different idea of when things have finished. Or just when most of the group have found their end, one or two will introduce a new action and things will kick-off again. Finding an end and committing to it is one of the signs that a group is really listening and working together as an ensemble – that the performers have a shared sense of rhythm. By this I do not mean that everyone needs to stop at once, or that there is a beat or sign that they are all counting or waiting for, so they know it is time to stop. For me, there is just a sense of when it is 'right' – a sense that many in this book have pointed to. There may be other ways to rationalize this, but at its most basic level, when it is 'right', we all simply know that it is the end. There is a sense of satisfaction, shared silence, a stillness, a suspension of time between this moment, and what follows.

there is always both a rhythm to be found and a particular actor to find it

–Peter Brook

GLOSSARY

accent An event that stands out or draws greater attention. In this sense, *accents* are commonly described as having more 'weight' or 'body' and often act as effective anchor points for attention. While the most common understanding of *accent* is of one event being louder than others (*dynamic accent*), a sudden drop in volume, a silence or a stillness can sometimes be just as effective in attracting attention.

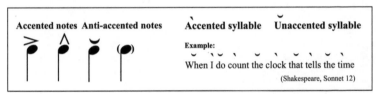

Figure G.1 Musical and spoken accent symbols.

We also find the term *accent* used to describe events that stand out due to their duration or displacement in time (*agogic accent*). This occurs most commonly in poetry, where a syllable occurring over a longer duration or after a longer pause is often perceived as receiving greater stress or emphasis. In regard to physical actions we might perceive an action as accentuated if its duration is prolonged or shortened, if it occurs at an unexpected moment or marks a change in quality or direction. Both dynamic and *agogic accents* are based on a change in the quality of a sound or action. Lerdahl and Jackendoff (1983) identify two further types of *accent*, resulting from a quality of structure and *metre*. *Accents* can occur due to the structural location of an event within a phrase (*structural accents*), with events at the beginning or end of a phrase or sequence (arrival or departure points) often standing out regardless of their individual characteristics.

Further, an *accent* can take place due to the location of an event within a perceived metric scheme (see *metre*). *Metric accents* form due to the formation of a repeated pattern of accented and unaccented events. A simple example of this is an alternating sequence of accent-unaccented-accented-unaccented and so on referred to as a *trochee*. Once established a pattern such as this will often continue to be experienced by an observer/participant, with certain parts of a phrase perceived as *accents* regardless of their duration, size or volume.

All *accents* can be considered as being relative to their context, with each event taking on different degrees of significance depending on its own characteristics in contrast to its context (*dynamic* or *agogic*), when it takes place within a sequence or phrase (*structural*), or when it takes place within an established metric framework (*metric*). See Lerdahl and Jackendoff (1983).

beat A pulsing or simple repeated rhythmic phrase or cycle. Often used interchangeably with the term *pulse*, or the musical term *tact*. A heartbeat consists of two alternating parts: *systole* and *diastole*. Similarly, any musical or physical sense of *beat* is also made up of two elements, the *pulse* (event) and the *interval* (space between the events). As director Ariane Mnouchkine says: 'Without stops, there can be no rhythm' (Richardson 2010:264). It is in the cyclic/alternating relationship between these two elements that a sense of a *pulsation, beat* and *rhythm* emerges. Actions or sounds occurring within the interval between two beats can be said to occur in the *off-beat*, often experienced most strongly half way between two *beats*.[1] See Flatischler (1992:31). The *beat* or *pulse* is often the foundation on which rhythmic structures and phrases can be formed, with the beat establishing the basic unit that is either grouped to form a metre or divided into further subdivisions.

Beat is also used by some practitioners to refer to an analytical segment, a unit, a phrase or development in a scene. These elements are identified by actors and directors in the process of analysing a script where scenes are broken down into their individual *beats*.[2] The term *beat* has also been adopted in dramatic texts and dramaturgy as a means of marking a brief duration of silence or stillness in the text or flow of actions, much like a *rest* within music (i.e. walk on stage – *beat* – turn to face audience – *beat* – speak text – *beat*). See Adams in Chapter 13.

communitas A term used by the anthropologist Victor Turner (1969) to describe an unstructured, emergent quality of camaraderie and union, often formed through the rhythmic interactions and shared intentions of a group in the context of a ritual or performance event. See Chapter 8.

contemplative running A practice developed by Nicolás Núñez during research undertaken as part of Grotowski's Theatre of Sources project in Poland in 1980. Núñez describes this as a 'meditation in motion'. This practice involves the motion of a group running through a space travelling in an anticlockwise direction, their bodies relaxed while their minds remain focused and attentive. See Chapter 10.

ecstasy (trance) Understood here as a technique of transforming or transgressing the familiar parameters of the self, while simultaneously remaining consciously present within one's experiences and actions. This is a term that has been interpreted in a wide variety of ways by theorists and practitioners working in the field of ritual and performance practices. See Part Four.

entrainment A principle of physics whereby two or more objects moving at similar frequencies synchronize with each other forming a unified (*coupled*) pattern of movement. The principle of *entrainment* was first identified by the scientist Christian Huygens in 1665 when he was working on a design for a nautical pendulum clock. He observed that two pendulums that were both mounted on the same wooden beam began to swing in unison after some time. Through their shared vibrations it seemed that these rhythms were able to interact and achieve a synchronous state (Sethares 2007:148).

Similar forms of *mutual coupling* have been observed in the firing of neurons in the brain, in the relationships between heart cells that synchronize to form a unified beating, in the unison flashing of fireflies and within the physical rhythms of human interactions including the movement of crowds and parent–infant synchronization. See Chapter 8, as well as Strogatz (2004) and Feldman (2007).

eurhythmics/eurhythmy A Greek term, translated literally as a *good* or *pleasing* form of rhythm. These terms were adopted by Dalcroze, Laban, Duncan and Steiner to describe their use of rhythmic physical forms within their practices. See descriptions in Chapters 2, 3 and 4.

follow-through A term used by Copeau to describe a quality of continuity in a performer's actions. Copeau associated the capacity for a performer to *follow-through* with an action with a sense of sincerity, simplicity and naturalness. See Chapter 1.

Kinaesthetic response A term used in *Viewpoints* to describe a bodily impulse that provides a catalyst for actions. A responsive quality of relationship by which the ensemble responds instantaneously to stimuli, without intentionally pre-planning or analysing these decisions. See Chapter 7.

luft-pause A musical term, derived from German, literally meaning a pause for breath, originally related to the playing of wind instruments or singing. This term is also used as a compositional device indicating a suspension in the rhythm of a piece of music similar to the use of a comma in speech. Meyerhold linked this term to the idea of *sub-text* in drama. See Chapter 5.

metre This term often suggests a steady *beat/pulse* (either heard or felt) that can be grouped into repeated units made up of *accented* and unaccented *beats*.

In poetry, *metre* is used to describe a grouping of accented and non-accented syllables (see Table 1.1), referred to through Greek terms such as *iambus* (unaccented, accented) and *trochee* (accented, unaccented). In Greek poetry these *accents* are often *agogic*, whereas in English poetry, metres are predominantly *dynamic* (see *accents*). These patterns of accented and unaccented syllables (referred to as feet) can be further grouped into repeated sequences with the first *accent* of each metric cycle often experienced as having more weight to it than the others (see *structural accents*). For example, a grouping of five *iambus accents* forms *an iambic pentameter*, a *metre* commonly used by Shakespeare (see Figure G.1 in *accent*).

In music, *metre* plays a similar role, establishing a framework or grouping of *accents* through and over which rhythmic phrases are performed and heard. These patterns establish expectations and shape the ways that music is heard and felt by listeners and performers. In both music and poetry, *metre* can either be expressed overtly or can be more ambiguous and/or subtle in nature, at times disappearing altogether. A metre can also change throughout a poem or musical composition. See Chapter 5 for discussion on the distinctions between *rhythm* and *metre*.

note values Drawing from Western musical practices, many theatre directors have adopted musical terms and forms of notation to describe and score the rhythms of their performances (see Chapters 3, 5 and 9). The following table outlines the hierarchical structure in which these notes can be located (the longest duration at the top) along with their names (both European and American).[3]

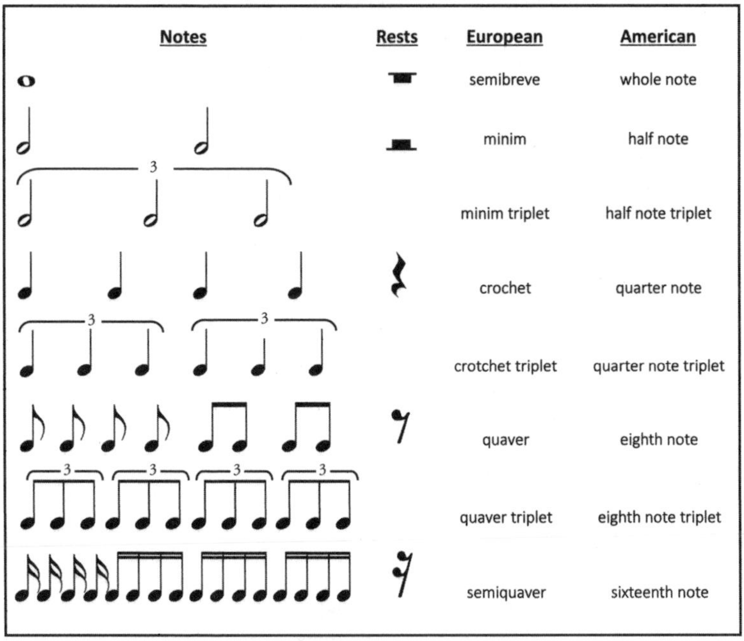

Notes	Rests	European	American
		semibreve	whole note
		minim	half note
		minim triplet	half note triplet
		crochet	quarter note
		crotchet triplet	quarter note triplet
		quaver	eighth note
		quaver triplet	eighth note triplet
		semiquaver	sixteenth note

Figure G.2 Note values: European and American names.

psychophysical A term used both in science and in actor training to refer to the unified relationship between mental and physical aspects. The term *psychophysical* gained popularity in the mid-nineteenth century, through the writings of German psychologist and philosopher Gustav Fechner. Like other scientists of his time, Fechner was looking to investigate the relationship between the 'mind' and 'physical body', with a view that these were in fact 'two sides of the same reality' (Hui 2008:32). Stanislavski adopted this term to discuss relationships between 'inner' and 'outer' aspects of his practice and the techniques associated with these relationships. More recently practitioners including John Britton (2013) and Phillip Zarrilli have used this term to discuss contemporary approaches to actor training which focus on 'the relationship between the physical/cognitive/perceptual elements woven simultaneously together and at play in embodied work' (Zarrilli 2008:29). See Chapter 3.

rakurz **(Russian)/** *raccourci* **(French)** Translated as 'short-cut', this term was used by Meyerhold, Eisenstein, Copeau and Decroux to describe condensed, intensified moments of performance. In Meyerhold's practice this often referred to an instantaneous moment of dynamic stillness or the way a single gesture could be seen to encapsulate the essence of a character or situation. Eisenstein described *raccourci* as 'an arrangement for maximum expressiveness, the essentiality of the movement, mechanically made acute' (Law and Gordon 1996:98). In the context of French mime this term has also been used to describe 'how a sequence is telescoped into a gesture' (Pavis 1999:333). See Chapter 5.

rhythm In performance, the term *rhythm* has a broad range of meanings that vary amongst practitioners and contexts. Here, many definitions of this term refer to a sense of form and/or a quality of motion, with different definitions varying the emphasis given to each of these aspects. *Rhythm* is also often associated with a sense of vitality and nuance, being seen in contrast to the supposedly fixed nature of *metre* or *tact*. However, there are also many practitioners who relate this term more closely to a quality of repetition and fixed form.

While the understandings and applications of rhythm in this field rarely conform to a stable set of frameworks, we can identify three processes that are commonly identified as *rhythm*:

1   the impression of temporal form arising from an action or sound;
2   the action/sound itself; and
3   the form or structure that an action/sound is said to follow.

Further, the term *rhythm* can also be used to describe a more general category of temporal phenomena, encompassing the above aspects.

score A term used to describe a preconceived performance structure or set of instructions. In some cases, a performance *score* may take a form similar to a musical *score* (as seen in Stanislavski, Meyerhold and Grotowski's practices; Chapters 3, 5 and 9).

Alternatively, this term can be used to describe a more choreographic structure of rehearsed movements or sounds. Within improvisation practices, the term *score* can also be used to refer to the set of parameters, guidelines, instructions or directives that the performers are working to. See Chapters 6 and 7 for examples of scores for improvisation.

simultaneity As a musical term, *simultaneity* commonly refers to a 'group of notes played at the same time' (Latham 2012), though a more general use of this term is applied in this book. Here simultaneity is defined as the perceived relationship of events that can be said to happen together in time, during the same timeframe, or share a common point in time (temporal axis). This includes events that are fully synchronized (i.e. they clapped their hands together), as well as those that are not fully synchronized but still share the same timeframe, or temporal axis (he danced during her monologue). See Schmiedtová (2004), Jammer (2006) and Vrobel et al. (2008).

In regard to the *scoring* of the dramaturgy or *mise-en-scène* of a performance we can describe *simultaneity* as the vertical temporal relationship of events (Figure 11.1). See Chapter 11 and Postlewait (1988), Pavis (2003), Meyer-Dinkgräfe (2006) and Barba (2010).

tempo In performance *tempo* is used to describe the speed or pace of an action, sound, character, scene, sequence or entire production. In musical notation *tempo* is often measured by the number of beats per minute (i.e.120 bpm) or alternatively it is represented through Italian, or French terms that describe not only the pace of a *rhythm* but also its feel or energetic quality (i.e. *grave* = slow and solemn, *adagio* = slow and stately, *andante* = a walking pace, *allegro* = quickly and bright).

David Roesner points out that while musical *tempo* is generally linked to the rate of a regular *beat*, in theatre *tempo* often emerges from a 'sense of expectation and realization or surprise' (2014:84). A gesture is often read as slow or fast relative to our expectations. This can come from having seen a similar gesture in the same performance or by comparing the speed that a gesture is performed to how it is normally executed in daily life.

The *tempo* of a performance often results from the combined impression of all the rhythmic elements of a piece. The way these relate to one another (and to our expectations) brings about a sense of speed or overall flow (see Epstein 1995:99).

Within performance discourses, *tempo* is often associated with an external sense of time passing, being linked to a sense of atmosphere or the energetic dynamics of a scene or a play. However, this principle does not hold true for all definitions of *tempo*. *Tempo* can equally be applied to the specific pace of an individual's actions or to an internal and variable pace that could exist within a single performer or be shared by an ensemble as a common *pulse*. See Chapter 3.

tempo-rhythm A term used by Stanislavski and subsequently by various other practitioners. While there are various interpretations of this term, most often it is used to suggest either the relationship between *tempo* and *rhythm* (at times seen as oppositional) or a more general sense of the pace and rhythmic qualities of a character, an action or a scene.

Referring to both *inner* and *outer tempo-rhythm*, Stanislavski established a body of exercises and approaches that looked to explore the interrelationship between the *inner* and *outer* aspects of a performer, often associated with psychological/imaginative and physical or externally prescribed elements of a performance (i.e. musical, textual or choreographic elements). See Chapter 3.

time bracket A term used by John Cage and Merce Cunningham to establish the duration of each action, behaviour or sound within a composition. Here, rather than measuring durations by musical bars or *notes*, these practitioners indicated the number of minutes and seconds a sound or action should occur for. Cage's musical composition *4:33* is perhaps the most famous example of this. In this piece the performer is required to sit in silence at a piano for four minutes and thirty-three seconds. See Chapter 2.

timing An aspect of *rhythm* that often relates to the use of duration, synchronicity and pace within a performance. A performer can be said to have a 'good' or 'bad' sense of *timing*, based on their effective use of these elements. *Timing* also often suggests a sense of personal expression, a characteristic that defines an individual performer, ensemble or director. See Goodridge (1999) for a discussion on the distinctions between *rhythm* and *timing* in performance.

tormos A term used within Meyerhold's Biomechanics training. This literally translates as 'brake', a mechanical term which referred to 'slowing the action of the machine by offering a resisting counter-force' (Pitches 2005:79). For a performer, this was a way of exerting control over an action as it was performed, allowing an action to be elongated or at its extreme, brought to the point of dynamic stillness. See Chapter 5.

tripartite rhythms A rhythmic system adopted within Meyerhold's Biomechanics training. This is a way of breaking movements down into three component parts. These are commonly referred to as *otkaz, posil, tochka* or *i, ras, dva* (and, one, two). In English these three parts are often described as preparation, realization and end. In the Biomechanical approach, this rhythmic scheme can be applied to every aspect of a performance from a single gesture to the development of a production as a whole. See Chapter 5.

Similar structures have been adopted by other practitioners including Dalcroze, Copeau and Laban as well as theorists including Langer, to describe the preparation, realization and resolution of action. We also see similar forms used within the Japanese performance practices of Noh and Kabuki represented by the structure of *jo, ha, kyu*. See Quinn (2005:127–30).

NOTES

Epigraph

1   Japanese text from Omote Akira (ed) (1978). Translation by Tom Hare from
    Zeami's treatise, 'A Mirror to the Flower' (1424) in Zeami (2008) *Zeami:
    Performance Notes*. Used here with permission from Columbia University
    Press.

Part One

1   Throughout this book, I will be using the terms 'actor', 'performer' and
    'theatre practitioner', separately as well as interchangeably. While I am
    not suggesting that these are entirely analogous terms, here as in other
    contemporary texts, I seek to 're-establish their affinity' (Read 2007:27)
    rather than isolate them as separate fields of study and practice. See also
    Cull (2012).
2   Meyerhold's methods and theories were publicly attacked by a directive
    from the RAPP that linked his work with that of Mikhail Chekhov and
    Andrei Bely ('rhythm as dialectics'). These accusations contributed to
    Meyerhold's approaches being rejected by the Soviet government, which
    ultimately led to his arrest and execution.

Chapter 1

1   See conversation with Karen Christopher in Chapter 13 for a further
    discussion of this phenomenon.
2   Sophie Gibson argues that Aristoxenus was responsible for establishing
    musicology as a field of science and for establishing music theory as a
    subject in its own right (2014:2).
3   The categorization of rhythmic forms in relationship to moods as well
    as natural or spiritual elements, can also be observed in other cultures

including Hindustani traditional and classical music, as well in various West African and Afro-Caribbean traditions. In these contexts specific rhythmic forms are linked to elemental qualities, *devatas* (Hindi), *òrìṣàs* (Yoruba). For a discussion of the associations between psychophysical states and Hindustani musical forms see Balkwill and Thomson (1999), and for details regarding relationships between drumming patterns and *òrìṣàs* in the Afro-Cuban *Lucumi* tradition see Schweitzer (2003).

4   This aspect is particularly pertinent when considering the prominent links between rhythmic training practices and political regimes, military training, industrialized labour and concepts of race and identity (see Golston 2008).

Chapter 2

1   In Greek, *Eu* is a prefix expressing notions of 'good', 'well' and 'pleasing'. The term *eurhythmy* was also adopted by Steiner, Dalcroze and Duncan, who used the terms *eurhythmy* and *eurhythmics* to describe their practices.

2   Translations of d'Udine's texts have been sourced from Richard Taylor's translation of Mikhail Yampolski's chapter 'Kuleshov's Experiments and the New Anthropology of the Actor' (1994).

3   On another occasion Stanislavski contradicted this usage of metronomes stating: 'A metronome and true creativeness cannot possibly coexist' (Stanislavski and Rumyantsev 1998:38).

4   These approaches take a particularly anthropocentric view of rhythm, understanding it primarily as a process of human perception. Following this line of thought, something is or is not rhythmic based on a human's capacity to experience it, rather than due to its essential qualities. Others including Deleuze and Guattari (1988), Laura Cull (2012) and Eleni Ikoniadou (2014) have looked to challenge this anthropocentric definition, arguing for a broader understanding and categorization of rhythm in both philosophy and the arts.

5   See description of 'time brackets' in Glossary.

Part Two

1   This part of the book is a reworking of on an article originally published in May 2014 under the title 'The Ins and Outs of Tempo-Rhythm' in the journal *Stanislavski Studies*, issue 2, vol. 2.

2   Recent articles that have discussed Stanislavski's interest in rhythm and music include Carnicke and Rosen (2013) and Frendo (2014).

Chapter 3

1   Experimentation with rhythm in musical productions and operas became a central element of work undertaken at MAT's Music Studio (from October 1919), later referred to as the Stanislavski Opera Studio (from 1924), then the Opera Studio-Theatre (1926) and finally the Stanislavski Opera Theatre (1928–39), with Meyerhold taking over as director briefly after Stanislavski's death (1938–39). Musical productions which Stanislavski directed during the latter part of his career include *Werther* (1921), *Evgeny Onegin* (1922), *The Secret Marriage* (1924), *A May Night* (1926–28), *Boris Godunov* (1928) and *Rigoletto* (1938). For more details, see Stanislavski and Rumyantsev (1998), Carnicke and Rosen (2013) and Frendo (2014).

2   James Lee lists a collection of prominent figures, amongst those who visited Hellerau to see Dalcroze's performance and training work: Sergei Rachmaninoff, Anna Pavlova, Harley Granville-Barker, Paul Claudel, Rainer Maria Rilke, Ernst Ansermet, Stanislavski, Bernard Shaw, Vaslav Nijinsky, Georges Pitoeff, Sergei Diaghilev, Max Reinhardt, Upton Sinclair, Darius Milhaud, Franz Werfel and Jacques Rouché (2003:115).

3   These classes were originally taught by Sergei Volkonski. Stanislavski's brother Vladimir Alekseev took over running these classes at MAT in the 1920s and 1930s.

4   The First Studio was established by Stanislavski in 1912 to aid him in his development of a new 'system' of acting. Practitioners involved in this period of work included Richard Boleslavsky, Evgeny Vakhtangov, Michael Chekhov and Maria Ouspenskaya, with Leopold Sulerzhitsky leading much of the research undertaken from 1912 to 1916 (Carnicke 2008:28).

5   See Mitter (1988) for a detailed discussion of relationships between 'inner' and 'outer' aspects within the work of Peter Brook.

6   Exercises similar to these can be seen in Meyerhold's work during this time (Leach 1993:114) and can also be observed in Grotowski's training practices in the early 1960s (Barba 1965:132). See examples in Chapters 5 and 9.

7   See Glossary for explanations of musical note values and names.

8   Translations of Stanislavski (1986a, b) texts have been made here with the help of Shawn Bodden.

9   Similar examples are offered in *Moscow Rehearsals* in which Norris Houghton describes a rhythmic scale from 1 to 10 that he observed being used in rehearsals between 1934 and 1935. This was used as a way of communicating the rhythm or energy level: rhythm 1 was that of a man who was almost dead, 5 was normal and 10 was extremely excitable to the point of almost jumping out of a window (Houghton 1936:61). A close comparison can also be made here with the 'seven levels of tension' exercises commonly attributed to Lecoq (Lecoq 2006:89).

10 A similar example of combining two rhythmic aspects into a single term can found in Decroux's use of the term 'Dynamo-rhythm', as found within his Corporeal Mime practices. This term has been defined as 'the collective qualities of physical movements, in all their complexity, which are linked to ... their outline or trajectory – their speed – their power or force' (Alaniz 2013:8).

Chapter 4

1 The original text from which Copeau copied these notes was written by Percy Ingham and published within a collection of writings compiled by Jaques-Dalcroze (1912).
2 Bing studied acting from 1905 to 1907 at the Conservatoire de Musique et de Déclamation and had previous experience as a professional actress in France before working with Copeau.
3 Copeau and Bing met Howarth early in 1917 in Geneva, where she was taking postgraduate classes at the Dalcroze School. Howarth was an English dancer and violinist who had studied on the theatre course at the Dalcroze School in Hellerau in 1910. Here she developed skills in pantomime, studying with Alexander Sulzman, as well as dance and physical therapy. Following her work with the Vieux-Colombier she became a choreographer for the Paris Opera.
4 Margaret Naumburg was instrumental in popularizing Dalcroze's eurhythmics and Alexander Technique in America as well developing her own approaches to education growing out of her training with Maria Montessori. Frost and Yarrow mark Bing's experiences at Naumburg's school as a key influence in the development of play-based approaches to drama teaching (2007:27).
5 Howarth offers her own account of time spent with the company in New York in a letter to Norman Paul written in 1960, in which she describes many of the challenges faced by the company at that time and some details of Copeau's approach to directing the company (Howarth 1960).
6 Similar exercises continue to be used within contemporary forms of actor training. See Berry (2013:79) and interview with Papi in Chapter 14.
7 Bing integrated the use of live music into her production of the Japanese Noh play, *Katan*, encouraging some of the students to play flutes and drums as part of the production.
8 Parallels can be seen here with Laban's work on movement analysis and more recent training approaches such as 'Viewpoints' (Chapter 7).
9 The descriptions in this section are based on student notes taken from classes at the Vieux-Colombier School between November 1922 and June 1923 (Kusler 1974:132, 166–7).

Chapter 5

1   For a detailed discussion of musicality in a range of theatre practices including those of Meyerhold, see Roesner (2014).

2   Actor Nikolai Brasilov wrote of his experiences of training with Meyerhold: 'Just as a pianist, before beginning to study some song, trains himself with exercises, the actor, too, before beginning to study a role must work on the technical training of his material' (Brasilov 1996:159).

3   See definition of *luft-pause* in Glossary.

4   These concepts echo strongly the guidance given by Aristotle in regard to the rhythms of prose. See 'Etymology of Rhythm' in Chapter 1.

5   See Hasty (1997) and London (2004) for a more detailed discussion of metre and rhythm in regard to musical composition and perception.

6   The philosophers Giles Deleuze and Félix Guattari further elucidate this distinction, stating: 'It is well known that rhythm is not meter or cadence: there is nothing less rhythmic than a military march. The tom-tom is not 1–2, the waltz is not 1,2,3, music is not binary or ternary … Meter, whether regular or not, assumes a coded form whose unit of measure may vary, but in a noncommunicating milieu, whereas rhythm is the Unequal or Incommensurable that is always undergoing transcoding. Metre is dogmatic, but rhythms is critical…. It is the difference that is rhythmic not the repetition, which nevertheless produces it: productive repetition has nothing to with reproductive metre' (Deleuze and Guattari 1988:345–6).

7   Pavis (2003) inverts this relationship somewhat, describing the structuring of time in performance as 'rhythm' and the changeable spontaneous elements as 'tempo'. See 'Tempo-rhythm – ins and outs' in Chapter 3.

8   The perception of rhythmic phrases, accents, groupings within uniform sequence of sounds is referred to as 'subjective rhythmization'. See London (2004:13) for further details.

9   Eisenstein claimed that while attending Meyerhold's directing workshops he failed the 'rhythmic gymnastics' class, claiming that this work was not on rhythm but focused rather on metrics and a metronomic sense of time. Eisenstein wrote: 'The same thing happened with dance. When I learned how to dance, I could not grasp certain figure-dances at all, and I was wildly delighted when the foxtrot appeared, where you can move however you like according to the sense of the music rather than the various steps' (Eisenstein 2010:321).

10 Bode was a student of Jaques-Dalcroze who went on to reject many aspects of eurhythmics and establish his own system of rhythmic gymnastics within Germany. His approach took a strong stance against the use of 'musical rhythm' within physical education and advocated for a more embodied, non-musical approach to rhythmic training. See Crespi (2014) and Toepfer (1997).

11 Pitches points out that if this sequence is underscored with a count of 'one, two, three', then the sense of intention and musicality is blurred (Pitches 2005:68). This counting system can be seen in descriptions by Braun (Meyerhold 1991:201) as well as Barba and Räuker (1997). Beginning this sequence with 'and' rather than a 'one' establishes a particular rhythmic quality. The use of 'and' suggests a sense of anticipation, with the 'one' receiving a stronger emphasis or point of accent and the 'two' suggesting some resolution.

Chapter 6

1 Karl Marx drew this concept from Hegelian philosophy and discussed it in detail within *The Poverty of Philosophy* ([1847] 2008:114–64).
2 The word ensemble can be understood here as referring to a group of performers as well as to the quality of relationship that (in)forms that group, what Britton refers to as the 'sense of ensemble-ness' that can emerge from training together or a shared history (Britton 2013:4).
3 For a detailed discussion of ensemble, see Britton (2013), a collections of writings from various practitioners and scholars on this subject.
4 Other examples of ball games used within the context of actor training can be found in numerous practices including those of Michael Chekhov (Petit 2009), Maria Knebel (Hodge 2010), Clive Barker (1977), Mladen Materic (Materic and Hulton 1997), Tony Cots and David Zinder (2002).
5 See Glossary and Chapter 8 for a definition and discussion of entrainment.

Chapter 7

1 I first worked with Viewpoints in 2003 as part of a month-long residency attended in Brisbane, Australia, with physical theatre company Zen Zen Zo. This workshop was led by Lin Bradley and Simon Woods, who studied Viewpoints and Suzuki work with the SITI company.
2 It is worth noting the ways Britton's work has also been strongly influenced by the American movement improvisation scene, primarily through his training with American-Australian improviser Al Wunder.
3 See Grotowski (1973) for another perspective on these issues.
4 An actor training approach developed by Tadashi Suzuki, drawing on elements of martial arts, Noh and Kabuki training (Suzuki 1986; Allain 2002).
5 Bogart and Landau also highlight the importance of working with contrasting inner and outer tempos, a concept with obvious correlations to Stanislavski's use of contrasting inner and outer tempo-rhythms, as well as aspects of Suzuki's work drawn from Japanese Noh theatre. An insightful discussion on the use of contrasting inner and outer elements within Noh

theatre and contemporary performance practices can be found in Yoshi
Oida's book *The Invisible Actor* (Oida and Marshall 1997:39–42).

6   A comparison can be made here to Bing's use of everyday associations (a
typewriter or an elevator) as tempo references (Chapter 4).

Part Four

1   A similar distinction between ecstasy and possession has been made
by both Eliade (1964:6) and Rouget (1985:19). Schechner also makes
the point that no performance is 'pure' ecstasy or possession. Rather,
the performer exists in a dialectic tension, shifting between these two
extremes of the spectrum (1988:175).

2   For a more detailed discussion of the characteristics of trance and ecstatic
states, see Buber (1996), Rouget (1985) and Zarrilli (2011).

Chapter 8

1   See Chamberlain, Middleton and Pla (2014) for a discussion of Buddhist
mindfulness and psychophysical performance.

2   In Núñez's practices we can observe the use of various elemental and
natural forms drawn from sacred practices in Mexico and Tibet. These
include elemental steps sourced from traditional Conchero dances and
the use of animal movements as a means of accessing specific modes of
consciousness. See Chapter 10 and Núñez (1996) for further details.

3   A link between stepping patterns and an individual's state of consciousness
can be observed in the mutual influence that repeated actions (such as
dance steps) and the vestibular system have on each other. Located within
the inner ear, the vestibular system is responsible for guiding one's sense of
equilibrium and spatial orientation (see Phillips-Silver and Trainor 2008).

4   See definition and background of entrainment in Glossary.

5   While Neher's findings have been cited and drawn on within a number of
other studies examining rhythm and altered states of consciousness, this
work has also been challenged by other scholars who have described
his research methods and findings as problematic and inconclusive. See
Rouget (1985).

6   Theta brainwaves occur between 4 and 8 Hz (beats per second) and are
often associated with drowsy, near unconscious states and the period just
before waking or sleeping. During theta activity it is often difficult to sustain
consciousness without any outside stimulation; yet it has been observed
that long-term meditators have been able to maintain self-awareness
during enhanced theta activity, suggesting that this is a capacity that can
be cultivated through practice (Jovanov and Maxfield 2012:40–2).

7 In general terms, the part of the brain known as the cortex is associated with cognitive processes including abstract thinking, language and counting, whereas sub-cortical areas of the brain such as the amygdala are seen to be related to the limbic system and to emotion, memory, instinctual behaviour and respiration.

8 It has been found that children as young as two and half years were able to show some synchronization in drumming to a steady beat, but only when that drumming occurred with a live partner in a social context (as opposed to a machine or a sound recording) (Kirschner and Tomasello 2009:311).

9 *Tloque Nahuaque* is the name of a Nahuatl deity referred to by Núñez as 'the God of Closeness and Togetherness' (1996:80). Núñez also refers to this element as being symbolic of the dialogue between and balancing out of oppositional energies such as contraction/expansion and centrifugal/centripetal forces (interview with author, November 2010). For footage of the *Tloque Nahuaque* 'dance', see the end of video documentation available at http://eilonmorris.com/support-3-3/.

Chapter 9

1 The term 'techniques' will be used throughout this and the following chapters to denote the technical abilities which a performer seeks to develop (performance techniques), as well as a more anthropological understanding of this term (body techniques). This later usage relates to what Marcel Mauss named 'techniques of the body'. These can be understood as forms of practical knowledge – encultured ways of using one's body that, while being rooted in one's physicality, are also seen as being cultivated through training or through the cultural norms and dispositions that we encounter. See Mauss (1973) and Crossley (2007).

2 Charles Dullin was one of the founding members of the Vieux-Colombier, along with Suzanne Bing. Dullin left the company soon after their return from New York and established his own theatre company, teaching and directing, amongst others, Jean-Louis Barrault, Etienne Decroux and Antonin Artaud.

3 *Expressive Man* was also a key text in Stanislavski's own development of rhythm exercises with both Stanislavski and Vakhtangov making various references to this foundational text (Stanislavski and Rumyantsev 1998; Stanislavski 2008; Malaev-Babel 2011).

4 A published account of rhythmic exercises undertaken by the Laboratory Theatre was written by Eugenio Barba and accompanied other descriptions of training exercises observed between 1959 and 1962, originally published in the Italian text *Alla Ricerca Del Teatro Perduto* [In Search of a Lost Theatre] (Barba 1965:129–37). While many of these descriptions went on to be published in *Towards a Poor Theatre*

(Grotowski 1969), the descriptions of rhythm exercises were edited out of this later text and remain available only in Barba's original (1965) Italian text and its Hungarian translation. The illustrations that follow are based on notation found in Barba's (1965) text (pp.132–3). These scores have been sourced from the Odin Teatret Archive and have been reproduced here with their permission.

5   See Glossary for a table of note values and their names.

6   Examples of exercises based on and inspired by the work of Delsarte and Dalcroze can be found in *Towards a Poor Theatre* (Grotowski 1969:133–46). In this selection of training descriptions, we can also observe clear links to Bing and Dullin's improvisation practices drawing on imaginative work with animal and plant associations.

7   Exercises such as these were inspired in part by Carlos Castaneda's descriptions of slow walking as well as other traditional walking meditation practices, with Grotowski also making reference to what he called the 'walk of power' (Grotowski 2001a:259, 263). See discussion in the following chapter for a discussion of Núñez's work with these practices.

8   See the following chapter for a discussion of 'verticality' in Grotowski and Núñez's practices.

9   In a revised translation Grotowski uses the phrase 'the waves of "old body" in the actual body' (Grotowski 2001a:299).

Chapter 10

1   Alternatively referred to as 'Contemplative Trot' (Núñez 1996:89).

2   Footage of 'contemplative running' filmed as part of my documentation of research undertaken in Mexico City in 2010 can be seen here: https://youtu.be/73RENOTUwMo. Footage of 'slow walking' taken from a workshop run by Núñez in the UK in 1999 can be seen here: https://youtu.be/qZh4OU8mjxU?t=1m26s and here: https://youtu.be/DvOlYYzUHnc?t=1m50s.

3   The use of similar forms of collective running can be found within the traditional practices of the Tarahumara tradition of Mexico and the Lung-Gom-Pa runners of Tibet. Meditative running forms can also be observed within other approaches to actor training, including the work of Gardzienice. Actor Mariusz Gołaj describes the use of 'night running' as a core aspect of the training work of Gardzienice. He sees this as 'naturalising him both by heightening his consciousness of nature – "the pulse of the earth and the shooting stars" – and that of natural human gestures and behaviour – "breathing, the next exercise, mutuality, the group"' (Allain 1998:65).

4   For a more detailed theoretical discussion on the mutable qualities of time, see Vrobel (2008).

Chapter 11

1 Over the past century the concept of simultaneity has gained increasing
   currency within the fields of science, philosophy, visual arts, music, dance
   and theatre. Recent scholarship on this subject includes Postlewait (1988);
   Jammer (2006); Meyer-Dinkgräfe (2006); Hughes (2007); Vrobel, Rössler
   and Marks-Tarlow (2008); Barba (2010).

2 As Einstein pointed out: 'We have to bear in mind that all our propositions
   involving time are always propositions about simultaneous events' ([1905]
   1989:141). In his definition of simultaneity published at the beginning of
   the twentieth century, Einstein proposed: 'If, for example "the train arrives
   here at 7 o'clock", that means, more or less, "the pointing of the small
   hand of my clock to 7 and the arrival of the train are simultaneous events"'
   (Einstein [1905] 1989:141).

3 See a discussion of this topic in Morris (2013).

4 For further discussion on the use of spoken syllables rather than counting
   in rhythm training, see Flatischler (1992). Drawing on Indian and other
   spoken musical training techniques, Flatischler uses spoken syllables
   such as Ta-Ki, Ga-Ma-La and Ta-Ke-Ti-Na to establish basic rhythmic
   groupings and cycles.

5 In more advanced versions of this exercise, we would fix the exact number
   of beats per journey around each circle (i.e. centre circle – twelve beats,
   middle circle – fifteen, outer circle – twenty). This task is considerably more
   challenging at the early stages of this training, so for at least the first few
   sessions participants are free to take as many steps as needed to get
   around each circle.

6 A detailed description of Huracán can be found within Morris (2013:
   147–54), with footage of these practices also available at http://eilonmorris
   .com/support-3-3/.

7 David Locke identifies this phenomenon occurring in West African Gahu
   rhythms, describing this as a type of 'gestalt flip' (1998:24). Justin
   London also references this phenomenon in his book Hearing in Time.
   Here he argues that while different performers within an ensemble may
   hear and think about a piece of music from differing perspectives (one
   hearing in 6/8, another in 3/2), perceptually it remains impossible for a
   single listener to sustain the perception of two differing metric frameworks
   simultaneously. When engaging with a complex polyrhythmic form a
   listener/performer 'will either (a) extract a composite pattern of all the
   rhythmic streams present, or (b) focus [on] one rhythmic stream and
   entrain to its meter' (2004:84).

Part Five

1   Papers from the conference of *Meter, Rhythm and Performance* held at the University of Vechta, Germany, in May 1999, offers a range of perspectives on poetic language in performance (Küper 2002). Kathleen George's (1980) book *Rhythm in Drama* also presents an analysis of various rhythmic forms found in dramatic texts. From a more practical perspective, many of Cicely Berry's exercises on voice and acting offer an introduction to methods of approaching work on both poetry and prose texts for performance (Berry 2013). A more theoretical examination of rhythm in relationship to language and text can be found in Henri Meschonnic (1982), Patrice Pavis (1991, 1999, 2003) and in the work of other theorists including Erika Fischer-Lichte (2008).

Chapter 12

1   Giving further emphasis to the plurality of rhythmic interpretations of language in performance, Mikhail Bakhtin's writings on 'utterance', 'dialogism' and carnival also challenge the notion of a singular understanding or voice within a performance text. Bakhtin suggested that contained within an 'utterance' is multiple layers of references and meanings: previous uses and current meanings (1986:93).

2   A movement towards a more individualized approach to rhythm can be seen within the field of music as well. Leonard Meyer's text *Emotion and meaning in music* (1961) provides us with a clear critique of early twentieth-century rhythm research, stating outright: 'Music is not a "universal language"', insisting rather that 'The languages and dialects of music are many' (1961:62).

3   A key influence on Stanislavski's approaches to text was Sergei Volkonski, who taught both speech and rhythm classes at the Moscow Art Theatre. See Chapters 2 and 9 for references to Volkonski's theories.

Chapter 13

1   *Crossing the Line* is the title of one of Adam's performance texts.

2   See Vrobel (2011:89) and discussions regarding simultaneity in Chapter 11.

Chapter 14

1   Translation by James Greene, used here with permission from Angel Books. This text can be found in Mandelshtam (1990).
2   A short extract from this performance can be seen online: https://vimeo .com/156066520.
3   *Orghast* was the first public performance presented by Brook's International Centre of Theatre Research in 1971. It was developed in collaboration with Ted Hughes and involved the invention of a language that Hughes named Orghast. The formation of this language emerged through improvisations that Brook and Hughes led with an international company of actors.
4   These exercises draw on Cicely Berry's work with poetic language, involving walking the grammar and structure of thoughts. See discussion on Berry in Chapter 12 and her writings (2013:79). See also Marshall (2001:77–79).

Part Six

1   Peter Brook, quoted by Shomit Mitter (1988:49).

Glossary

1   The concept of *beat* and *off-beat* also corresponds to the Classical Greek understanding of *thesis* [basis] (the foot touching the ground or the hand beating a drum) and *arsis* (the foot or the hand lifting up) (Aristoxenus [c. 370 BC] 1990).
2   It is suggested that this usage comes from a miscomprehension of the term 'bits' used by Russian acting teachers in America in the 1920s. This term can be understood as a translation of the Russian term *kusok*, meaning a piece or section of something (Carnicke 2008:214).
3   Images of musical notes in all figures have been sourced from http:// linkwaregraphics.com/music/.

REFERENCES

Abbott, J. (2007) *The Improvisation Book*. London: Nick Hern Books.

Alaniz, L. (2013) 'The Dynamo-Rhythm of Etienne Decroux and His Successors'. *Mime Journal*, 24 (1), pp. 1–50.

Allain, P. (1998) *Gardzienice: Polish Theatre in Transition*. London: Routledge.

Allain, P. (2002) *The Art of Stillness: The Theatre Practice of Tadashi Suzuki*. London: Methuen Drama.

Allain, P. (ed.) (2009) *Grotowski's Empty Room*. London: Seagull Books.

Allen, D. (1999) *Performing Chekhov*. London: Routledge.

Aristotle (1991) *The Art of Rhetoric*. London: Penguin Classics.

Aristoxenus (1990) *Aristoxenus Elementa Rhythmica Book II and the Additional Evidence for Aristoxenean Rhythmic Theory*. Oxford: Clarendon Press.

Armstrong, F. (1992) *As Far as the Eye Can Sing*. London: Women's Press.

Bakhtin, M. M. (1986) *Speech Genres and Other Late Essays*. Austin: University of Texas Press.

Baldwin, J. (2013) 'The Accidental Rebirth of Collective Creation: Jacques Copeau, Michel Saint-Denis, Léon Chancerel and Improvised Theatre', in: K. Syssoyeva & S. Proudfit (eds), *A History of Collective Creation*. New York: Palgrave Macmillan, pp. 71–96.

Balkwill, L. & Thompson, W. (1999) 'A Cross-Cultural Investigation of the Perception of Emotion in Music: Psychophysical and Cultural Cues'. *Music Perception: An Interdisciplinary Journal*, 17 (1), pp. 43–64.

Barba, E. (1965) *Alla ricerca del teatro perduto [In Search of a Lost Theatre]*. Padova: Marsilio Editori.

Barba, E. (1972) 'Words or Presence'. *The Drama Review: TDR*, 16 (1), pp. 47–54.

Barba, E. (2010) *On Directing and Dramaturgy: Burning the House*. London: Routledge.

Barba, E. & Räuker, R. (1997) *Meyerhold's Etude: Throwing the Stone*. Exeter: University of Exeter Arts Documentation Unit.

Barba, E. & Savarese, N. (2006) *A Dictionary of Theatre Anthropology: The Secret Art of the Performer*. 2nd edition. London: Routledge.

Barker, C. (1977) *Theatre Games: A New Approach to Drama Training*. London: Methuen.

Beacham, R. C. (1985) 'Appia, Jaques-Dalcroze, and Hellerau, Part One: "Music Made Visible"'. *New Theatre Quarterly*, 1 (2), pp. 154–164.

Becker, J. (1994) 'Music and Trance'. *Leonardo Music Journal*, 4, pp. 41–51.

Becker, J. (2012) 'Rhythmic Entrainment and Evolution', in: J. Berger & G. Turow (eds), *Music, Science, and the Rhythmic Brain: Cultural and Clinical Implications*. Abingdon: Routledge, pp. 49–72.

Belgrad, D. (2014) 'Bebop as Cultural Alternative', in: Ajay Heble & Rebecca Caines (eds), *The Improvisation Studies Reader: Spontaneous Acts*. London: Routledge, pp. 223–235.

Benedetti, J. (1982) *Stanislavski: An Introduction*. Revised. London: Methuen Drama.

Benedetti, J. (1998) *Stanislavski and the Actor: The Final Acting Lessons, 1935–38*. London: Methuen Drama.

Benveniste, É. (1971) *Problems in General Linguistics*. Coral Gables, FL: University of Miami Press.

Berger, J. & Turow, G. (2012) *Music, Science, and the Rhythmic Brain: Cultural and Clinical Implications*. Oxon: Routledge.

Berry, C. (1973) *Voice and the Actor*. London: Harrap.

Berry, C. (2013) *From Word to Play: A Handbook for Directors*. London: Oberon Books.

Bing, S. (1920) *Translation by Norman H. Paul of Suzanne Bing's Undated Paper on "Bodily Technique" Using Music as Exercises*. Canterbury: Jacques Copeau Archive, University of Kent.

Blacking, J. (1989) *'A Commonsense View of All Music': Reflections on Percy Grainger's Contribution to Ethnomusicology and Music Education*. Cambridge: Cambridge University Press.

Blair, R. (2008) *The Actor, Image, and Action: Acting and Cognitive Neuroscience*. Abingdon: Routledge.

Bogart, A. & Landau, T. (2005) *The Viewpoints Book: A Practical Guide to Viewpoints and Composition*. New York: Theatre Communications Group.

Boleslavsky, R. (1987) *Acting the First Six Lessons*. New York: Routledge.

Brasilov, N. (1996) 'Profile of the Actor Graduating from the Meyerhold State Theatre School', in: A. Law & M. Gordon (eds), *Meyerhold, Eisenstein and Biomechanics: Actor Training in Revolutionary Russia*. London: McFarland & Co, pp. 151–161.

Brecht, B. (1964) *Brecht on Theatre*. London: Methuen.

Britton, J. (2010a) 'What Is It? The "It"-ness of Ensemble', in: *Encounter Ensemble Symposium*, University of Huddersfield, 16 September 2010. Available Online: http://eprints.hud.ac.uk/id/eprint/8616 (Accessed 12 May 2012).

Britton, J. (2010b) *Research Outline. Ensemble Physical Theatre-John Britton*. Available Online: https://ensemblephysicaltheatre.wordpress.com/research -scholarship/ (Accessed 21 February 2016).

Britton, J. (ed.) (2013) *Encountering Ensemble*. London: Methuen Drama.

Brook, P. (2009) *With Grotowski: Theatre Is Just a Form*. G. Banu, G. Ziółkowski & P. Allain (eds). Wrocław: The Grotowski Institute.

Buber, M. (1996) *Ecstatic Confessions: The Heart of Mysticism*. P. Mendes-Flohr (ed.). Syracuse: Syracuse University Press.

Bücher, K. (1899) *Arbeit und Rhythmus*. Leipzig: B.G. Teubner.

Carnicke, S. M. (2008) *Stanislavsky in Focus*. 2nd edition. Abingdon: Routledge.

Carnicke, S. M. & Rosen, D. (2013) 'A Singer Prepares', in: A. White (ed.), *The Routledge Companion to Stanislavsky*. Abingdon: Routledge, pp. 120–138.

Chamberlain, F., Middleton, D. & Pla, D. (2014) 'Buddhist Mindfulness and Psychophysical Performance', in: *International Symposium for Contemplative Studies*, 30 October – 2 November 2014, Boston, MA. (Unpublished). Available Online:http://eprints.hud.ac.uk/23013/ (Accessed 5 July 2016).

Chekhov, M. (2002) *To the Actor: On the Technique of Acting*. London: Routledge.

Copeau, J. (1970) 'Notes on the Actor', in: H. Krich Chinoy & T. Cole (eds), *Actors on Acting*. New York: Crown Publishers, pp. 218–223.

Copeau, J. (1990) *Copeau: Texts on Theatre*. J. Rudlin (ed.), Trans. N. Paul. London: Routledge.

Copeau, J. & Bing, S. (1920) *Translation by Norman H. Paul of Copeau's Notebook on the "Ecole du vieux colombier" about the Creation of the School on 1915, with Notes by Suzanne Bing*. Canterbury: Jacques Copeau Archive, University of Kent.

Cowan, M. (2007) 'The Heart Machine: "Rhythm" and Body in Weimar Film and Fritz Lang's Metropolis'. *Modernism/Modernity*, 14 (2), pp. 225–248.

Crespi, P. (2014) 'Rhythmanalysis in Gymnastics and Dance: Rudolf Bode and Rudolf Laban'. *Body & Society*, 20 (3–4), pp. 30–50.

Crossley, N. (2007) 'Researching Embodiment by Way of "Body Techniques"'. *The Sociological Review*, 15 (55), pp. 80–94.

Cull, L. (2012) *Theatres of Immanence*. Houndmills, Basingstoke: Palgrave Macmillan.

D'Aquili, E. G. (1985) 'Human Ceremonial Ritual and the Modulation of Aggression'. *Zygon*, 20 (1), pp. 21–30.

Delaumosne, D., Arnaud, A., Delsarte, F. & Géraldy M. D. (1893) *Delsarte System of Oratory*. New York: E.S. Werner.

Deleuze, G. (1990) *Expressionism in Philosophy: Spinoza*. Trans. M. Joughin. Cambridge: Zone Books.

Deleuze, G. & Guattari, F. (1988) *A Thousand Plateaus: Capitalism and Schizophrenia*. London: The Athlone Press.

Doğantan-Dack, M. (2006) 'The Body Behind Music: Precedents and Prospects'. *Psychology of Music*, 34 (4), pp. 449–464.

D'Udine, J. (1912) *Iskusstvo i zhest [Art and Gesture]*. Trans. S. Volkonski. St. Peterburg: Izdanie 'Apollona'.

Duncan, I. (1928) *The Art of the Dance*. New York: Theatre Arts, Inc.

Dunkelberg, K. (2008) 'Grotowski and North American Theatre: Translation, Transmission, Dissemination'. Unpublished PhD Thesis. New York: New York University.

Einstein, A. (1989) *The Collected Papers of Albert Einstein: The Swiss Years, Writings, 1900–1909*. West Sussex: Princeton University Press.

Eisenstein, S. (2010) *Writings, 1934–1947: Sergei Eisenstein Selected Works.* R. Taylor (ed.). London: I.B. Tauris.

Eliade, M. (1964) *Shamanism: Archaic Techniques of Ecstasy*. Revised English edition. Princeton, NJ: Princeton University Press.

Ellis, S. (2010) 'The Body in the Voice': Interview with Cicely Berry. *American Theatre*, 27 (1), pp. 34–36, 121–122.

Epstein, D. (1995) *Shaping Time: Music, the Brain, and Performance*. New York: Schirmer Books.

Evans, M. (2006) *Jacques Copeau*. Abingdon: Routledge.

Fachner, J. (2011) 'Time Is the Key', in: E. Cardeña & M. Winkelman (eds), *Altering Consciousness: Multidisciplinary Perspectives*. Santa Barbara, CA: ABC-CLIO, pp. 355–376.

Feldman, R. (2007) 'Parent–Infant Synchrony: Biological Foundations and Developmental Outcomes'. *Current Directions in Psychological Science*, 16 (6), pp. 340–345.

Fischer-Lichte, E. (2008) *The Transformative Power of Performance: A New Aesthetics*, Abingdon: Routledge.

Flatischler, R. (1992) *The Forgotten Power of Rhythm: Taketina*. Mendocino, CA: Life Rhythm.

Frendo, M. (2014) 'Stanislavsky's Musicality: Towards Physicalization'. *Studies in Musical Theatre*, 8 (3), pp. 225–237.

Frost, A. & Yarrow, R. (2007) *Improvisation in Drama*. 2nd edition. New York: Palgrave Macmillan.

George, K. (1980) *Rhythm in Drama*. Pittsburgh: University of Pittsburgh Press.

Gibson, S. (2014) *Aristoxenus of Tarentum and the Birth of Musicology*. London: Routledge.

Goebbels, H. (2012) '"It's All Part of One Concern": A "Keynote" to Composition as Staging', in: D. Roesner & M. Rebstock (eds), *Composed Theatre: Aesthetics, Practices, Processes*. Bristol: Intellect Books, pp. 111–120.

Golston, M. (2008) *Rhythm and Race in Modernist Poetry and Science*. New York: Columbia University Press.

Goodridge, J. (1999) *Rhythm and Timing of Movement in Performance: Dance Drama and Ceremony*. London: Jessica Kingsley Publishers.

Gordon, M. (1988) *The Stanislavsky Technique: Russia*. New York: Applause Theatre Book Publishers.

Grimes, R. (2001) 'The Theatre of Sources', in: R. Schechner & L. Wolford (eds), *The Grotowski Sourcebook*. Abingdon: Routledge, pp. 271–282.

Grotowski, J. (1969) *Towards a Poor Theatre*. E. Barba (ed.). London: Methuen.

Grotowski, J. (1973) 'Holiday'. *The Drama Review: TDR*, 17 (2), pp. 113–135.

Grotowski, J. (1978) 'The Art of Beginner' [statement at ITI conference in Warsaw in 4 June 1978]. *International Theatre Information,* Paris, Spring/Summer 1978, pp. 7–11.

Grotowski, J. (1987) 'Tu es le fils de quelqu'un [You Are Someone's Son]'. *The Drama Review: TDR*, 31 (3), pp. 30–41.

Grotowski, J. (1988) 'Performer', in: *Centro per la Sperimentazione e la Ricerca Teatrale*. Privately distributed pamphlet. Pontedera, Italy: Workcenter of Jerzy Grotowski, pp. 36–41.

Grotowski, J. (1989) 'The Art of Beginner'. Trans. J. Chwat. *The Act*, 1 (3), pp. 6–7.

Grotowski, J. (1995) 'From the Theatre Company to Art as Vehicle', in: *At Work with Grotowski on Physical Actions*. 1st edition. London: Routledge, pp. 115–135.

Grotowski, J. (1997) 'A Kind of Volcano', in: Bruno De Panafieu, Jacob Needleman & George Baker (eds), *Gurdjieff*. New York: Continuum International Publishing Group, pp. 87–106.

Grotowski, J. (2001a) 'Theatre of Sources', in: R. Schechner & L. Wolford (eds), *The Grotowski Sourcebook*. Abingdon: Routledge, pp. 252–270.

Grotowski, J. (2001b) 'Interview with Grotowski', in: R. Schechner & L. Wolford (eds), *The Grotowski Sourcebook*. Abingdon: Routledge, pp. 271–282.

Gumbrecht, H. (1988) 'Rhythm and Meaning', in H. Gumbrecht and K. Pfeiffer (eds), Trans. W. Whobrey, *Materialities of Communication*, Stanford: Stanford University Press, pp. 170–182.

Hasty, C. (1997) *Meter as Rhythm*. Oxford: Oxford University Press.

Hobsbaum, P. (2006) *Metre, Rhythm and Verse Form*. London: Routledge.

Hodge, A. (2010) *Actor Training*. Abingdon: Taylor & Francis.

Hodgson, J. (2016) *Mastering Movement: The Life and Work of Rudolf Laban*. 1st edition. Abingdon: Routledge.

Houghton, N. (1936) *Moscow Rehearsals: The Golden Age of the Soviet Theatre*. New York: Grove Press.

Howarth, J. (1960) *Letter from Jassmin [sic] Howarth to Norman Paul about Her Collaboration with Copeau as a Practitioner of Eurhythmics*. (Annotated by N. Paul). Copeau Archive, Canterbury: University of Kent.

Hughes, G. (2007) 'Envisioning Abstraction: The Simultaneity of Robert Delaunay's "First Disk"'. *The Art Bulletin*, 89 (2), pp. 306–332.

Hui, A. (2008) 'Hearing Sound as Music: Psychophysical Studies of Sound Sensation and the Music Culture of Germany, 1860–1910'. Unpublished PhD Thesis, University of California, Los Angeles.

Ikoniadou, E. (2014) *The Rhythmic Event: Art, Media, and the Sonic*. London: MIT Press.

Jammer, M. (2006) *Concepts of Simultaneity from Antiquity to Einstein and Beyond*. Baltimore: Johns Hopkins University Press.

Jaques-Dalcroze, É. (1912) *The Eurhythmics of Jaques-Dalcroze*. London: Constable & Company Ltd.

Jaques-Dalcroze, É. (1967) *Rhythm, Music and Education*. Revised edition. London: The Dalcroze Society Inc.

Jones, R. (1986) 'Attentional Rhythmicity in Human Perception', in: J. Evans & M. Clynes (eds), *Rhythm in Psychological, Linguistic and Musical Processes*. Springfield: Charles C. Thomas Publisher Ltd, pp. 13–40.

Jovanov, E. & Maxfield, M. C. (2012) 'Entraining the Brain and Body', in: J. Berger & G. Turow (eds), *Music, Science, and the Rhythmic Brain: Cultural and Clinical Implications*. Abingdon: Routledge, pp. 31–48.

Kirillov, A. (2015) 'The Theatrical System of Michael Chekhov', in: M. Mathiue & Y. Meerzon (eds), *The Routledge Companion to Michael Chekhov*. Abingdon: Routledge, pp. 40–56.

Kirschner, S. & Tomasello, M. (2009) 'Joint Drumming: Social Context Facilitates Synchronization in Preschool Children'. *Journal of Experimental Child Psychology*, 102 (3), pp. 299–314.

Koritz, A. (2001) 'Drama and the Rhythm of Work in the 1920s'. *Theatre Journal*, 53 (4), pp. 551–567.

Kozintsev, M. (1987) 'A Child of the Revolution', in: L. Schnitzer, J. Schnitzer & M. Martin (eds) *Cinema in Revolution: Heroic Era of Soviet Films*, New York: Da Capo Press, pp. 89–108.

Kumiega, J. (1985) *The Theatre of Grotowski*. London: Methuen.

Küper, C. (ed.) (2002) *Meter, Rhythm, and Performance: Metrum, Rhythmus, Performanz*. Papers from conference held at the University of Vechta, Germany, May 1999, New York: Peter Lang.

Kusler, B. (1974) 'Jacques Copeau's Theatre School: L'Ecole Du Vieux-Colombier, 1920–29'. Unpublished PhD Thesis, University of Wisconsin.

Laban, R. (1920) *Die Welt des Tänzers: Fünf Gedankenreigen*. Stuttgart: Walter Seifert.

Laban, R. (1980) *The Mastery of Movement*. Plymouth: Macdonald and Evans.

Laban, R. (2014) 'Eurhythmy and Kakorhythmy in Art and Education'. *Body & Society*, 20 (3–4), pp. 75–78.

Laban, R. & Lawrence, F. C. (1942) *Laban Lawrence Industrial Rhythm – Lilt in Labour*. Manchester: Paton Lawrence & Co.

Landau, T. (1995) 'Source-Work, the Viewpoints and Composition: What Are They?', in: M. Dixon & J. Smith (eds), *Anne Bogart: Viewpoints*. Lyme: Smith and Kraus, pp. 13–30.

Langer, S. (1953) *Feeling and Form*. London: Routledge.

Latham, A. (2012) 'Simultaneity', in: *The Oxford Companion to Music. Oxford Music Online*. Available Online: http://www.oxfordmusiconline.com /subscriber/article/opr/t114/e6203 (Accessed 13 March 2012).

Lavy, J. (2005) 'Theoretical Foundations of Grotowski's Total Act, Via Negativa, and Conjunctio Oppositorum'. *The Journal of Religion and Theatre*, 4 (2), pp. 175–188.

Law, A. & Gordon, M. (1996) *Meyerhold, Eisenstein and Biomechanics: Actor Training in Revolutionary Russia*. London: McFarland & Co Inc.

Leach, R. (1993) *Vsevolod Meyerhold*. Cambridge: Cambridge University Press.

Lecoq, J. (2006) *Theatre of Movement and Gesture*. D. Bradby (ed.). London: Taylor & Francis.

Lee, J. W. (2003) *Dalcroze by Any Other Name: Eurhythmics in Early Modern Theatre and Dance*. Texas: Texas Tech University.

Lerdahl, F. & Jackendoff, R. (1983) *Generative Theory of Tonal Music*. London: MIT Press.

Lex, B. (1979) 'The Neurobiology of Ritual Trance', in: E. D'Aquili (ed.), *The Spectrum of Ritual: A Biogenetic Structural Analysis*. New York: Columbia University Press, pp. 117–151.

Locke, D. (1998) *Drum Gahu: An Introduction to African Rhythm*. Tempe, AZ: White Cliffs Media.

London, J. (2004) *Hearing in Time: Psychological Aspects of Musical Meter: Psychological Aspects of Musical Meter*. New York: Oxford University Press.

Love, L. (2002) 'Resisting the "Organic"', in: Phillip B. Zarrilli (ed.), *Acting (Re) considered: A Theoretical and Practical Guide*. 2nd edition. Abingdon: Routledge, pp. 227–290.

Maffei, V., Indovina, I., Zago, M., La Scaleia, B., Bosco, G., Lacquaniti, F. & Gravano, S. (2015), 'Gravity in the Brain as a Reference for Space and Time Perception'. *Multisensory Research*, 28 (5–6), pp. 397–426.

Malaev-Babel, A. (ed.) (2011) *The Vakhtangov Sourcebook*. Abingdon, Oxfordshire: Taylor & Francis.

Malloch, S. & Trevarthen, C. (eds) (2008) *Communicative Musicality: Exploring the Basis of Human Companionship*. Oxford: Oxford University Press.

Mandelshtam, O. (1990) *The Eyesight of Wasps, Poems*. Second Impression edition. London: Angel Books.

Marshall, L. (2001) *The Body Speaks: Performance and Physical Expression*. London: Methuen.

Martin, J. (2004) *The Intercultural Performance Handbook*. London: Routledge.

Marx, K. (2008) *The Poverty of Philosophy*. New York: Cosimo Classics.

Materic, M. & Hulton, P (1997) *Organic Sequences in the Theatre*. Exeter: Arts Archives [DVD].

Mauss, M. (1973) 'Techniques of the Body'. *Economy and Society*, 2 (1), pp. 70–88.

McNeill, W. H. (1995) *Keeping Together in Time: Dance and Drill in Human History*. Cambridge: Harvard University Press.

Merlin, B. (2007) *The Complete Stanislavsky Toolkit*. London: Nick Hern Books.

Meschonnic, H. (1982) *Critique du Rythme: Anthropologie Historique du Langage*, Lagrasse: Verdier.

Meyer, L.B. (1961) *Emotion and Meaning in Music*. London: University of Chicago Press.

Meyer-Dinkgräfe, D. (2006) 'Simultaneity, Theatre and Consciousness', in: R. Ascott (ed.), *Engineering Nature: Art and Consciousness in the Post-Biological Era*. Bristol: Intellect, pp. 247–251.

Meyerhold, V. (1981) *Meyerhold at Work*. P. Schmidt (ed.), Manchester: Carcanet New Press.

Meyerhold, V. (1991) *Meyerhold on Theatre*. E. Braun (ed.), London: Methuen.

Meyerhold, V. (1998) *Meyerhold Speaks, Meyerhold Rehearses*. A. Gladkov (ed.), Amsterdam: Harwood Academic.

Michon, P. (2011) 'A Short History of Rhythm Theory Since the 1970s'. *Rhuthmos* website. Available Online: http://rhuthmos.eu/spip .php?article462 (Accessed 7 June 2016).

Michon, P. (2016) 'Could Rhythm Become a New Scientific Paradigm for the Humanities?', in: *Rhythm as Pattern and Variation: Political, Social & Artistic Inflections*, 23 April 2016. London: Goldsmiths College.

Middleton, D. (2001) 'At Play in the Cosmos: The Theatre and Ritual of Nicolás Núñez'. *TDR – The Drama Review*, 45 (4), pp. 42–63.

Middleton, D. (2008) '"Secular Sacredness" in the Ritual Theatre of Nicolás Núñez', *Performance Research: A Journal of the Performing Arts*, 13 (3), pp. 41–54.

Miner, J. B. (1903) 'Motor, Visual and Applied Rhythms: An Experimental Study and a Revised Explanation'. *The Psychological Review: Monograph Supplements*, 5 (4), pp. 1–106.

Mitter, S. (1988) 'Inner and Outer: "Open Theatre" in Peter Brook and Joseph Chaikin', *Journal of Dramatic Theory and Criticism*, 3 (1), pp. 47–70.

Mitter, S. & Shevtsova, M. (2004) *Fifty Key Theatre Directors*. Abingdon: Routledge.

Molik, Z. & Campo, G. (2010) *Zygmunt Molik's Voice and Body Work: The Legacy of Jerzy Grotowski*. Abingdon: Routledge.

Morris, E. (2009) 'Sources of Rhythm: An Anthropocosmic Enquiry', in: *Grotowski: After – Alongside – Around – Ahead*. 15 June 2009. University of Kent: Available Online: http://hud.academia.edu/EilonMorris /Papers/1686130/Sources_of_Rhythm_An_Anthropocosmic_Enquiry (Accessed 28 July 2012).

Morris, E. (2013) 'Via Rhythmós: An Investigation of Rhythm in Psychophysical Actor Training'. Unpublished PhD Thesis, University of Huddersfield.

Nisenson, E. (2009) *Ascension: John Coltrane and His Quest*. New York: Da Capo Press.

Núñez, N. (1996) *Anthropocosmic Theatre: Rite in the Dynamics of Theatre*. D. Middleton (ed.), Trans. R. Fitzimons. Amsterdam: Routledge.

Núñez, N. (2016) *Swimming in the Inner Source*. Audio Recording from workshop run at Huddersfield University, 31 May–1 June 2016.

Oida, Y. & Marshall, L. (1997) *The Invisible Actor*. Abingdon: Routledge.

Omote A. (ed.) (1978) *Zeami Zenchiku (Nihon shisô taikei, v. 24)*. Tokyo: Iwanami shoten.

Osiński, Z. (1986) *Grotowski and His Laboratory*. New York: PAJ Publications.

Osiński, Z. (2009) 'Grotowski and the Reduta Tradition', in: P. Allain (ed.), *Grotowski's Empty Room*, London: Seagull Books, pp. 19–54.

Overlie, M. (2006a) 'The Six Viewpoints', in: A. Bartow (ed.), *Training of the American Actor*, New York: Nick Hern Books, pp. 187–221.

Overlie, M. (2006b) *The SSTEMS: The Six Viewpoints*, Available Online: http://www.sixviewpoints.com/Theory_3.html (Accessed 19 June 2016).

Pavis, P. (1991) *Theatre at the Crossroads of Culture*. London: Routledge.

Pavis, P. (1999) *Dictionary of the Theatre: Terms, Concepts and Analysis*. Toronto: University of Toronto Press.

Pavis, P. (2003) *Analyzing Performance: Theater, Dance and Film*. Trans. D. Williams, Ann Arbor: The University of Michigan Press.

Penman, J. & Becker, J. (2009) 'Religious Ecstatics, "Deep Listeners", and Musical Emotion'. *Empirical Musicological Review*, 4 (1), pp. 49–70.

Petit, L. (2009) *The Michael Chekhov Handbook: For the Actor*. Abingdon: Routledge.

Phillips-Silver, J. & Trainor, L. (2008) 'Vestibular Influence on Auditory Metrical Interpretation'. *Brain and Cognition*, 67 (1), pp. 94–102.

Phillips-Silver, J., Aktipis, C. A. & G. A. Bryant (2010) 'The Ecology of Entrainment: Foundations of Coordinated Rhythmic Movement'. *Music Perception: An Interdisciplinary Journal*, 28 (1), pp. 3–14.

Piette, A. (1997) 'In the Loneliness of Cities: The Hopperian Accents of David Mamet's "Edmond"'. *Studies in the Humanities*, 24 (1), pp. 43–51.

Pitches, J. (2003) *Vsevolod Meyerhold*. London: Routledge.

Pitches, J. (2005) *Science and the Stanislavsky Tradition of Acting*. Abingdon: Routledge.

Postlewait, T. (1988) 'Simultaneity in Modern Stage Design and Drama'. *Journal of Dramatic Theory and Criticism*, 3 (1), pp. 5–28.

Prattki, T. (2016) *LISPA, Berlin Prospectus 2016*. Available Online: http://www.lispa.co.uk/pdf/Lispa-devising-theatre-and-performance-2016.pdf (Accessed 1 May 2016).

Quinn, S. F. (2005) *Developing Zeami: The Noh Actor's Attunement in Practice*. Honolulu: University of Hawaii Press.

Read, A. (2007) *Theatre, Intimacy and Engagement: The Last Human Venue*. Basingstoke: Palgrave Macmillan UK.

Ribot, T. A. (2006) *The Psychology of the Emotions*. Whitefish: Kessinger Publishing Company.

Richardson, H. (2010) 'Ariane Mnouchkine and the Theatre du Soleil', in: A. Hodge (ed.), *Actor Training*. Abingdon: Taylor & Francis, pp. 250–267.

Rios, D. & Katz, F. (1975) 'Some Relationships between Music and Hallucinogenic Ritual. The "Jungle Gym" in Consciousness'. *Ethos*, 3 (1), pp. 64–76.

Roach, J. (1993) *The Player's Passion: Studies in the Science of Acting*. New edition. Ann Arbor: The University of Michigan Press.

Roesner, D. (2014) *Musicality in Theatre: Music as Model, Method and Metaphor in Theatre-Making*. Farnham: Ashgate.

Rogers, C. M. (1966) 'The Influence of Dalcroze Eurhythmics in the Contemporary Theatre'. Unpublished PhD Thesis, Louisiana State University.

Rosenbaum, D. A. (1998) *Timing of Behavior: Neural, Psychological, and Computational Perspectives*. Cambridge: Massachusetts Institute of Technology Press.

Rössler, O. E. (1998) *Endophysics: The World as an Interface*. Singapore: World Scientific.

Rouget (1985) *Music and Trance: A Theory of the Relations Between Music and Possession*. Chicago: Chicago University Press.

Rowell, L. (1979) 'Aristoxenus on Rhythm'. *Journal of Music Theory*, 23 (1), pp. 63–79.

Ruckmich, C. A. (1913) 'The Rôle of Kinaesthesis in the Perception of Rhythm'. *The American Journal of Psychology*, 24 (3), pp. 305–359.

Rudlin, J. (1986) *Jacques Copeau*. Cambridge: CUP Archive.

Sachs, C. (1952) 'Rhythm and Tempo: An Introduction'. *The Musical Quarterly*, XXXVIII (3), pp. 384–398.

Sakai, K., Hikosaka, O., Miyauchi, S., Takino, R., Tamada, T., Iwata, N. K. & Nielsen, M. (1999) 'Neural Representation of a Rhythm Depends on Its Interval Ratio'. *The Journal of Neuroscience*, 19 (22), pp. 10074–10081.

Sauer, D. K. & Sauer, J. A. (eds) (2003) *David Mamet: A Research and Production Sourcebook*. Westport: Praeger.

Schechner, R. (1988) *Performance Theory*. London: Routledge.

Schmidt, P. (1978) 'Discovering Meyerhold: Traces of a Search'. *October, 7: (Soviet Revolutionary Culture)*, pp. 71–82.

Schmiedtová, B. (2004) *At the Same Time: the Expression of Simultaneity in Learner Varieties*. New York: Mouton de Gruyter.

Schögler, B. & Trevarthen, C. (2007) 'To Sing and Dance Together: From Infants to Jazz', in: S. Bråten (ed.), *On Being Moved: From Mirror Neurons to Empathy*. Philadelphia: John Benjamins Publishing, pp. 281–302.

Schweitzer, K. G. (2003) 'Afro-Cuban Bata Drum Aesthetics: Developing Individual and Group Technique, Sound and Identity'. Unpublished PhD Thesis: University of Maryland. Available Online: http://www.lib.umd.edu/drum/bitstream/1903/55/1/dissertation.pdf (Accessed 22 October 2008).

SCUDD (2013) 'Introducing Alba Technique-a new tool for actors (Workshop)'. Email Correspondence.

Sethares, W. (2007). *Rhythm and Transforms*. Madison: Springer.

Shawn, T. (1954) *Every Little Movement: A Book About Francois Delsarte*. Pittsfield: Eagle Print and Binding.

Shepherd, S. (2006) *Theatre, Body and Pleasure*. Abingdon: Taylor & |Francis.

Spychalski, T. & Ziółkowski, G. (2015) 'On the Long and Winding Road: Teo Spychalski Talks to Grzegorz Ziółkowski', in: P. Allain (ed.), *Voices from Within: Grotowski's Polish Collaborators*. Polish Theatre Perspectives, pp. 150–160. Available Online: https://culturehub.co/works/On_the_Long_and_Winding_Road (Accessed 29 May 2016).

Stanislavski, K. (1952) *My Life in Art*. London: Routledge.

Stanislavski, K. (1967) *Stanislavsky: On the Art of the Stage*. 2nd edition. London: Faber & Faber.

Stanislavski, K. (1986a) *Iz Zapisnykh Knizhek* [Notebooks] *(Volume I)*. Vladimir Prokof'ev (ed.). Moscow: VTO.

Stanislavski, K. (1986b) *Iz Zapisnykh Knizhek* [Notebooks] *(Volume II)*. Vladimir Prokof'ev (ed.). Moscow: VTO.

Stanislavski, K. (2008) *An Actor's Work: A Student's Diary*. Abingdon: Routledge.

Stanislavski, K. (2010) *An Actor's Work on a Role*. Abingdon: Routledge.

Stanislavski, K. & Rumyantsev, P. (1998) *Stanislavski on Opera*. Abingdon: Routledge.

Strasberg, L. (1965) *Strasberg at the Actors Studio: Tape-recorded Sessions*. R. Hethmon (ed.), New York: Viking Press.

Strogatz, S. H. (2004) *Sync: The Emerging Science of Spontaneous Order*. London: Penguin Books.

Suzuki, T. (1986) *The Way of Acting: The Theatre Writings of Tadashi Suzuki*. New York: Theatre Communications Group.

Thaut, M. (2007) *Rhythm, Music, and the Brain: Scientific Foundations and Clinical Applications*. Abingdon: Routledge.

Tian, M. (2008) 'Re-Theatricalizing the Theatre of the Grotesque: Meyerhold's "Theatre of Convention" and Traditional Chinese Theatre', in: *The Poetics of Difference and Displacement*. Hong Kong: Hong Kong University Press, pp. 61–82.

Toepfer, K. (1997) *Empire of Ecstasy: Nudity and Movement in German Body Culture, 1910–1935*. Berkely: University of California Press.

Toporkov, V. O. (1998) *Stanislavski in Rehearsal*. London: Routledge.

Turner, V. (1969) *The Ritual Process: Structure and Anti-structure*. London: Routledge.

Vaitl, D. et al. (2005) 'Psychobiology of Altered States of Consciousness'. *Psychological Bulletin*, 131 (1), pp. 98–127.

Vakhtangov, E. (1947) 'Preparing for the Role: From the Diary of E Vakhtangov', in: T. Cole (ed.), *Acting: A Handbook of the Stanislavski Method*. New York: Crown, pp. 116–124.

Volkonski, S. (1913) *Vyrazitel'nyĭ Cheloviek: Stsenicheskoe Vospitanĭe Zhesta: Po Delsartu* [Expressive Man: Shaping Stage Gesture (Following Delsarte)]. St. Peterburg: Apollon.

Vrobel, S. (2008) 'Fractal Time: Extended Observer Perspectives', in: S. Vrobel, O. Rössler & T. Marks-Tarlow (eds), *Simultaneity: Temporal Structures and Observer Perspectives*. Hackensack NJ: World Scientific, pp. 3–14.

Vrobel, S. (2011) *Fractal Time: Why a Watched Kettle Never Boils*. London: World Scientific.

Vrobel, S., Rössler, O. E. & Marks-Tarlow, T. (eds) (2008) *Simultaneity: Temporal Structures and Observer Perspectives*. Hackensack, NJ: World Scientific.

Waterman, E. (2014) 'Improvised Trust', in: A. Heble & R. Caines (eds), *The Improvisation Studies Reader: Spontaneous Acts*. Abingdon: Routledge. pp. 59–62.

Weibel, P. (2008) 'Simultaneity – The Next Revolution in Physics', in: S. Vrobel, O. Rössler & T. Marks-Tarlow (eds), *Simultaneity: Temporal Structures and Observer Perspectives*. Hackensack, NJ: World Scientific. pp. v–viii.

Wetzsteon, R. (2001) 'David Mamet: Remember That Name', in: L. Kane (ed.), *David Mamet in Conversation*. Ann Arbor: University of Michigan Press, pp. 9–16.

Whyman, R. (2008) *The Stanislavsky System of Acting: Legacy and Influence in Modern Performance*. Cambridge: Cambridge University Press.

Whyman, R. (2013) *Stanislavski: The Basics*. Abingdon: Routledge.

Williams, D. (1991) *Peter Brook and the 'Mahabharata': Critical Perspectives*. London: Routledge.

Woodbury, L. J. (1962) 'The Director's Use of Rhythm'. *Educational Theatre Journal*, 14 (1), pp. 23–28.

Woolf, V. (1980) *The Letters of Virginia Woolf, Volume III, 1923–1928*. N. Nicolson & J. Trautmann (eds.), New York: Harvest Books.

Wundt, W. (1897) *Outlines of Psychology*. Trans. C. Judd, London: Williams & Norgate.

Yampolsky, M. (1994) Kuleshov's Experiments and the New Anthropology of the Actor, in: R. Taylor & I. Christie (eds), *Inside the Film Factory: New Approaches to Russian and Soviet Cinema*. London: Routledge, pp. 31–50.

Zarrilli, P. (2007) 'An Enactive Approach to Understanding Acting'. *Theatre Journal*, 59 (4), pp. 635–647.

Zarrilli, P. (2008) *Psychophysical Acting*. Abingdon: Routledge.

Zarrilli, P. (2011) 'Altered Consciousness in Performance: West and East', in: E. Cardeña & M. Winkelman (eds), *Altering Consciousness: Multidisciplinary Perspectives*. Santa Barbara, CA: ABC-CLIO, pp. 301–326.

Zarrilli, P. (2013) 'Psychophysical Training and the Formation of an Ensemble', in: J. Britton (ed.), *Encountering Ensemble*. London: Methuen Drama, pp. 369–380.

Zeami, M. (2008) *Zeami, Performance Notes*, T. Hare (ed. and trans), New York: Columbia University Press.

Zinder, D. (2002) *Body Voice Imagination: A Training for the Actor*. London: Routledge.

Zinman, T. (1992) 'Jewish Aporia: The Rhythm of Talking in Mamet', *Theatre Journal*, 44 (2), pp. 207–215.

INDEX

Note: The letter 'n' following locators refers to notes and the bold locators refer to glossary and headings.

accent(s) 4, 54, 91, 251 n.7
  attention to 146
  between 103, 186
  definition of **240–1**
  marking 189
  metric 188, 205
  musical 145
  perception of 251 n.8
  physical 187
  syllables 227, 242–3
actualized instant 140, 168, 174–7.
  See also here and now
Adams, Judith 7, 209–12, 216
Aeschylus 8
Alba Emoting Technique 38–9
Alekseev, Vladimir 249 n.3
Alexander Technique 250 n.4
alternation 10, 28, 29, 179, 183, 192,
  240–1
Ang Gey Pin 236
animal 57, 84, 91, 133, 145, 154, 164
  aspect 164
  associations 255 n.6
  imitation of 81–2, 139, 253 n.2
  territory 19
Ansermet, Ernst 249 n.2
Appia, Adolphe 53, 80, 236
Aristotle 9, 10, 20–1, 20
Aristoxenus 9–10, 185, 247 n.2,
  258 n.1
Armstrong, Frankie 225–30

Arnshtam, Lev 29
Artaud, Antonin 91, 143, 236,
  254 n.2
attention 112, 117, 140–1, 172, 179,
  183, 193
  and accent 240
  on ensemble 113, 115, 133, 193
  flickering 183, 191
  and movement 101, 119, 169,
    173, 186–8
  on the present 170, 174–7, 191
  and simultaneity 182–3, 185–6,
    256 n.7
  sustained 165, 166, 177–8, 193–6
  synchronized 146
audience 15–17, 41, 65, 103, 179,
  213–16
  attention 20, 184–5
  communication with 12–14, 29,
    38, 50, 51, 64, 202–7, 212,
    219, 222
  expectations 21, 37, 75, 107,
    122, 129
  synchronization 33, 140, 143,
    145–6 (See also entrainment)
Australia 109, 252 n.1, 252 n.2
authentic 35–8, 150–1, 203

Bakhtin, Mikhail 257 n.1
Barba, Eugenio 12, 16, 29–30, 155–7,
  245, 252 n.11, 254–5 n.4

Barrault, Jean-Louis 91, 254 n.2
Barthes, Roland 220
beat(s)
    definition of **241**
    dramatic 183, 258 n.2
    heart 30, 63–4, 147, 157, 241
    internal 66
    in language 201, 212, 221
    metric 39, 102–4
    musical 122, 126, 146, 228
    number of 62, 64, 88, 188–94,
        234, 256 n.5
    off-beat 103–4, 186, 192, 258 n.1
    pause 211
    per minute 245
    per second 147, 253n.6
    pulsing 16 (*See also* pulse)
    steady 10, 30, 61, 129, 242
    subdivision of 69
    synchronising 33, 242, 254 n.8
    underlying 236
Beck, Jessica 38–9
Becker, Judith 139–40, 149–51
Beckett, Samuel 14, 206
Belgrade, Daniel 112
Benedetti, Jean 60, 62–3
Benveniste, Émile 8
Berry, Cicely 14, 204–6, 221,
    250 n.6, 257 n.1, 258 n.4
Bing, Suzanne 76, 254 n.2, 255 n6.
    See also Copeau, Jacques
    ball games 86, 90, 116–17
    Dramatic Instinct 85–6
    Katan 250 n.7
    Musique Corporelle **87–92**
    New York 83–5
    teaching children 80–4, 87
    Vieux-Colombier (company) 77,
        83
    Vieux-Colombier (school) 85–91
    voice and text training 86–7
bit (*kusok*) 258 n.2
Blacking, John 145
Bloch, Susana 38

Bodden, Shawn 249 n.8
Bode, Rudolf 28, 104, 251 n.10
body 9, 12, 28, 30, 32, 34–6, 49,
    53, 59, 64, 84, 104, 123, 132,
    141, 164, 173. 229. *See also*
    brain
    awareness of 134, 169, 174,
        175–7, 183, 191
    bodily 34–5, 38, 101, 165
    culture 26–7
    and language 98, 204, 210, 212,
        218, 221, 223
    limbic system 147–8, 254 n.7
    memory 159–60, 164, 255 n.9
    and mind 27, 48, 52, 55–6, 142,
        169, 171–2, 244
    muscularity 29, 145, 205
    neurophysiological 146–8 (*See*
        also psychophysical)
    poetry and 217
    synchronization of 145
    techniques 78, 84, 112, 163, 165,
        168, 235, 254 n.1
    vestibular system 253 n.3
Bogart, Anne 76, 121–36, 160, 196,
    228, 252 n.5
Boleslavsky, Richard 7, 11, 249 n.4
Boris Godunov 69, 249 n.1
boundary loss 139, 141, 150, 172,
    179, 194, 195
brain 50, 144–8, 210, 215, 242. *See
    also* body
    amygdala 254 n.7
    right hemisphere 144
    sub-cortical 147–8, 254 n.7
    theta waves 147, 253–4 n.6
Bread in the Bone 237
breath 16, 20, 29, 47, 50, 59, 91,
    103, 139, 158, 217, 255 n.3
    awareness of 183, 186
    cardiovascular 147
    control 127, 147
    duration of 88
    and emotion 38, 63

ensemble 17, 119
luft-pause 100, **242**
pranic breathing 63–4
synchronization of 145, 146–8,
    157, 169
of the text 29
and voice, 86, 205, 207, 211,
    218, 220–1, 223, 229
Brecht, Bertolt 17, 236
    Brechtian theory of rhythm (Pavis)
        201–3
    gestus 202
Britton, John 76, 244
    ball game **116–19**, 175, 192
    Duende 109, 237
    energetic 109, 116, 118–19
    Self-With-Others 112–13, 181, 196
Brook, Peter 3, 16, 236, 239, 249 n.5
    Orghast 218–19, 258 n.3
Bruce, Lenny 21
Bücher, Karl 31
Burrows, Jonathan 237

Cage, John 39, 246
Calonarang 147
Cardeña, Etzel 176
Carnicke, Sharon 248 n.2, 249 n.1
Castaneda, Carlos 168, 255 n.7
The Cat and the Old Rat 81
chaos 41, 191, 194, 223
character 8, 48, 65–9, 81–2, 85, 112
    qualities 13, 22, 118, 135
    role 11, 15, 19, 20–1, 27, 35, 55,
        87, 141, 182–3, 206, 244
Chekhov, Anton 67
Chekhov, Michael 33, 65, 140, 236,
    247 n.2, 249 n.4, 252 n.4
The Cherry Orchard 67
children 19, 112
    condition of childhood 161, 165
    education 80–4
    infants 17, 146, 229, 242
    teenagers 85–7
    toddlers 254 n.8

Chinese Opera 96–7, 99, 153
Christopher, Karen 21, 212–16
Cieślak, Ryszard 158
circus 102
Claudel, Paul 249 n.2
Coe, Chris 225–30
Coltrane, John 115
comedy 21, 201
communitas 17, 145, 149–51,
    178–9, 195, 196, 241
Complicite 237
consciousness 29, 50, 164, 235
    altered states of 139–42, 143–51,
        157, 162–3, 162, 165, 171–2,
        175–7, 178–9, 196, 253 n.5,
        255 n.3
    awareness 141, 147, 162, 164,
        170–2, 183, 210
    dual 113, 176
    subconsciousness 50, 132
    unconscious 19, 37, 103, 169,
        213, 253 n.6
Constable, Paule 40
Copeau, Jacques 28, 53, 77–87, 91,
    202, 236, 246, 250 n.1. *See
    also* Bing, Suzanne
    ball games 86, 117
    breath 29
    continuous/discontinuous
        14–15
    follow-through 14, 242
    raccourci 101, **244**
    Vieux-Colombier (company) 77,
        78, 80, 83, 84, 91, 250 n.3,
        254 n.2
    Vieux-Colombier (school) 85–91,
        250 n.3
counterpoint. *See under* simultaneity
Craig, Gordon 80
Cuba 181, 247–8 n.3
Cull, Laura 247 n.1, 248 n.4
    immanent authorship 124–5
    plurality of presents 195
Cunningham, Merce 39, 246

D'Aquili, Eugene 149
Dalcroze. *See* Jaques-Dalcroze, Émile
dance 4, 32, 40, 87, 234, 250 n.3,
    251 n.9
    Afro-Caribbean 153, 164
    animal 139, 145, 164
    Central American 153, 253 n.2
    Conchero 253 n.2
    ecstatic 139, 253 n.3
    ensemble 113–14, 149–51
    fairy 157
    of the Furies 81
    Indian 153
    Manitoulin 162
    modern 28, 33, 34
    Osip Mandelstam 218
    sacred 143–51, 153, 160–2,
        163–5, 165, 168
    Salpuri 147
    of Shiva 153
    theory 106
    of thought 50
    Tibetan mosastic 167
    Tloque Nahuaque 150, 254 n.9
    training 52–3, 56, 79, 84, 85, 88,
        92, 189
    yanvalou 164
Dambhala 164
Dead Souls 67
Decroux, Étienne 91, 236, 244, 250
    n10, 254 n.2
deep listening 140
Deleuze, Gilles 19, 103, 141–2, 248
    n.4, 251 n.6
Delsarte, François 11, 27, 32–3, 34,
    39, 154–5, 157, 203, 255 n.6
Democritus 8
devising 12, 77, 121, 126–7, 155–60,
    187–8, 236
Diaghilev, Sergei 249 n.2
directing 98, 100–1, 104, 107, 121,
    123, 124–5, 133–4, 201, 209,
    221–4, 234–6
Doğantan-Dack, Mine 34
Dorcy, Jean 91

dramaturgy 19–20, 127, 206, 224,
    233, 241, 245
drumming 144, 146–7, 148, 162,
    168, 247–8 n.3, 250 n.7, 254
    n.8, 258 n.1
D'Udine, Jean, 32, 248 n.2
Dullin, Charles 85, 91, 154, 236, 254
    n.2, 255 n.6
Duncan, Isadora 27, 28, 34, 59, 99,
    104, 203, 242, 248 n.1
duration 10, 11, 88, 91, 99, 213–15
    agogic accents 240
    extended 162, 168, 171, 177–9
    journeying 186–8
    note 156, 243
    and simultaneity 182
    Viewpoints **129–31**
dynamics 58, 68, 86, 87, 116–19,
    144, 187, 240, 242
dynamo-rhythm 250 n.10

ecstasy 30, **139–42**, 144, 149–51,
    163, 165–6, 194–5, **241–2**,
    253 n.1, 253 n.2
Edmond 206
Einstein, Albert 256 n.2
Eisenstein, Sergei 103–4, 236, 244,
    251 n.9
Elevator Repair Services 124, 237
Eliade, Mercia 139, 253 n.1
Elliott, Hilary 184
The Embezzlers 68
embodiment 20, 65, 83–4, 139,
    157–60, 223
    embodied sense of rhythm 56,
        102, 120, 165–6, 185–92
    embodied understanding 5, 23,
        167–8, 204–5, 234, 237
    of language 204–6, 208, 212,
        220–4
    of rhythmic principles 89–93, 136
emotion/mood 8, **13–15**, 32–3, 36,
    38–9, **49–51**, 60–7, 81, 91,
    97, 202, 212, 254 n.7
endo-perspective 185

ensemble 61–2, 64–6, 68, 123–5, 135–6
  aesthetic 23
  defining **113–14**
  ensemble/group rhythm 18, 23, 118, 132, 136, **149–51**
  training 12, 17–18, 76, 85–7, 109–20, 121, 129–35
entrainment 18, 118, **145–51**, 168, 176–8, 194–5, **242**. *See also* synchronization
erscheinung 28
eurhythmics. See under Jaques-Dalcroze, Émile
eurhythmy. See under Laban, Rudolf
Evgeny Onegin 249 n.1

Fechner, Gustav 244
Ferdinandov, Boris 33
Fersen, Alexander 143
film-making 33, 36, 103. *See also* video design
First World War 53, 80
Fischer-Lichte, Erika 19–20, 39, 204
Flatischler, Reinhard 181, 241, 256 n.4
France 28, 77, 101, 181, 220, 244, 250 n.2
Frost, Anthony 75, 250 n.4

games 77, 79, 80–1, 84, 86, 89–90. *See also* play
  ball games 86, 90, **116–19**, 175, 252 n.4
Gardzienice Theatre Association 236, 255 n.3
Garoute, Tiga 163
Gastev, Alexi 31
Gaudete 220, 222–3
Gaulier, Philippe 91, 236
George, Kathleen 257 n.1
Germany 31, 53, 242, 244, 251 n.10, 257 n.1
gesture 14, 34, 59, 69, 98–9, 101, 106, 116, 121, 123, 129, 132–3, 155–7, 187, 202, 244, 245, 255 n.3

Giannoti, Elana 218
Glück, Christopher 81
Goat Island 124–5, 213, 237
Goebbels, Heiner 98
Gołaj, Mariusz 255 n.3
Goodridge, Janet 12, 14, 246
Gordon, Mel 11, 55
Granville-Barker, Harley 249 n.2
gravity 34–5, 51, 101, 191
  centre of 32, 169
Greece
  Ancient Greek 4, 8–12, 141, 199, 242, 248 n.1, 258 n.1
  music 9, 88
  theatre 8, 10, 85, 218–19
Greene, James 217, 258 n.1
Grimes, Roland 162
Grotowski, Jerzy 16
  animal aspect 164
  art as vehicle 164
  conjunctio oppositorum 158–9, 163
  improvisation 75, 154
  Laboratory Theatre 57, 155, 157
  movement which is repose 163, 171, 174, 196
  Objective Drama 163–5
  organic v mechanic 30–1
  physical scores 155–60
  plastiques **158–60**
  running 163, 170
  slow walking 162–3, 255 n.7 (*See also* Núñez, Nicolás)
  Theatre of Sources 161–3, 168–9
  verticality 141, 163, **173–4**
  warrior 144
Guardia, Helena 167
Guattari, Félix 19, 103, 248 n.4, 251 n.6
Gumbrecht, Hans Ulrich 4

habit 32, 56, 62, 97–8, 117, 125, 129–31, 134–5, 161, 162, 169–70, 178–9
Haiti 161, 163–4
Hamlet 65

here and now 170–1, **174–8**, 182,
    191. *See also* actualized
    instant; presence; simultaneity
Hobsbaum, Philip 102
Hoeing 228–9
Houghton, Norris 249 n.9
Howarth, Jessmin 83–5
Hughes, Ted 220, 258 n.3
Huygens, Christian 242

Ikoniadou, Eleni 248 n.4
immanence 124, 132, 141–2
improvisation 36, 47, **75–6**, 77, 85,
    87–8, 91–3, 107, **135–6**, 175,
    178, 189, 196, 238
    ensemble 109, 111–16, 121,
        123–5, 124, 129–34, 134–5
    in music 76, 95–9, 111–16, 228–9
    score 159–60, 245
impulse 32, 58, 117, 131–2, 134,
    144, 159–60, 175, 229, 242
India 51, 153, 161, 247–8 n.3
inner rhythm 47–8, 51, 55–6, 63, 83,
    90, 145–8, 160, 171, 229
International Centre of Theatre
    Research 258 n.3
Italy 80, 229

Jackendoff, Ray 240–1
Japan 22–3, 99, 246, 247, 250 n.7,
    252–3 n.5
Jaques-Dalcroze, Émile 27, 28, 32–3,
    59, 99, 104, 157, 251 n.10
    eurhythmics 52–4, 60, 65–6, 69,
        78–81, **83–5**, 89, **242**, 248
        n.1, 251 n.10
    Hellerau 53, 249 n.2, 250 n.3
    tripartite rhythm **246** (*See also*
        under Meyerhold, Vsevolod)
Jarrett, Keith 114
jo, ha, kyu 246
Judson Church Theatre 124

Kinaesthetic response (Viewpoints)
    131–2
kineseos taxis 9

Komissarzhevsky, Fyodor 47
Kozintsev, Grigori 26–7
Kuleshov, Lev 33, 248 n.2
Kusler, Barbara 87
kusok (bit) 258 n.2

Laban, Rudolf 27
    effort analysis 31
    effort and recovery 28
    eurhythmy 28, **242**, 248 n.1
    Greek metres 13
    tripartite rhythm **246** (*See also*
        under Meyerhold, Vsevolod)
Landau, Tina 76, 121–35, 196
Langer, Susanne 106, 187, 246
language. *See also* voice
    as action 202, 204, 205, 207
    poetic 10, 13–14, 102–3, 201,
        204–6, 207–8, 217–24, 225,
        226–30, 240, 242–3, 258 n.4
    prose 10, 205
Lawrence, Fredrick 31
laws of rhythm 28, 34–5, 55–6, 100,
    203
Lecoq, Jacques 7, 16, 91, 236
    seven levels of tension 249 n.9
Lee, James 249 n.2
legato 100–1
Lerdahl, Fred 240–1
Lex, Barbara 144
lighting 19, 35, 39–41, 58
Lili 47
live streaming 37
Living Theatre 124, 236
Locke, David 256 n.7
London, Justin 256 n.7
London International School of
    Performing Arts (LISPA) 91
Lorre, Peter 202
Love, Lauren 36
A Lover's Discourse 220
Lung-Gom-Pa 255 n.3

Mamet, David 206–7
Mandafounis, Ioannis 218

Mandelstam, Osip 217–18
Mann ist Mann 202
Marceau, Marcel 91
Marriage 27
Marthaler, Christopher 236
Martin, John 11
Maxfield, Melinda 146
A May Night 249 n.2
mechanical 3–4, 26, **30–3**, 40–2,
        48–51, 53–8, 89, 100–4, 141,
        146, 157–9, 171, 205
Medea 219
meditation 143, 171, 183, 241,
        253 n.1, 255 n.2, 255 n.7
Mei Lanfang 97
Merlin, Bella 11
Meschonnic, Henri 257 n.1
metaphysical 35, 48, 173
metre 106–7, 178, 193, 201, **242–3**
    a-metrical 9
    as distinct from rhythm **101–4**,
        251 n.6, 251 n.9
    Greek 10, 13, 242
    mechanical 30, 102–3
    musical 243
    poetic 10, 201, 205, 227, 242–3
metronomes, 33, 54, 61, 65–6, 69,
        248 n.3
Mexico 161, 167, 181, 253 n.2, 255
        n.2
Meyer, Leonard 257 n.2
Meyerhold, Vsevolod 3–4, 15–16,
        247 n.2, 249 n.1
    breath 29
    ensemble 18
    factory workers 32
    grotesque 22
    improvisation 95–6, 98–9
    luft-pause 100, **242**
    musical accompaniment 96–100,
        120
    musicality 22, 96
    musical training 96, 251 n.2
    rakurz 101, 244
    regarding Dalcroze 53, 99, 251 n.9

    regarding Stanislavski 45, 97
    rhythm v metre 101–4
    tempo 97, 100
    tormos 100, **246**
    tripartite rhythm **104–6**, 246,
        252 n.11
Michon, Pascal 25
Middleton, Deborah 150, 169, 171,
        174
Milhaud, Darius 249 n.2
mirroring exercise 89
Mnouchkine, Ariane 241
Molik, Zygmunt 57
monoideism 148
monotony 16, 144, 162
Montessori, Maria 250 n.4
A Month in the Country 67
Morris, Eilon
    Britton 109
    Núñez 167–8
    Orbits 181–96
Mosca, Roberta 218
Moscow Art Theatre (MAT) 18, 53,
        64. *See also* Stanislavski,
        Konstantin
Moscow Conservatoire 47
Mudra Space Awareness 183
music 16, 19
    accompaniment 29, 47, 89, 96,
        109–11, 119, 120, 125–7,
        135, 157
    Afro-Caribbean 153, 163–4, 181,
        247-8 n.3
    ancient Greece 8–10, 13
    and emotion 49
    ensemble **113–14**
    Hindustani 153, 247–8 n.3,
        256 n.4
    jazz 16, **110–13**, 114–15, 120
    as metaphor/model 34, 67,
        110–16, 119
    and movement 9, 52–4, 59–62, 79,
        81, 83, 87–91, 97–101, 102–4
    musicology 9, 25, 247 n.2
    opera 47–8, 59, 69–70, 97, 98–9

terminology 39, 54–9, 61–2, 65–6, 69, 83–4, 100–1, 122, 156, 189, 227–8, 240–6
training 29, 52–3
West African 194, 247–8 n.3, 256 n.7
musicality 12, 19, 22, 96, 100, 111, 120, 188, 201, 203, 205–6, 251 n.1
Myers, Bruce **217–20**, 224

Nahuatl 167
natural 15, 27–8, 32, 34, 36, 57, 59, 78, 81, 98, 141, 145, 150, 154–5, 210–11, 242, 255 n.3. *See also* organic
naturalistic 27, 36, 97–8
Naumburg, Margaret 84, 250 n.4
Neher, Andrew 147, 253 n.5
Nigeria 161
Nijinsky, Vaslav 249 n.2
Noh Theatre 22, 96–7, 153, 246, 250 n.7, 252 n.4, 252 n.5
Nübling, Sebastian 236
Núñez, Nicolás 143, 144
    actualized instant 140, 168, 174–7
    Anthropocosmic Theatre 167, 177
    contemplative running **170–2**, 190–2, 255 n.1, 255 n.2
    Huracán 190–1, 256 n.6
    slow walking 168–72, 255 n.7, 255 n.2 (*See also* Grotowski, Jerzy)
    Taller de Investigación Teatral (TRW) 167, 168, 181
    Theatre of Sources 163
    verticality **173–4**

OBRA Theatre Co. 220–4, 237
Odin Teatret 30, 236
Oida, Yoshi 252–3 n.5
Old Vic Theatre School 167
Open Theatre 124
organic **27–42**, 49, 51, 55, 141, 145, 158, 161, 164, 203. *See also* natural
    whole 8, 9

ornamentation theory (Pavis) 201
Orphée 81
Osiński, Zbigniew 154
Ouspenskaya, Maria 249 n.4
Overlie, Mary 121–3

Papi, Kate **220–4**
Paul, Norman 250 n.5
Pavis, Patrice 20, 57–8, 184, 201–3, 251 n.7
    definition of rhythm 11
Pavlov, Ivan 49
Pavlova, Anna 249 n.2
Paxton, Steve 124
Phillips-Silver, Jessica 118
Pieśń Kozła 237
Piette, Alain 206
Pinter, Harold 14, 206
Pitches, Jonathan 95, 104–5, 252 n.11
Pitoeff, Georges 249 n.2
Plato 9–11, 42
play 3, 59, 70, 76, 80–7, 89–90, 92–3, 153, 161, 186, 210, 250 n.4. *See also* games
playwrighting 7, 14, 29, 201, 203, 206–7, 209–12
Poland 161, 167, 168, 170, 241
postdramatic theatre 36
The Poverty of Philosophy 252 n.1
presence 65, 140, 141, 144–5, 161, 164, 174, 194, 195
psychophysical **15**, 17, 38, 45, **48–51**, 63, 112–13, 112, 144, 148, 168, 174, 179, 205, 244
pulse 33, 61, 67, 102–3, 110, 126–7, 144, 153, 186, 190, 192, 221, 228–9, 236, 241–2, 245, 255 n.3. *See also* beat

The Queen of Spades 99

Rachmaninoff, Sergei 249 n.2
Ramacharaka (Atkinson, William) 51
real. *See* authentic
real-time 36

Reduta Theatre Company 154
Reinhardt, Max 249 n.2
repetition 10–11, 18, 22, 29–30, 32,
    90, 102–4, 106, 110, 121,
    132–4, 143–4, 149–50, 162,
    177–8, 179, 194, 244, 251 n.6,
    253 n.3. *See also* monotony
rhein 8
rhythmisierung 31
Ribot, Theodule 15, 49
Rigoletto 249 n.1
Rilke, Rainer Maria 249 n.2
Robar, Maud 163
Roesner, David 12, 22, 111–12, 129,
    245
Rössler, Otto 185
Rouché, Jacques 249 n.2
Rouget, Gilbert 148, 253 n1, 252 n.5
Ruckmich, Christian 25–6
Rumyantsev, Pavel 65
Russia 3, 18, 25, 28, 31, 48, 52, 97,
    234, 258 n.2
Russian Association of Proletarian
    Writers (RAPP) 3, 247 n.2
rythmós 8–12

Sachs, Curt 4
Saint-Denis, Michel 91
Saint-Denis, Ruth 27
San Francisco Mime Troupe 124
Saratoga International Theatre
    Institute (SITI) 126, 237
Schechner, Richard 141, 253 n.1
schema 8
Schleef, Einar 204
score 62, 65, 97, 99, 100, 103,
    155–6, 158–60, 158, 187–90,
    221, 243, **244–5**
Second City 124
The Secret Marriage 249 n.1
Seeger, Pete 226
seven levels of tension 249 n.9
Shakespeare, William 14, 112, 212,
    219, 240, 243
Shaw, Bernard 249 n.2
Shiva 153

simultaneity 19–20, 181–5, 188, 237,
    245, 256 n.1
    counterpoint 64–6, 69, 100, 111,
        126, 195, 204, 236
    Einstein's definition of 256 n.2
    polyrhythm 195–6
Sinclair, Upton 249 n.2
singing 163
Sleeping Beauty 87
song 87–8, 144, 160, 212, 225–30
    vibratory 163–5
    work 17, 32, 229
Spychalski, Teo 161
staccato 100–1
Stanislavski, Konstantin **43**, 97, 154,
        155, 202, 234–5, 246, 249 n.1,
        249 n.2, 249 n.3, 249 n 4
    as if 229
    camel/ox rhythm 20
    clock metaphor 33, 146
    definition of rhythm 10–11
    ensemble 18
    eurhythmics **52–4**, 59–60
    First Studio 51, 55, 249 n.4
    given circumstances 56, 63–4,
        157
    here and now 175
    levels of rhythm 68, 249 n.9
    Music/Opera Studio 59, 249 n.1
    opera **47–8**, 69–70, 249 n.1
    organic 36, 49, 51
    prana 51, 63–4, 69, 183
    psychophysical technique 15,
        48–51, 63, 244 (*See also*
        psychophysical)
    repetition 32
    rhythm as a foundation 45
    speech 207–8
    standing in rhythm 68–9
    tempo (*See* tempo-rhythm)
    through-lines 182–3
    universality 35, 51
Steiner, Rudolf 242, 248 n.1
Strasberg, Lee 22–3, 167
subjective rhythmization 103, 251 n.8
sub-text 99, 103–4, 107, 208, 242

Sulerzhitsky, Leopold 249 n.4
Sulzman, Alexander 250 n.3
Suzuki, Tadashi 126–7, 252 n.4
swing 110, 111, 113
Switzerland 80, 81
synchronization 18, 33, 102, 146,
    157. *See also* entrainment
    de-synchronization 19–20, 41, 99
syncopation 52, 68, 145, 147, 228
systole and *diastole* 241
Szpakiewicz, Mieczysław 154

tact 241, 244. *See also* beat; pulse
Ta-Ke-Ti-Na 181, 256 n.4
Tanner, Phil 226
Tarahumara 255 n.3
Taylor, Frederick 31
Teatr Chorea 237
technology 39. *See also* mechanical
teilspannungen 28
temperament 97
tempo 17, 22, 37, **54–9**, 56–9, 61–2,
    67–9, 70–1, **89**, 99, 126, 127,
    128–9, 168–9, 178–9, 188,
    201–2, 235, **245**. *See also*
    tempo-rhythm; timing
    acceleration 20, 56, 86, 117, 144,
        156–7, 179
    deceleration 56, 100, 246
    established norms 21, 22–3
    external 55–7
    innate 221
    internal 20, 57–8
    justification 48
    mechanical 30
    musical descriptions 100
    temperament 97
    Viewpoints 121, **128–9**, 130
tempo-rhythm 17, 47, **54–9**, 70–1,
    159, 164, 183, 235, **245–6**
    contrasting **64–6**, 69–70, 204,
        252 n.5
    emotion 50
    Grotowski 164
    inner **63–4**, 68–9
    outer **60–2**, 89, 97, 155

in speech 207–8
training, 59–60
territory **19–21**, 23, 119, 136, 151,
    172, 174, 194, 196
Théâtre du Soleil 236
thesis and *arsis* 10, 258 n.1
thesis, antithesis and *synthesis* (Marx)
    114
Thevenaz, Paulet 83
Tibet 253 n.2
    Tibetan Institute of Performing
        Arts 167
timing 4, 11, 14, 31, 34, 39, 56, 61,
    98–9, 103, 111, 201, 226,
    246. *See also* tempo
    micro-timing 107
    personal/cultural tendencies 56,
        97, 122, 129–30, 136
Tristan and Isolde 99
Turgenev, Ivan 67
Turner, Victor 151, 241

United Kingdom 25, 31, 167, 181
United States of America 25–6, 31,
    52, 83–4, 123–4, 167, 206,
    250 n.4 252 n.2
universal 3, 27, 33–8, 38–9, 51, 79,
    149, 203, 234, 237, 257 n.2
ur-rhythm 160
U Theatre 237

Vakhtangov, Yevgeny 55–7, 59, 154,
    249 n.4, 254 n.3
verbatim theatre 37
versification theory (Pavis) 201
verticality 141, 163, **173–4**
    temporal (*See* simultaneity)
video design 39–41
Viewpoints **121–35**, 175, 196, 242,
    250 n.8
Villard, Jean 86, 91
visual arts 39, 90, 92, 134, 226, 233,
    256 n.1
voice 20, 47–8, 68, 103, 107, 164,
    183, 189, 199, 201–3, 204,
    209, 212, 217–24

training 81, 85–91, 85–7, 98, 204–6, 219
utterance 203 (*See also* language; song)
Volkonski, Sergei 27, 39, 203, 249 n.3, 257 n.3
Expressive Man 154–5, 254 n.3
Vrobel, Susie 216

walking 61, 64, 81–2, 110, 126, 128, 130–2, 186–90, 210, 220–1, 229, 255 n.7
slow 162–3, **168–70**, 172, 255 n.2
Warner, Leo 40–1
Weibel, Peter 182
Weill, Kurt 202
Werfel, Franz 249 n.2
Werther 249 n.1
West Africa 148, 194, 247–8 n.3, 256 n.7

Whyman, Rose 4, 55
Wilson, Robert 19–20
wohlfluss 28
Woodbury, Lael 10
Woolf, Virginia 212
Wooster Group 124, 237
Worley, Lee 183
Wunder, Al 252 n.2
Wundt, Wilhelm 15

Yarrow, Ralph 75, 250 n.4
Yiddish 218
yoga 35, 48, 50–1, 63, 143, 163, 171

Zaporah, Ruth 124
Zarrilli, Phillip 17–18, 143, 244
Zeami Motokiyo 247 n.1
Zen Zen Zo 252 n.1
Zinman, Toby 206
Zmysłowski, Jacek 170
ZU-UK 237